scientific
allocation
of water
resources

# ENVIRONMENTAL SCIENCE SERIES

Asit K. Biswas, *Editor*
Department of Environment, Ottawa, Canada

## Published

Scientific Allocation of Water Resources
Nathan Buras

## In Preparation

Dynamics of Fluids in Porous Media
Jacob Buras

Systems Approach to Water Management
Asit K. Biswas, *Editor*

# scientific allocation of water resources

water resources development and utilization – a rational approach

## Nathan Buras

The Lowdermilk Faculty
of Agricultural Engineering

Technion—Israel Institute
of Technology, Haifa

american elsevier
publishing company, inc.
NEW YORK

AMERICAN ELSEVIER PUBLISHING COMPANY, INC.
52 Vanderbilt Avenue, New York, N.Y. 10017

ELSEVIER PUBLISHING COMPANY
335 Jan Van Galenstraat, P.O. Box 211
Amsterdam, The Netherlands

International Standard Book Number 0-444-00104-2

Library of Congress Card Number 70-158630

Copyright © 1972 by American Elsevier Publishing Company, Inc.

All rights reserved.
No part of this publication may be reproduced,
stored in a retrieval system, or transmitted
in any form or by any means, electronic,
mechanical, photocopying, recording,
or otherwise, without the prior
written permission of the publisher,
American Elsevier Publishing Company, Inc.,
52 Vanderbilt Avenue, New York, New York 10017.

*Printed in the United States of America*

# Contents

Preface . . . . . . . . . . . . . . . . . . . . . . . . . . . . ix

**CHAPTER 1**

**Introduction** . . . . . . . . . . . . . . . . . . . . . . . . . 1

A. Historical Background . . . . . . . . . . . . . . . . . . 1
B. Water Resources Engineering . . . . . . . . . . . . . . 6
References . . . . . . . . . . . . . . . . . . . . . . . . . 12

**CHAPTER 2**

**The Systems Approach to Water Resources Problems** . . . . 15

References . . . . . . . . . . . . . . . . . . . . . . . . . 27

**CHAPTER 3**

**Problems in Water Resources Engineering** . . . . . . . . . 30

A. Development Problems . . . . . . . . . . . . . . . . . 30
B. Design Problems . . . . . . . . . . . . . . . . . . . . 36
C. Operational Problems . . . . . . . . . . . . . . . . . 41
D. Recapitulation . . . . . . . . . . . . . . . . . . . . . 47
References . . . . . . . . . . . . . . . . . . . . . . . . . 48

**CHAPTER 4**

**Some Probabilistic Methods Applied in Water Resources** . . . 52

A. Statistical Applications . . . . . . . . . . . . . . . . . 52
B. Stochastic Processes and Water Storage . . . . . . . . . 55
C. Storage Control Problems . . . . . . . . . . . . . . . 72
References . . . . . . . . . . . . . . . . . . . . . . . . . 81

## CHAPTER 5
### Applications of Linear Programming . . . . . . . . . . . . . . 84
A. General . . . . . . . . . . . . . . . . . . . . . 84
B. Water Quality Management . . . . . . . . . . . . . . . 85
C. Design and Operation of Reservoirs . . . . . . . . . . . 93
D. Aquifer Management . . . . . . . . . . . . . . . . . 105
E. Summary . . . . . . . . . . . . . . . . . . . . . 112
References . . . . . . . . . . . . . . . . . . . . . . 112

## CHAPTER 6
### Dynamic Programming . . . . . . . . . . . . . . . . . . 114
A. Sequential Decision Processes . . . . . . . . . . . . . 114
B. Recurrence Relationships . . . . . . . . . . . . . . . 115
C. The Principle of Optimality . . . . . . . . . . . . . . 119
D. One-Dimensional Allocation Processes . . . . . . . . . . 120
E. Multidimensional Allocation Processes . . . . . . . . . . 123
F. Optimization in Space . . . . . . . . . . . . . . . . 125
G. Optimization in Time . . . . . . . . . . . . . . . . 126
H. Conclusion . . . . . . . . . . . . . . . . . . . . 139
References . . . . . . . . . . . . . . . . . . . . . . 141

## CHAPTER 7
### Applications of Dynamic Programming in Water Resources Engineering . . . . . . . . . . . . . . . . . . . . . . 142
A. General . . . . . . . . . . . . . . . . . . . . . 142
B. General Design Applications . . . . . . . . . . . . . . 143
C. Storage Regulation . . . . . . . . . . . . . . . . . 149
D. Conjunctive Use of Surface and Groundwater Resources . . . . 155
E. Multistructure and Multipurpose Systems . . . . . . . . . 171
F. Pumped Storage . . . . . . . . . . . . . . . . . . 176
References . . . . . . . . . . . . . . . . . . . . . . 179

## CHAPTER 8
### Simulation Methods for the Design of Water Resource Systems 182
A. Introduction . . . . . . . . . . . . . . . . . . . . 182
B. The Monte Carlo Method . . . . . . . . . . . . . . . 183
C. Generation of Synthetic Streamflow Data . . . . . . . . . 187
D. Examples of Simulation Studies . . . . . . . . . . . . 189
References . . . . . . . . . . . . . . . . . . . . . . 192

**CHAPTER 9**
**Conclusion** . . . . . . . . . . . . . . . . . . . . . . . . . 193
Reference . . . . . . . . . . . . . . . . . . . . . . . . . . 197
Author Index . . . . . . . . . . . . . . . . . . . . . . . . 199
Subject Index . . . . . . . . . . . . . . . . . . . . . . . . 203

# PREFACE

The field of water resources engineering, a newcomer to technology fifteen years ago, a mere bud on the ever-branching tree of applied knowledge, has shown a spectacular growth. There is almost no area of scientific endeavor, whether physical sciences or social sciences, that does not contribute to the expansion of this field and is not touched by it. As in many other fields of science and technology, the rapid growth of water resources engineering was accompanied by an information explosion of considerable proportions. As in most explosive phenomena, fragments of varying qualitative and quantitative properties have been scattered in many different directions. So far, not many attempts have been made (with a few notable exceptions) to bring together the knowledge generated in this field in a form useful to the researcher or practicing engineer. The present volume intends to perform this function, by surveying the state of the art of water resources engineering while this information explosion is still in progress.

This book is oriented primarily toward students in their last year of undergraduate studies or first year of graduate work. But in addition to students pursuing a formal program of studies in water resources, development planning, or other interdisciplinary channels, engineers and planners will also find the book a valuable reference manual. For the treatment of water resources here embraces a broad spectrum of issues: quantity aspects as well as quality aspects within a systems approach.

Thus the book opens with a definition of the field of water resources engineering, emphasizing its natural and social sciences components. This introduction points out the complexity of most problems in this field, a situation that requires a broad approach to their analysis and solution. Such an approach is offered by systems engineering, which is briefly described and illustrated in the context of the design and operation of water resources systems.

Problems in water resources engineering are discussed next. They are grouped into three broad categories: development, design, and operation problems. The first group includes engineering, economic, and management problems. The second is made up of the comprehensive water resources planning, problems of basic data for design, the stochastic aspects of reservoir design, and water resources planning in metropolitan areas. In the third group, operating rules and some techniques for their optimization are included.

The analysis and solution of these problems are attained through the application of operations research methods. Probability techniques, including Markov chains and queuing, have been successfully applied, especially in problems connected with water storage. A separate chapter is devoted to linear programming, an operations research technique widely used in water resources engineering.

The design and operation of water resources systems are, almost always, sequential decision processes. The method of analysis best suited for this type of process is undoubtedly dynamic programming. Some basic ideas of dynamic programming are presented briefly, followed by a chapter showing the application of this method in water resources engineering. The examples shown are related to the derivation of optimal operating procedures for a fairly wide variety of systems, from relatively simple ones (single-purpose, single-structure) to complex systems involving many structures, several purposes, and surface water and groundwater.

Before concluding the monograph, a separate chapter deals with simulation techniques. Perhaps a case could be made against including simulation in a volume dealing with the scientific allocation of water resources. However, the widespread use of simulation, and the increasingly sophisticated methods used in it, seem to be sufficient justification for introducing methods such as Monte Carlo and synthetic hydrology.

This book is an outgrowth and an extension of a research project on the application of mathematical analysis in water resources engineering, which started in the mid-sixties and was supported by the Ford Foundation: this support is gratefully acknowledged. Other research grants, provided by the Israeli Ministry of Agriculture and by the United States Department of Agriculture also assisted the preparation of the manuscript: thanks are also offered to them.

Authors of books, like everyone else, never work in a vacuum. Conversations with colleagues, seminars with students, and teaching courses in water resources engineering provided much of the stimulus necessary for the writing of the book, and the kind of constructive criticism that refines some of the ideas, concepts, and methods presented in it. In particular, Theodore Herman, a graduate student and close collaborator, contributed substantially in the assembly of the material pertinent to the application of the operations research techniques in water resources engineering.

While mentioning the assembly of materials, thanks are given to the American Society of Civil Engineers, the Harvard University Press, and Tahal Ltd., for permission to publish material originally copyrighted by them.

Mr. and Mrs. Gabriel Mohos took charge of typing the manuscript and did the drawings. This important support is acknowledged with thanks.

But certainly the most essential encouragement came from my wife Netty and our son Nir, who put up with all the trials and tribulations, inconveniences, and time taken from the family and given to the manuscript, which made it all possible. To them is this book dedicated.

NATHAN BURAS

Chapter 1

# INTRODUCTION

## A. HISTORICAL BACKGROUND

Man's quest for a better use of the available water is as old as mankind itself. His understanding of the phenomena connected with the occurrence of water in nature is relatively recent, and until about 150 years ago it was rather limited. Nevertheless, man has tried to offer plausible explanations about the natural hydrological processes, at a level of sophistication commensurate with the general *niveau* of scientific development at the time.

Perhaps one of the earliest mentions of water is in the first chapter of Genesis. Starting with the second verse, the Bible echoes what may well be one of the oldest myths of mankind, in an attempt to explain the origins of water on earth. Paradise itself, the Garden of Eden, was imagined to be a place in which water was plentiful (Genesis 2: 10 *et seq.*). Four rivers originated in it, irrigating the lands of the Ancient World. This, in a way, is related to the foci of civilization of the Near East, which developed along rivers and in their alluvial plains: Tigris and Euphrates in Mesopotamia, Nile in Egypt, and Jordan in Israel. Philosophers in ancient Greece considered water as one of the four elements of the universe, the other three being earth, air, and fire.

It seems that some basic principles of hydraulic engineering were discovered on the banks of the Nile as early as several centuries before the present era. Later, the Romans adopted them through Ptolemaic Egypt [1] for application in constructing bridges and aqueducts. The latter have been considered by many to be Rome's greatest engineering achievement.

With the fall of Rome, the western world was plunged into the penumbra of the Dark Ages, from which it emerged only with the advent of the Renaissance. Modest advances in the utilization of waters can be detected in the fourteenth century [2]. Waterpower was used in sawmills, a rather complicated pump was constructed, and well boring was recorded for the first time.

From that point on, sciences related to water expanded rapidly. Daniel Bernoulli applied the concept of conservation of matter to hydrodynamics in 1738. At about the same time, d'Alembert showed that Newton's third law of motion applies equally well to moving bodies (hence, to flowing water) as to bodies at rest. Toward the end of the eighteenth century, Chézy derived the formula (which bears his name to this day) describing the flow of water in open channels. An important landmark in the development of modern thought in relation to water problems is the treatise published by Darcy in 1856 regarding the flow of water in a porous medium [3]. The research — empirical, applied, and basic — spread to touch on most problems in hydrology, hydraulics, and their engineering aspects. A concise summary of the historical development of scientific thinking related to hydrosphere can be found in the first section of Chow's monumental *Handbook of Applied Hydrology* [4].

As the understanding of the natural phenomena related to the hydrological cycle increased due to the progress of hydrology and hydraulics, the need began to be felt to augment the scope of the analysis offered by these descriptive sciences with elements of decision theory. Out of this grafting of decision sciences on the descriptive sciences emerged water resources engineering.

Among the earliest comprehensive formulations of problems in water resources development, utilization, and conservation was the report of the United States' President's Water Resources Policy Commission in 1950 [5]. This report gave impetus to further investigations in the sphere of public administration [6, 7], and generated (in an indirect way, perhaps) sufficient interest to start research activities at a number of universities.

In 1955, a water resources program was initiated at Harvard University [8]. The purpose of this program was to develop a methodology for planning and designing complex, modern water resource systems. From the outset, it was recognized that these systems exhibit certain fundamental engineering aspects, as well as broad economic and social overtones. The methodology developed aimed, first, to enable a preliminary screening of alternatives in a systems context in order to identify promising measures suitable for further analysis; and, second, to analyze in detail systems of such alternatives leading to the identification of an optimal design or designs [9–12]. New techniques for relating economic objectives, engineering analysis, and governmental planning were evolved. These techniques, which are appropriate for both the preliminary screening and the detailed analysis, fall into two classes: analytical models and digital computer simulation models. Considerable progress was made in both directions [13–16].

## Introduction

At about the same time that the Harvard Water Program got under way, and quite independently from it, a number of workers at the University of California began studying the problem of optimization of water resource systems. The earliest mention of concern in this area is perhaps a problem suggested by W. A. Hall in the book on dynamic programming by R. E. Bellman [17, page 143]. Research in water resources engineering gained momentum with the establishment of the University of California Water Resources Center on December 1, 1957. One of the first products of this effort was a fundamental paper [18] showing the analysis of sequential multistage decision processes in water resources engineering, through the application of dynamic programming. The study of dynamic programming as an optimization technique in water resources engineering was continued. Increasingly complex systems were analyzed, including pumped-storage schemes [19].

Another landmark in the rapid growth of water resources engineering in the last decade is the Western Resources Conference. Starting in 1959, a number of universities in Colorado (the University of Colorado, Colorado State University, and the Colorado School of Mines) organized yearly conferences at which problems of development and utilization of natural resources were debated. Thus in 1959, the conference theme was focused on building toward a continuous program of graduate study and research in the conservation and development of the resources of the western United States with special emphasis on water [20]. In 1960, the conference concentrated on the estimation of projected water requirements, and on ways to meet future demands [21]. The 1961 conference considered the land–water complex within the context of planning for regional growth [22]. After discussing mineral and energy resources in 1962, the conference considered in 1963 the development, utilization, and conservation of water resources [23]. The 1964 conference had a broad horizon of issues and methodology in resources research, but returned in 1965 to specific problems of water research: economic analysis, water management, evaluation problems, water reallocation, political and administrative problems, hydrology and engineering, and research programs and needs [24].

The increased research and educational activity in a number of American universities prompted the establishment of the Universities Council on Hydrology (UCOH) in 1963 [25], which transformed itself about two years later into the University Council on Water Resources (UCOWR).

Under the impetus of the work done at the universities, and following additional studies by various governmental bodies, the United States Congress passed in 1964 the Water Resources Research Act. This legislation enabled the establishment of water resources research centers in colleges and universities in all of the United States. In these centers, basic research in water resources is promoted and conducted.

Research in water resources engineering is done in a host of institutions throughout the world. In almost every country and region one can find centers of research activity. These have become almost too numerous to be described in detail. However, we should mention at least three of them: the Water Research Association in England; Centre de Recherches et d'Essais de Chatou d'Electricité de France; the Technion–Israel Institute of Technology.

The Water Research Association is active in a number of problems of water resources engineering and management in England. Considerable effort is directed toward the analysis of storage problems, and to the derivation of operating rules for reservoirs [26].

In France, at the Electricité de France, the major research effort in water resources engineering is directed toward storage problems. The operation of power stations connected with impounding dams necessitates the application of probability theory for the analysis of the hydrological input to the station [27]. The use of Markov processes in the analysis make possible the establishment of rational operating rules for multiple-purpose reservoirs [28].

At the Technion–Israel Institute of Technology, work in several aspects of water resources engineering has been done for some time. During the earlier stages of development of Israel, when the demand for water was relatively low, the major problem was that of controlling excess water, which caused many unfavorable drainage situations [29]. Later, as irrigated agriculture expanded and water supplies became scarce at several localities in different seasons, the economic aspects of water supply systems were stressed [30]. More recently, as practically the whole country is supplied by water from a single national scheme, the systems approach to water resources engineering was introduced [31]. In this approach, various mathematical analytical techniques are employed.

The development of water resources has almost always had a marked impact upon regional economic growth and overall progress. We can also state the converse: whenever plans for regional development have been made, water resources systems served very often as a central core around which other regional natural resources were developed. This is particularly true for

## Introduction

land resources and agricultural development [32]. In this respect, it is sufficient to survey some of the better-known development projects in various parts of the world, and the truth of this statement becomes at once obvious.

The North American continent, especially the United States, is replete with examples. Take, for instance, the lower part of the Colorado river. The development of water resources within this river basin had far-reaching effects well beyond the basin boundaries. The growth of the Imperial Valley could not have been possible without the large quantities of water diverted from the Colorado River. Millions of acres of land, which otherwise would have remained useless desert, were transformed into fertile fields. In fact, much of the amazing progress registered in California can be linked directly with the development of water resources [33].

Another example illustrating the impact of water resources upon the development of other natural resources is the Tennessee Valley Authority [34]. Within this broad and varied river basin, water was instrumental not only in increasing agricultural output, but also, by supplying relatively inexpensive hydroelectric power, in giving significant impetus to the development of regional industries, particularly mining (aluminum) and manufacturing (chemical fertilizers).

Similar examples can be cited from other parts of the world. The Indus Valley in the Indian subcontinent is a case in point. The harnessing of a mighty river by British engineers some hundred years ago through the construction of the largest irrigation project in the world transformed the greater part of the Tharr desert into the granary of India. Land resources that lay idle since the beginning of time were put to use and made productive by the addition of water. A vast, relatively empty area became within a few decades a region teeming with millions of people. The impact of water on the development of land resources in the Indus Valley was very spectacular. Almost as spectacular are the problems that exist today in this valley [35], problems that are linked to the management and the mode of utilization of water resources. The introductory chapter to a discussion on the scientific allocation of water resources is hardly the place to elaborate on the difficulties encountered today in the Indus Valley. Suffice it to say that to a large extent these difficulties are also a result of ignoring (or neglecting, or both) certain aspects of water resources management at the time when the project was planned and designed. In other words, application of the principles of systems engineering [36] might have helped in designing a more comprehensive water resources system.

Today, the concept of comprehensive planning for water and other natural resources within a geographical region gains acceptance rapidly. Almost no planning agency, national or international, considers economic development separately from the development of water resources within the region in question. Conversely, many large engineering offices that are especially active in water resources development are expanding their staff so as to be able to deal with water resource projects in a much broader context [**37**]. Then the regional water plan becomes the nucleus around which other economic activities requiring engineering design (e.g., transportation systems) are planned.

The scientific, professional, and technical literature on water resources is rapidly increasing in quantity. We can almost say that there is an information explosion in progress. This information explosion presents certain problems to the professional man, scientist, and student active in the field of water resources. Although there is at least one internationally recognized scientific periodical in this field (*Water Resources Research*), much material appears in a host of other publications. The present volume, while disclaiming omniscience of the entire field of water resources, surveys the state of the art in at least one corner of it. In this way it hopes to fulfill a need that was felt by some water resources engineers.

## B. WATER RESOURCES ENGINEERING

Natural resources, like many other items appearing under a common heading, can be classified in a number of different ways. A convenient classification is that which distinguishes between *renewable* and *nonrenewable* natural resources. Renewable resources usually undergo changes that repeat themselves in a cyclical pattern. For example, atmospheric carbon (in the form of $CO_2$) may be incorporated into plant tissue through the process of photosynthesis; then it may be ingested by animals, only to be released back to the atmosphere (again mostly as $CO_2$) through their metabolic processes.

Fossil fuels and mineral ores are considered nonrenewable resources. When adequate amounts are found, they are exploited through extraction, the process being termed mining.

In fact, it is rather difficult to draw a hard and fast boundary between renewable and nonrenewable resources. In the first place, it is inconceivable that the so-called nonrenewable resources eventually vanish from the world.

## Introduction

On the contrary, after they are transformed through various technological processes and used by man, they will return to nature in a changed form and, eventually after a long time, may be mined anew. It seems, therefore, that all resources go in nature through cycles, and the only difference is the speed with which these transformations occur. Relatively rapid transformations are connected with what we term renewable resources; those which involve millenia, with nonrenewable ones.

Water is a renewable resource that follows in nature a path called the *hydrological cycle*. The details of the hydrological cycle are described and analyzed at length in texts on hydrology [38–40]. It will suffice to point out that the oceans are considered the sources of all water on earth. The continuous stream of energy originating in the sun and reaching this planet causes the evaporation of water from the oceans. Meteorological processes result in the precipitation of part of the atmospheric water vapor. Water then reaches the ground as liquid (rain, dew) or in solid state (snow, hail), and eventually finds its way back to the ocean, thus closing the hydrological cycle.

Man has always tried to tap the hydrologic cycle at one or more points, in order to utilize the water for a variety of purposes. For example, from the earliest times man had diverted surface streams for his use, whether for irrigation, domestic use, or navigation. Groundwater has also been exploited from the dawn of civilization. An early description of groundwater exploitation appears in the Bible in connection with the expansion of Isaac's household in the northern Negev (Genesis 26: 13–33). His shepherds dug wells and came in conflict with a neighboring tribe, competing for the same limited resource. The friction continued until a more abundant supply was developed by digging wells in the vicinity of Beersheba.

Man's attempts to take advantage of certain aspects of the hydrological cycle gave rise to water resources projects of a wide range of sophistication. In their simplest form, such projects are nothing more than primitive facilities for the storage of rainwater in cisterns, for human consumption and domestic use. Vestiges of such primitive (but clever) water resource systems were discovered in the Negev [41]. In their most sophisticated form, water resources projects involve a complex of multiple-purpose structures that regulate streamflows, recharge groundwater aquifers, generate hydroelectric power, protect highly industrialized and urbanized areas against flooding, satisfy recreational needs of large numbers of people, and may also attain other objectives. (Multiple-purpose projects are defined [42] as "... engineering works which serve more than one principal purpose, and where the value of benefits accruing from each such purpose is commensurate with the portion of total costs alloted to it.") In between these two extremes—primitive water storage facilities and intricate multiple-purpose projects—there are many possible ways in which water resources may be developed and utilized. Each of these ways represents a solution to a programming problem, that is, a problem that demands the optimization of a given criterion, subject to a set of constraints.

It is easy, therefore, to realize that the increasing complexity of water resource systems gives rise to a host of problems connected with the development, control, allocation, treatment, utilization, and re-use of water. The analysis and solution of these problems form the field of *water resources engineering*.

The main problem in water resources engineering, and perhaps *the* problem in its most general formulation, arises from the fact that water is often available at times, in locations, and of a quality different from those which define the demand for it. In addition to this, the amounts of water available may be at variance with those required for certain economic activities. Considering this situation, which can be characterized by the maldistribution of water in time and in space coupled with its often undesired quality, three major questions arise:

1. What system has to be built in order to minimize the discrepancy existing between the natural supply of water (in time, space, and quality) and the demand for it?

2. To what extent should the water resource be developed, and how extensive should be the region serviced by the system?

3. Once it is built, how should the system be operated so as to achieve a given set of objectives in the best possible way?

The order in which these questions are presented here corresponds largely also to the chronological sequence in which their answers were attempted. First, man tried to understand the natural hydrological phenomena, and to build storage and conveying structures for water. This activity generated the branch of science called hydrology, and hydraulic engineering. The state of art and knowledge in this domain has been surveyed recently in handbooks and monographs [4, 43, 44].

The second and the third questions have occupied engineers, economists, and planners for quite some time in the past 70 to 80 years. They were brought into sharper focus about a quarter of a century ago, when we began to

## Introduction

recognize the specificity of the problems raised by the development and utilization of natural resources (water included) as contrasted with other production processes [45]. Massé defined *resources* as the sum total of goods that can be used for the maintenance and improvement of standards of living. The distinction was made between the problems posed by the development and utilization of resources as opposed to those raised by industrial production processes, or by the transportation of goods. Emphasis was placed on the time element, which appears to affect markedly the development of natural resources.

The analysis and solution of these problems have advanced at an increased rate since the advent of the high-speed electronic computers. The growing sophistication of computing machinery has not only made possible the rapid and accurate performance of tedious and repetitious calculations, but has also been a catalytic factor in the evolution of several mathematical theories and methods. Some of these methods were applied in the design of water resource systems, and many more are potentially adaptable to it. Conversely, not all of the sophisticated mathematical methods are seen to be of immediate practical use in water resources engineering.

Quite often the problems encountered in planning water resources development are rather complex. Take, for example, the question of objectives. How should we define the objective to the attainment of which we build and operate a water resource system? A comprehensive discussion of this aspect of water resources development may be found elsewhere [12, 34]. But the complexity of water resources development problems stems also from the wide range of the possible values that factors involved in their solution may take. These factors are both structural and nonstructural, hardware and software. To name a few: reservoirs and inflows; aquifers and operating policies; wells and water quality control criteria; groundwater recharge facilities and flood plain zoning regulations. Many of these factors can be expressed in quantitative terms; others have yet to be quantized. Still other factors may never be amenable to much more than a qualitative description.

The interdisciplinary nature of water resources engineering emerges clearly from the foregoing discussion. Indeed, this broad field of engineering straddles the area where natural sciences and social sciences overlap (see Figure 1.1). (We should mention, of course, that there are no hard and fast boundaries between natural and social sciences.) This overlap extends from pure (basic) sciences to their application. Water resources engineering (again, with

*Scientific Allocation of Water Resources*

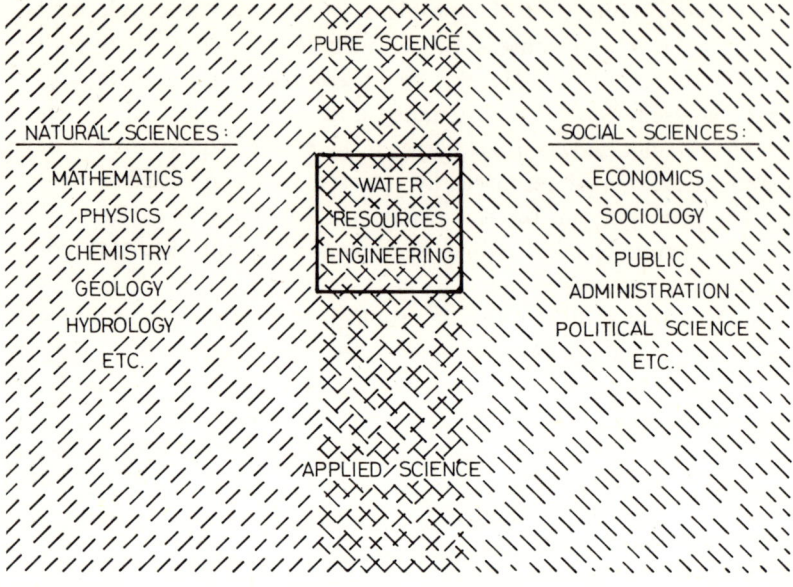

FIGURE 1.1. The relation of water resources engineering to natural and social sciences.

ill-defined boundaries) covers the overlap and extends also into the realms of natural and social sciences. It incorporates parts of many disciplines (agricultural engineering, civil engineering, economics, law, and others), but it is impossible to identify any one of them with water resources engineering. For example, it would be false to claim that "hydraulic engineering" and "water resources engineering" are interchangeable terms. The former refers to a very specialized branch of civil engineering, whereas the latter deals with the overall development and utilization of one of the most essential natural resources. We can, however, detect in water resources engineering close affinities with the following traditional disciplines.

(i) *Agricultural Engineering*. One aspect of agricultural engineering deals with the maintenance and control of an adequate moisture regime within the root zone of cultivated lands [46]. Problems of irrigation and drainage fall under this heading, including storage of water on farms and allocation of water to different fields within one farming enterprise [47]. Other aspects of agricultural engineering that pertain to water resources are watershed management, soil and water conservation, and land reclamation.

*Introduction*

(ii) *Civil Engineering*. A number of engineering disciplines are included under this heading. Of these, two are of particular importance to water resources engineering: hydraulic engineering and sanitary engineering. The former pertains to the hydraulic and structural design of dams, outlets, canals, diversions, pipelines, and power-generating facilities, as well as to river regulation and navigation works (harbors, locks, and bridges) [48]. The latter deals with the quality of water supplied for domestic and industrial uses, and with disposal, treatment, reclamation, and re-use of waste waters [49].

(iii) *Hydrology*. Basic to the analysis and solution of problems in water resources engineering is applied hydrology [4]. Its primary function is the quantitative evaluation of the supply of water in a water resource development project. On the basis of existing records, applied hydrology can yield estimates of future streamflows with specified probabilities. These probabilities reflect the uncertainty faced by the decision makers in water resource development, from the determination of optimal size of various structural elements to operating policies. The uncertainty is often translated in terms of risk, especially when economic evaluations are performed.

(iv) *Chemical Engineering*. Improvement of the mineral quality of water (desalination) borrows heavily from chemical engineering. It involves problems of heat and mass transfer, thermodynamics, and other energy relationships, many of them irreversible [50].

(v) *Economics*. It has been implied that water resources engineering is "an attempt to consummate the marriage of engineering and economics" [10, page **134**]. In order to perform such a "marriage," the quantitative aspects of economics become more heavily involved. Econometrics, decision theory, programming methods, and other operations research techniques link the two disciplines.

(vi) *Public Administration*. Water resource projects are very often planned, designed, built, and operated subject to one or more institutional constraints. Whether it is an irrigation district or a drainage authority, a flood control district or a valley authority (TVA), the type of organization and its administration will influence markedly the outputs from a water resource system. An excellent example of such a situation in which organizational structure and performance affect a large region is the California Water Project [33].

(vii) *Law*. There is hardly one water resource project in which legal overtones are absent. Concepts and doctrines are continually developing, and are translated into law at one time or another [51]. For example, the riparian rights to water in streams, the beneficial use concept, and the appropriation doctrine are quite evident in the design of many water resource systems and in their modes of operation [52]. In many instances, the allocation of water resources among users, purposes, and sectors depends on the existing legal framework. A case in point is the debate over whether the construction of hydroelectric features in multipurpose projects by the private sector would be preferred to public construction from an economic standpoint [53]. In this debate the legal arguments have a preponderant weight.

From the foregoing discussion it becomes quite clear that water resources engineering is a complex discipline with many facets. One of its most most important qualities is that it integrates several areas from natural and social sciences in the analysis and solution of problems involved in the development and utilization of water resources of a given region. From this, it also follows that water resources engineers must be (or are becoming by necessity) generalists in the true sense of the word. However, just as system analysts in other fields are proficient in at least one discipline, so is the water resources engineer an expert in one of the sciences that blend to form the water resources engineering.

## REFERENCES

1. W. Durant, *Caesar and Christ*. Simon and Schuster, New York, 1944.
2. W. Durant, *The Reformation*. Simon and Schuster, New York, 1957.
3. H. Darcy, *Les Fontaines Publiques de la Ville de Dijon*. V. Dalmont, Paris, 1856.
4. V. T. Chow (ed.), *Handbook of Applied Hydrology*. McGraw-Hill, New York, 1964.
5. *A Policy for the American People*, Report of the President's Water Resources Policy Commission, Vol. 1: General Report; Vol. 2: Ten Rivers in America's Future; Vol. 3: Water Resources Law, U.S. Government Printing Office, Washington, D.C., 1950.
6. *Report on Water Resources*, prepared for the Commission on Organization of the Executive Branch of the Government by the Task Force on Water Resources and Power, 3 vols., U.S. Government Printing Office, Washington, D.C., 1955.
7. *Water Resources Policy*, Presidential Advisory Committee on Water Resources Policy, U.S. Government Printing Office, Washington, D.C., 1955.
8. M. M. Hufschmidt, "The Harvard Program: A Summing Up," *Water Research* (A. V. Kneese and S. C. Smith, eds.), pp. 441–455. Johns Hopkins Press, Baltimore, Maryland, 1966.
9. A. Maass and M. M. Hufschmidt, "In Search of New Methods of River System Planning," *J. Boston Soc. Civil Engineers* **46**(1959), 99.
10. A. Maass and M. M. Hufschmidt, "Toward Better River System Planning," *Resources*

## Introduction

*Development, Frontiers for Research, Western Resources Conference, 1959* (Z. S. Pollak, ed.), pp. 133–179. University of Colorado Press, Boulder, Colorado, 1960.

11. M. M. Hufschmidt, J. V. Krutilla, J. Margolis, and S. A. Marglin, *Standards and Criteria for Formulating and Evaluating Federal Water Resources Developments*, Report of Panel of Consultants to the Bureau of the Budget, Washington, D.C., 1961.
12. A. Maass, M. M. Hufschmidt, R. Dorfman, H. A. Thomas, Jr., S. A. Marglin, and G. M. Fair, *Design of Water-Resource Systems*. Harvard University Press, Cambridge, Massachusetts, 1962.
13. S. A. Marglin, *Approaches to Dynamic Investment Planning*. North-Holland Publ., Amsterdam, 1963.
14. M. B. Fiering, "Multivariate Technique for Synthetic Hydrology," *Proc. Amer. Soc. Civil Engineers* **90**(1964), No. HY5.
15. R. Dorfman, "Formal (Mathematical) Models in the Design of Water-Resource Systems," *Water Resources Research* **1**(1965), 329.
16. M. M. Hufschmidt and M. B. Fiering, *Simulation Techniques for Design of Water-Resources Systems*. Harvard University Press, Cambridge, Massachusetts, 1966.
17. R. E. Bellman, *Dynamic Programming*. Princeton University Press, Princeton, New Jersey, 1957.
18. W. A. Hall and N. Buras, "The Dynamic Programming Approach to Water Resources Development," *J. Geophysical Research* **66**(1961), 517.
19. W. A. Hall and T. G. Roefs, "Hydropower Project Output Optimization," *Proc. Amer. Soc. Civil Engineers* **92**(1966), No. PO1, 67.
20. F. S. Pollak, ed., *Resources Development: Frontiers for Research*. University of Colorado Press, Boulder, Colorado, 1960.
21. H. L. Amoss, ed., *Water: Measuring and Meeting Future Requirements*. University of Colorado Press, Boulder, Colorado, 1961.
22. H. L. Amoss and R. K. McNickle, eds., *Land and Water: Planning for Economic Growth*. University of Colorado Press, Boulder, Colorado, 1962.
23. R. K. McNickle, ed., *Water: Development, Utilization, Conservation*. University of Colorado Press, Boulder, Colorado, 1964.
24. A. V. Kneese and S. C. Smith, eds., *Water Research*. Johns Hopkins Press, Baltimore, Maryland, 1968.
25. D. K. Todd, "Inter-University Conference in Hydrology," *Trans. Amer. Geophysical Union* **44**(1963), 491.
26. *Proc. Reservoir Yield Symposium*, Water Research Association, Medmenham, England, 1966.
27. J. Bernier and H. Roux, "L'Application du Calcul des Probabilités aux Problèmes d'Exploitation des Réservoirs," *La Houille Blanche* **20**(1965), 431.
28. J. Bernier, *La Gestion des Réservoirs à Buts Multiples*, Electricité de France, Chatou, 1966.
29. J. Breuer, "Swamp Drainage in Palestine," *J. Assoc. Engineers and Architects in Palestine* **3**(1942), No. 3 (in Hebrew).
30. S. Irmay, "Calcul Economique des Réseaux de Distribution d'Eau," *La Houille Blanche* **9**(1954), 135.
31. N. Buras, "Conjunctive Operation of a Surface Reservoir and a Ground Water

Aquifer," *Symposium on Surface Waters*, Publication No. 63 of the IASH, pp. 492–501. Gentbrugge, Belgium, 1963.

32  D. K. Todd, ed., *Impact of Water on Land*, Report No. 9, Water Resources Center, University of California, Los Angeles, 1966.

33  J. S. Bain, *Northern California Water Industry*. Johns Hopkins Press, Baltimore, Maryland, 1966.

34  J. V. Krutilla and O. Eckstein, *Multiple Purpose River Development*. Johns Hopkins Press, Baltimore, Maryland, 1958.

35  H. A. Thomas, Jr., and R. P. Burden, *Indus River Basin Studies*. Harvard University, Division of Engineering and Applied Physics, Cambridge, Massachusetts, 1965 (mimeographed).

36  A. D. Hall, *A Methodology for Systems Engineering*. Van Nostrand, Princeton, New Jersey, 1962.

37  Tahal, Water Planning for Israel, Ltd., Tel Aviv, private communication, 1968.

38  R. K. Linsley, Jr., M. A. Kohler, and J. L. H. Paulhus, *Applied Hydrology*. McGraw-Hill, New York, 1949.

39  R. J. M. De Wiest, *Geohydrology*. Wiley, New York, 1965.

40  D. K. Todd, *Ground Water Hydrology*. Wiley, New York, 1959.

41  M. Evenari, L. Shanan, M. Tadmor, and Y. Aharoni, "Ancient Agriculture in the Negev," *Science* **133**(1961), 979.

42  J. G. Brown, ed., *Hydro-Electric Engineering Practice*, 3 vols. Blackie, London, 1958.

43  R. K. Linsley and J. B. Franzini, *Water-Resources Engineering*. McGraw-Hill, New York, 1964.

44  E. Kuiper, *Water Resources Development*. Butterworth, London, 1965.

45  G. P. Massé, *Les Réserves et la Régulation de l'Avenir dans la Vie Économique*, 2 vols. Hermann, Paris, 1946.

46  T. Herman, *The Planning of Moisture Control Systems for Poorly Drained Soils Using Systems Engineering*, M. S. thesis, Technion–Israel Institute of Technology, Haifa, Israel, 1966.

47  W. A. Hall and N. Buras, "Optimum Irrigated Practice Under Conditions of Deficient Water Supply," *Trans. Amer. Soc. Agricultural Engineers* **4**(1961), No. 1, 131.

48  C. V. Davis, ed., *Handbook of Applied Hydraulics*. McGraw-Hill, New York, 1952.

49  G. M. Fair, J. C. Geyer, and D. A. Okun, *Water and Wastewater Engineering*, 2 vols. Wiley, New York, 1968.

50  K. S. Spiegler, ed., *Principles of Desalination*. Academic Press, New York, 1966.

51  M. McDonough, "The Legal Kaleidoscope," *Water Policy Conference*, Report No. 3, University of California Water Resources Center, Los Angeles, 1961.

52  C. D. Clark, "Our Complex Water Laws and Water Use Customs," *Water Law, Politics, and Economics*, Oregon State University Water Resources Research Institute, Corvallis, Oregon, 1965.

53  A. F. Pillsbury, ed., *Water Resources Center Annual Report*, Report No. 14, University of California Water Resources Center, Los Angeles, 1968.

Chapter 2

# THE SYSTEMS APPROACH TO WATER RESOURCES PROBLEMS

The design of a water resource system is so complex a problem that a broad approach is required to its analysis and solution. Among the factors playing a major role are water demands, water supply, available technology, management framework, and data-gathering facilities. All of them have to be attuned to each other and to a set of objectives which are either spelled out explicitly or included implicitly in the formulation of the problem [1]. This broad perspective of water resource problems requires a novel approach.

Perhaps the most important advance made in recent years in water resources was the adaptation of systems engineering to the analysis of problems in this field [2]. Systems engineering, which is sometimes called (incorrectly) operations research, is, in a sense, the attacking of a complex problem on a broad front. Variables describing components or states of a system can be defined, and relationships between them represented, through equations in a mathematical model. These relationships, whether linear or nonlinear, can be properly evaluated by a variety of techniques, some of which have been made possible by the advance in computer science.

However, if the problems were reducible to a set of mathematical expressions, there would have been no need to invent systems engineering: perhaps numerical analysis would have been sufficient in many cases. But in water resources problems there are also many social and political factors that must be given due consideration. When there is no realistic way to assign values to these factors, their effect upon the system as a whole can be evaluated by handling them as constraints. In short, anything as complex as the effects of water resources development on the total environment of man in a region requires a broad overall approach. The systems approach has made remarkable progress in the analysis of components and subsystems from which the synthesis of the complete system may be possible. This entire operation is aimed at producing a whole series of alternatives which can be ranked in accordance with a given criterion, and in which the beneficial and/or detrimental effects of each is clearly defined.

In more specific, and perhaps better focused, terms, we can state that the systems engineering approach attempts to shorten the time lag between the appearance of needs (e.g., increased demand for water) and the production of new hardware and/or software (operating procedures) that satisfy these needs [3]. Since it is rather difficult to offer a clear, unambiguous, and sharp one-sentence definition, the functions of systems engineering will be discussed briefly in the succeeding paragraphs.

Systems engineering is, in fact, an extension of the scientific method [4], and it introduces into it a certain degree of formalism, which channels the thinking and guides it through the maze stretched between formulation of objectives and performance of the designed hardware. This process can be divided into five phases:

(i) *Statement of Objectives.* Perhaps the most difficult of all functions of systems engineering is that of defining the objectives to be attained through the design of the new system. The objectives are formulated by the decision makers within the relevant organizational structure (national government, local government, company management, etc.) in cooperation with the systems engineering team that will design the necessary facilities [5].

(ii) *Exploratory Studies.* The nature of this phase varies from specific case to specific case. In some instances, it is a reconnaissance survey in a resource development project: field data are collected for the appraisal of amounts of water that can be made available toward the fulfillment of the objectives. In other instances, it consists of creating an extensive background of information on which the project can be based, so that the problem can be attacked with proper scope and breadth.

(iii) *Feasibility Studies.* If the results of the previous phase warrant it, a detailed study of the specific project, problem, or area of need is initiated. The freest possible imagination is encouraged to invent alternative systems that can satisfy the objectives [6]. Each alternative must be worked out in sufficient detail to permit its evaluation in terms of system performance, cost, quality, and so on. These evaluations are then compared for the selection of the best system. Finally, the results of this phase are communicated to the decision-making body in a formal report that draws one of three conclusions: (1) a specific system will solve the problem; (2) additional field and/or laboratory work is needed on particular alternatives before a sound conclusion can be reached; (3) within the existing economic and technological circumstances, the project should not be pursued further.

(iv) *Development Planning*. This phase begins only after a decision has been made that the project will be undertaken. This implies that the decision-making group has appropriated the necessary funds for the construction. It is only then that detailed designs of components are made and specifications for bids drawn up.

(v) *Current Engineering*. The performance of the system has to be monitored continuously, so as to improve its mode of operation and produce better designs for similar systems in the future.

The application of systems engineering to planning of water resources systems was formulated recently [7]. In general, the main objective of a water resources development project, whether public or private, is considered to be the maximization of the regional welfare, where the term "region" is employed to denote a geographical area ranging in size from a small farming field to an extensive river basin. This primary objective is liable to be interpreted in several ways [8]: (a) the attainment of economic efficiency [9]; (b) the generation of income redistribution in the region; (c) the stimulation of full employment [10]; (d) the promotion and support of economic growth; (e) the achievement of a certain intangible and/or nonquantifiable objective, such as settlement of nationally desirable areas, defense, or preservation of natural wilderness; (f) the attainment of other goals.

Whatever the interpretation given to the prime objective, the following three problems have to be solved in conjunction with each other [11].

1. Criteria for the optimal design (physical dimensions) of dams, reservoirs, groundwater recharge facilities, power plants, pumping stations, canals, pressure conduits, and so on, must be determined.

2. Target outputs for irrigation water, hydroelectric power, level of flood control—in other words, the scale of the development activity—must be determined.

3. An optimal operating policy, that is, a schedule indicating volumes of water to be kept in storage or released from storage facilities at given points in time, has to be established.

Now, assuming that the outcome of each of the foregoing three problems can be expressed as "benefit" $B$ (under this assumption, "costs" are negative benefits), we can say that $B$ is a function of three sets of variables: $X_1$, the physical dimensions of the system commensurate with the relevant hydrological conditions; $X_2$, the scale of development; $X_3$, the operating policy; where $X_i$ may be multidimensional vectors. Thus

$$B = f(X_1, X_2, X_3). \qquad (2.1)$$

Speaking geometrically, $B$ is the response surface in a multidimensional space, and the problem is then to find its highest peak within the range of admissible values of $X_i$. Hopefully, the systems engineering approach will provide the techniques through which this fundamental problem in water resources can be solved.

We hasten to mention that the $X_i$ vectors are not independent: in fact, strong correlations exist between them, and their separation is somewhat artificial. For example, the design and operating criteria interact very strongly; one depends very much on the other. Nevertheless, we elect to deal with each of these problems separately, maximizing $B$ in terms of one or two of the $X_i$ and considering either or both of the other two as parameters. For example, the following is an objective function in which the design criteria and the scale of development appear explicitly:

$$\max B = R(I) - K(I). \qquad (2.2)$$

Here $B$ represents the present value of net benefits (in monetary units); $R(I)$ is the present value (in monetary units) of $I$ volume units of water supplied yearly to an irrigated area; $K(I)$ is the investment (in monetary units) necessary for the construction of a system capable of supplying $I$ volume units of water per year. In this case, $I$ is the unknown, the value of which has to be determined so as to maximize $B$. The solution of equation (2.2) will determine simultaneously the physical criteria for designing the system $K(I)$ and the scale of development $R(I)$ where $I$ is given in volume units per year. The operating policy appears nowhere in equation (2.2), and it is quite conceivable that different values of $I$ maximizing $B$ can be found when different operating rules are applied to the system. Thus, equation (2.2) is solved under the condition that the operating policy is a parameter.

Equation (2.2) may be written in a number of different variations, depending on which of the primary objectives are to be attained. Of the goals listed earlier, let us concentrate on the first two: economic efficiency and income redistribution. The systems approach to this problem considers the following elements. Let $n$ water resources projects have a span of $T$ years of economic life. Every year project $j$ ($j = 1, 2, \ldots, n$) generates $B_{jt}$ ($t = 1, 2, \ldots, T$)

gross benefits. During the same (*t*th) year, project $j$ costs $M_{jt}$ monetary units for its operation and maintenance. Also, project $j$ requires a total investment $K_j$ for its construction. Hence, in order to attain economic efficiency, the following criterion must be maximized [12].

$$Z = \sum_{j=1}^{n} \sum_{t=1}^{T} \frac{B_{jt} - M_{jt}}{(1+i)^t} - \sum_{j=1}^{n} K_j \qquad (2.3)$$

where $i$ is the prevailing interest rate.

This model represents a rather simplified version of reality, mostly because $B_{jt}$ represent only primary (direct) system benefits. However, very often water resources development generates opportunities of economic growth external to the water resource system itself. The benefits from such external opportunities are referred to as *secondary benefits* [9].

If the secondary benefits are introduced into the model, it will represent a different situation. For when we attempt to evaluate the desirable effects of a water resource system by taking into account *all* the benefits (primary and secondary), we account, in fact, for the total direct income generated by the project within the area it services. This situation can be handled in either of two ways: either maximize total income under the condition of economic efficiency, that is, maximize

$$Z = \sum_{j=1}^{n} \sum_{t=1}^{T} \frac{(B_p + B_s)_{jt} - M_{jt}}{(1+i)^t} - \sum_{j=1}^{n} K_j \qquad (2.4)$$

subject to

$$\sum_{j=1}^{n} \sum_{t=1}^{T} \frac{B_{pjt} - M_{jt}}{(1+i)^t} - \sum_{j=1}^{n} K_j \geqslant 0, \qquad (2.5)$$

where $B_p$ and $B_s$ are primary and secondary benefits, respectively; or maximize economic efficiency with the total income as a constraining condition, that is, maximize

$$Z = \sum_{j=1}^{n} \sum_{t=1}^{T} \frac{B_{pjt} - M_{jt}}{(1+i)^t} - \sum_{j=1}^{n} K_j \qquad (2.6)$$

subject to

$$\sum_{j=1}^{n} \sum_{t=1}^{T} \frac{(B_p + B_s)_{jt}}{(1+i)^t} \geqslant B_r, \qquad (2.7)$$

where $B_r$ is a specified level of benefit in the region $r$ under development.

Since the investments $K_j$ are usually made by national governmental agencies and the benefits accrue to fairly restricted regions, it is clear that the two models represented by equations (2.4) through (2.7) deal with the income redistribution of the region as viewed from a wider (national) perspective.

The models presented above, which can easily be recognized as linear programming models, make tacitly a very important assumption: the investments $K_j$ are not constrained by any budgetary limitations. In fact, this is seldom so. Regional development of water resources is a complex process lasting several years and requiring rather careful allocation of the available budgets. This introduces additional constraints into the model but, on the other hand, allows for the simultaneous evaluation of several (or many) projects which may be considered under the development program of the region.

Assume an $M$-year development plan. Under this plan, yearly budgets $D_m$, $m = i, 2, \ldots, M$, are provided for the water resources projects. Let there be $n$ projects under consideration, which can be constructed in yearly stages $x_{mj}$, $j = 1, 2, \ldots, n$. Since $x_{mj}$ can be only an integer ($0 \leqslant x_{mj} \leqslant 1$), the problem becomes one of linear integer programming [13]. If the yearly investment required for project $j$ is $d_{mj}$, the budgetary constraint can be written as

$$\sum_{j=1}^{n} d_{mj} x_{mj} \leqslant D_m. \qquad (2.8)$$

If we delve into this problem a little further, we see that an additional condition has to be satisfied: that is, stage $m$ in the construction of the project cannot be started before stage $m - 1$ has been completed. Thus

$$x_{m-1, j} - x_{mj} \geqslant 0. \qquad (2.9)$$

The model can be enlarged to consider competing (mutually exclusive) alternatives of development. Suppose, for example, that out of a group of projects $j \in J$ only one may be constructed. Then

$$\sum_{j \in J} x_j \leqslant 1. \qquad (2.10)$$

This model can further be refined to include cases where the unused budget in any one year can be carried over to the next year.

The principles of systems engineering have been applied to a wide variety of problems in the water resources field [14]. Of these, problems connected with aquifer management show perhaps the broadest range within which systems engineering was adapted and applied [15]. To illustrate these applications, three examples will be offered:

**1. Southern California**

Management of groundwater resources in Southern California for the purpose of supplying with water an extensive metropolitan area presents numerous problems of various degrees of complexity [16–19]. In this project, the underlying postulate is that the total usable water supply can be increased by coordinated operation of surface and underground water resources. Aquifers are, therefore, viewed as elements of larger systems of water supply, and their utilization has to be optimized before deriving conjunctive operating rules.

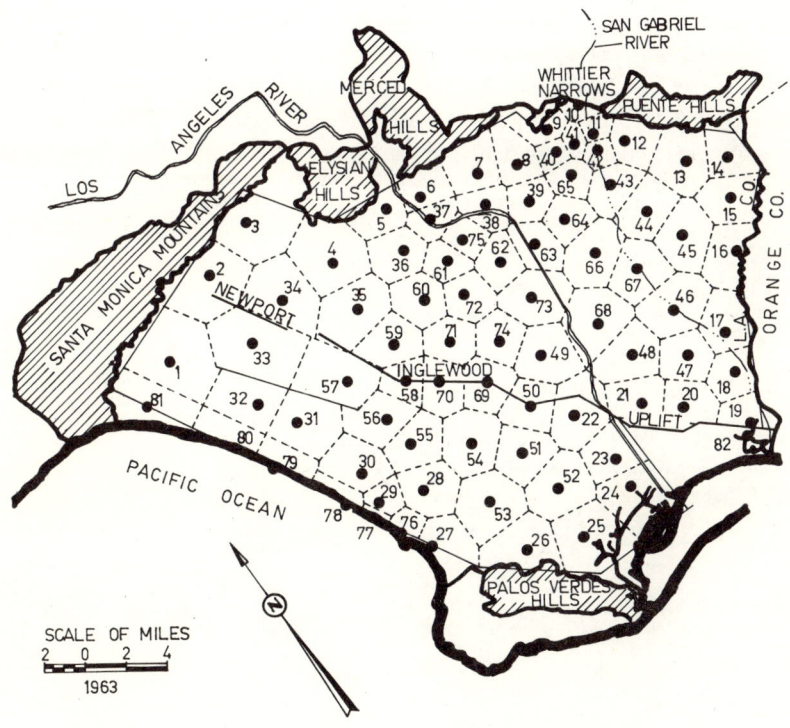

FIGURE 2.1. The Los Angeles groundwater basin (after [17]).

In the analysis of the aquifers operation, simulation was used for the derivation of operating policies. In order to set up the simulation model, however, certain hydrological parameters of the aquifers had to be determined quantitatively. For this purpose, a laboratory study based on field data was conducted. Considering the flow of water through porous media to be analogous to the flow of electricity through conductors, the transmissibility and storativity of the groundwater basin in its different sections were determined by means of an analog computer. Figure 2.1 shows the division of the Los Angeles basin into sections. The storativity of each such section was represented on the computer by a capacitance, while the transmissivities between adjacent sections were represented by resistances. The currents in the various branches of the analog network corresponded to flow rates of water, and the voltages to water level elevations. A typical resistor–capacitor network is given in Figure 2.2. The field data, consisting of rates of pumpage and recharge, were fed into the computer (by means of current generators) and the value of the resistors and capacitors were adjusted so as to yield the voltage drops corresponding to the measured water level elevations. At this stage, the electronic circuit developed into a network analyzer.

Having so determined storativity and transmissivity in different portions of the aquifer (two hydrological parameters that hardly lend themselves to

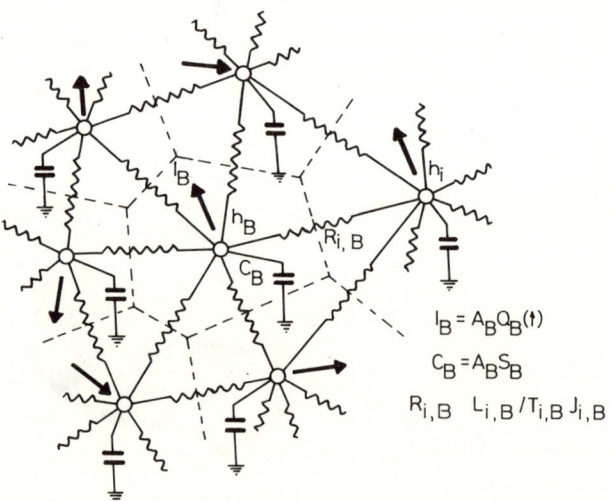

FIGURE 2.2. Typical resistor–capacitor network (after [17]).

direct quantitative measurement), the behavior of the aquifer was simulated on a digital computer using different schedules of pumping and recharge. Thus a number of operating policies were evaluated in terms of the dynamic response of the aquifer.

The results of these studies were used for the determination of the optimal operation rules for the coordination of surface and subsurface water resources and facilities. Again, a digital computer was used for the evaluation of a number of operating rules, and the policy having minimum annual costs was considered to be optimal.

**2. Indus Valley**

Part of the Indus river system was developed to form the largest irrigation scheme in the world. Approximately 16,000 km of canals had been installed to irrigate over 9,000,000 hectares (ha). This irrigation project covers the greater part of a vast plain covered with fine-textured alluvial soil overlaying a coarser subsoil extending tens of meters downward to the rock bottom of an ancient rift valley.

The development of the irrigation project began more than 80 years ago. Most of the canals were excavated through the surface soil to the more previous underlaying fine sand, so that a large proportion of the surface water diverted through these canals seeped underground. The subsoil, which forms an extensive aquifer, was continuously filled by the leaking irrigation canals, so that the groundwater table rose all the time. In many areas, this rise was estimated to be approximately 30 cm per year. The result was that in much of the Indus Valley the groundwater elevation was near the soil surface, which under the prevailing climatic conditions, caused an acute soil salinity problem. Recently, this problem became so serious that a major effort was undertaken for its analysis and solution [20–25]. An important part of this effort was taken by the hydrological studies made by the Harvard Water Resources Group [26].

The hydrological studies are focused on aquifer utilization and management, including mining of groundwater. The situation is shown diagramatically in Figure 2.3. The aquifer complex underlying the entire area is considered to be divided into two layers: the bottom layer, in which relatively saline water is found; and an upper layer through which the movement of higher quality water continuously recharging the aquifer takes place. This division indicates the necessity of operating each layer of the aquifer in a different

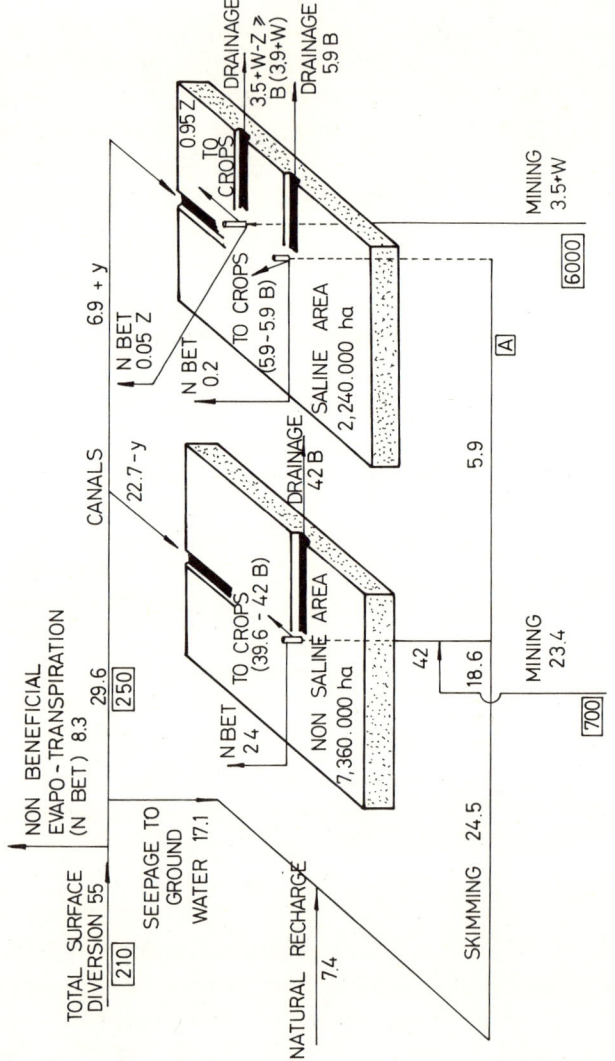

FIGURE 2.3. Schematic representation of the aquifer management problem in the Indus Valley (after [26]).

manner: the top layer is being "skimmed," thus providing relatively good quality water for irrigation; while the bottom layer is being "mined" for the purpose of generally lowering the water tables in the Indus Valley.

Recognizing that the aquifer is but one element in a rather complex system, we should also realize that its operation differs in relation to the other components of the system. Thus, dividing the entire irrigated land (9.6 million ha) into a nonsaline area (7.36 million ha) and a saline area (2.24 million ha), the utilization of groundwater and the operation of the aquifer is different in each of these two divisions. In both cases, a certain proportion $B$ of the pumped water has to be removed from the region through surface drainage in order to contribute to the lowering of the water tables and to alleviate the salinity problems. Furthermore, the pumped groundwater has to be diluted by higher quality surface (canal) water, in order to control the salt balance within the root zone of the irrigated lands.

Thus three nonnegative decision variables have been defined in the mathematical model used in the analysis of the Indus Valley studies:

$Y$ = flow of canal water diverted from the nonsaline to the saline area to dilute the pumpage, in $10^9$ m$^3$ per year;

$Z$ = the amount of saline groundwater to be diluted with surface water and applied to crops in the saline area, in $10^9$ m$^3$ per year;

$W$ = the rate of mining of groundwater in the saline area in excess of the rate of $3.5 \times 10^9$ m$^3$ per year required to prevent the movement of saline groundwater into the nonsaline area, in $10^9$ m$^3$ per year.

The optimization studies were carried out with a number of hydrological (and also economic) parameters, two of which are shown in Figure 2.3:

$A$ = concentration of total dissolved solids in the water recharging the aquifer in the saline area, in parts per million (ppm);

$B$ = fraction of groundwater to be pumped directly into surface drains and removed from the region.

In the Indus Valley studies, systems engineering was used as a problem-identification tool, rather than a problem-solving tool. Mathematical models were constructed for the various components of a complex hydroagronomic system, which were evaluated through simulation.

## 3. Israel

Many of the major groundwater aquifers in Israel are integrated operationally within the national water scheme. Here, too, the operational problems have quantitative as well as qualitative aspects.

The quantitative aspects refer to the functions of the aquifer as a source of water and as storage facility. In fact, some early analysis of the Israel Water Plan indicated plainly that in order to develop large quantities of water, storage space in excess of that available on the surface has to be utilized [27]. This additional storage space is provided, in part, by an extensive complex of aquifers, both in Turonian–Cenomanian limestone and in Pliocene–Pleistocene sandstone. However, in order to make best use of the underground storage, the pumpage from the aquifers has to be coordinated with releases of water from surface sources. A conceptual framework for the conjunctive operation of a surface reservoir and an aquifer (representing the entire hydrogeological complex) was proposed [28], as shown in Figure 2.4.

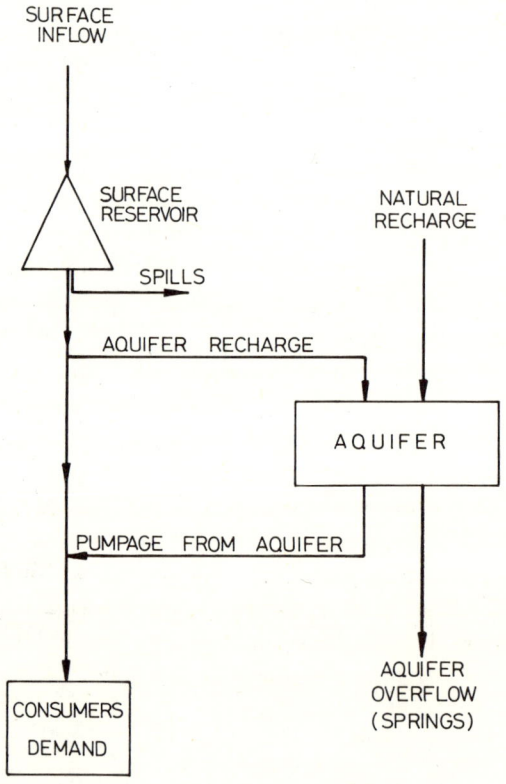

FIGURE 2.4. Schematic representation of a surface–groundwater system.

The qualitative aspects can be divided into two headings: (a) management of aquifers under conditions of relatively rapid salination; and (b) use of aquifers with high quality water in which more saline surface waters are stored.

One of the Pliocene–Pleistocene coastal aquifers in the southern part of Israel was investigated in more detail [29]. It was observed that the mineral content of the aquifer water was steadily increasing in time, the increase being estimated at more than 10 ppm of total dissolved solids per year. In order to utilize the groundwater after a certain salinity threshold were exceeded, two alternatives were studied: (a) desalination of the aquifer waters (through electrodialysis), as needed; and (b) importation of high quality water for diluting the local supplies.

The use of aquifers in conjunction with more saline surface water was analyzed in a general way [30]. The rather complicated field problem was reduced to a simpler physical formulation, in which a number of aquifers were lumped together into a single system component. The mathematical formulation referred to a sequential decision problem, which was analyzed through dynamic programming [31]. The state of the system at the outset of any stage was described by a three-dimensional vector showing the amount of water available in a surface reservoir, the amount of water in the aquifers, and the salinity of the surface water. Optimal operating policies were derived at monthly intervals, allowance being made for the stochastic characteristics of the inflows into the surface reservoirs.

To conclude this chapter, we emphasize again that systems engineering is, in fact, a modern elaboration of the classical scientific method. The various phases involved in the analytical process leading from the formulation of a problem to its solution and the implementation of the solution are more clearly defined through the systems approach. Mathematical techniques, collectively termed operations research, are used for the analysis and solution of problems. The application of systems engineering to water resources problems is only in its initial exploratory stage. Further research could improve and refine the analytical techniques used [32].

## REFERENCES

1 A. K. Biswas, "Basic Criteria in Water Resources Planning and Development," *Water and Water Engineering* **69**(1965), No. 838, 505.
2 A. F. Pillsbury, *Water Resources Center Annual Report*, Water Resources Center, University of California, Los Angeles, 1965.

3 A. D. Hall, *A Methodology for Systems Engineering.* Van Nostrand, Princeton, New Jersey, 1962.
4 R. L. Ackoff, S. K. Gupta, and J. S. Minas, *Scientific Method: Optimizing Applied Research Decisions.* Wiley, New York, 1962.
5 V. C. Hare, Jr., *Systems Analysis: A Diagnostic Approach.* Harcourt Brace Jovanovich, New York, 1967.
6 J. R. Dixon, *Design Engineering.* McGraw-Hill, New York, 1966.
7 M. M. Hufschmidt, "Field-Level Planning of Water-Resource Systems," *Water Resources Research* **1**(1965), 147.
8 V. T. Chow, "System Design by Operations Research," in *Handbook of Applied Hydrology* (V. T. Chow, ed.), Section 26-II. McGraw-Hill, New York, 1964.
9 J. V. Krutilla and O. Eckstein, *Multiple Purpose River Development.* Johns Hopkins Press, Baltimore, Maryland, 1958.
10 A. Maass, M. M. Hufschmidt, R. Dorfman, H. A. Thomas, Jr., S. A. Marglin, and G. M. Fair, *Design of Water-Resource Systems.* Harvard University Press, Cambridge, Massachusetts, 1962.
11 N. Buras, "Conjunctive Operation of Dams and Aquifers," *Proc. Amer. Soc. Civil Engineers* **89**(1963), No. HY6, 111.
12 A. Maass and M. M. Hufschmidt, "Report on the Harvard Program of Research in Water Resources Development," in *Resources Development: Frontiers for Research* (F. S. Pollak, ed.). University of Colorado Press, Boulder, Colorado, 1960.
13 G. Hadley, *Nonlinear and Dynamic Programming.* Addison-Wesley, Reading, Massachusetts, 1964.
14 N. Buras, Dynamic Programming in Water Resources Development," *Advances in Hydroscience* **3**(1966), 372–412.
15 N. Buras, "Systems Engineering and Aquifer Management," *Symposium of Haifa*, Publication No. 72, pp. 466–473. International Association of Scientific Hydrology, Haifa, 1967.
16 L. C. Fowler, "Ground-Water Basin Operation," *Proc. Amer. Soc. Civil Engineers* **90**(1964), No. HY4, 51.
17 H. N. Tyson, Jr., and E. M. Weber, "Computer Simulation of Ground-Water Basins," *Proc. Amer. Soc. Civil Engineers* **90**(1964), No. HY4, 59.
18 R. Y. D. Chun, L. R. Mitchell, and K. W. Mido, "Optimum Conjunctive Operation of Ground-Water Basins," *Proc. Amer. Soc. Civil Engineers* **90**(1964), No. HY4, 79.
19 V. E. Valantine, "Optimum Ground-Water Basin Management," *Proc. Amer. Soc. Civil Engineers* **90**(1964), No. HY4, 97.
20 The White House—Department of Interior Panel on Waterlogging and Salinity in West Pakistan, *Report on Land and Water Development in the Indus Plain*, The White House, Washington, D.C., 1964.
21 M. Ghulam, "Waterlogging and Salinity in the Indus Plain: A Critical Analysis of Some Major Conclusions of the Revelle Report," *Pakistan Development Review* **4**(1964), No. 3.
22 R. Dorfman, R. Revelle, and H. A. Thomas, Jr., "Waterlogging and Salinity in the Indus Plain: Some Basic Considerations," *Pakistan Development Review* **5**(1965), No. 2, 331.

23 A. Nazir, "Waterlogging and Salinity in the Indus Plain: Comment," *Pakistan Development Review* 5(1965), No. 2, 371.
24 J. M. Eaton, "Waterlogging and Salinity in the Indus Plain: Comment," *Pakistan Development Review* 5(1965), No. 2, 381.
25 M. Ghulam, "Waterlogging and Salinity in the Indus Valley: Rejoinder," *Pakistan Development Review* 5(1965), No. 2, 393.
26 H. A. Thomas, Jr., and R. P. Burden, *Indus River Basin Studies*, Harvard University, Cambridge, Massachusetts, 1965 (mimeographed).
27 B. V. Dean and N. Buras, *Effective Control and Economic Scheduling of Lake Kinneret Pumping Operations*, Publication No. 282, Tahal, Tel Aviv, 1963.
28 N. Buras, "Conjunctive Operation of a Surface Reservoir and a Ground Water Aquifer," *Symposium on Surface Waters*, Publication No. 63, pp. 492–501. International Association of Scientific Hydrology, Haifa, 1963.
29 H. Lahmi and E. Gazith, *Desalination and Mixing of Water in the Coastal Plain for the Maintenance of Constant Salinity Levels*, Tahal Report, 1963 (in Hebrew).
30 N. Buras, "Operation of a Complex Water-Resources Utilization System," *Intern. Conf. Water for Peace*, Washington, D.C., 1967.
31 R. E. Bellman and S. E. Dreyfus, *Applied Dynamic Programming*. Princeton University Press, Princeton, New Jersey, 1962.
32 P. O. Wolf, "Notes on the Management of Water Resources," *J. Inst. Water Engineers* 20(1966), No. 2, 95.

# Chapter 3

# PROBLEMS IN WATER RESOURCES ENGINEERING

## A. DEVELOPMENT PROBLEMS

### 1. Introduction

Regional planning and development includes the activities connected with planning and design of water resource systems. The necessity of integration of these systems within broader regional development plans has long been recognized and repeatedly stressed [1]. Nevertheless, development of water resources presents a number of aspects that are specific enough to warrant a more extensive discussion. Two of these will be presented in the sections that follow.

The development of water resources (or, for that matter, of any natural resource) can be formulated in terms of matrix transformations. If we can describe the occurrence of water resources and their properties by a matrix, the development process is simply transforming this matrix into another one which is related to the objectives of the development project [2]. The properties of the naturally occurring water may be described by a matrix $S$ consisting of three vectors: $L$ (location), $T$ (quantitative availability in time), and $Q$ (quality). Thus

$$S = \begin{bmatrix} L \\ T \\ Q \end{bmatrix}. \qquad (3.1)$$

The location vector $L$ has three kinds of components, $x$, $y$, and $z$, which determine the spatial extent of the resource. In the case of surface waters, $x$ and $y$ represent the actual location of the dam or of the diversion, the $z$ coordinate showing the amount of pumpage necessary to deliver the water to where it is needed, or the difference in elevation through which flowing water can generate power. When dealing with groundwater, it is conceivable that the location of the resource is to be represented by a family of $x_i$, $y_i$, and $z_i$ coordinates, which will define the extent and the thickness of the aquifers:

$$\mathbf{L} = (x_1, x_2, \ldots, x_n; y_1, y_2, \ldots, y_n; z_1, z_2, \ldots, z_n). \tag{3.2}$$

The time vector $\mathbf{T}$ consists of parameters of the probability distributions of the quantitative occurrence of the resource in time: means $\mu_i$, standard deviations $\sigma_i$, serial correlation coefficients $\rho_i$, coefficients of symmetry $\alpha_i$, of kurtosis $\beta_i$, and so on, of periodical flows. If the periods under consideration are years, then

$$\mathbf{T} = (\mu, \sigma, \rho, \alpha, \beta). \tag{3.3}$$

When shorter periods of time are considered (months, for example),

$$\mathbf{T} = (\mu_1, \ldots, \mu_{12}; \sigma_1, \ldots, \sigma_{12}; \rho_1, \ldots, \rho_{12}; \alpha_1, \ldots, \alpha_{12}; \beta_1, \ldots, \beta_{12}). \tag{3.4}$$

The quality vector $\mathbf{Q}$ has also a number of elements, such as $q_b$, the biological quality; $q_m$, the mineral quality; $q_h$, caloric quality; and so on:

$$\mathbf{Q} = (q_b, q_m, q_h, \ldots). \tag{3.5}$$

The development of water resources amounts, in fact, to the transformation of the original state matrix $\mathbf{S}$ into another matrix $\mathbf{S}^*$ in which the elements of the vectors $\mathbf{L}$, $\mathbf{T}$, and $\mathbf{Q}$ assume desired (or desirable) values:

$$\mathbf{S}^* = \begin{bmatrix} \mathbf{L}^* \\ \mathbf{T}^* \\ \mathbf{Q}^* \end{bmatrix}. \tag{3.6}$$

The vector $\mathbf{L}^*$ indicates the new location at which water is desired; $\mathbf{T}^*$ pertains to the time distribution of the quantities in demand for water and water derivatives; and $\mathbf{Q}^*$ represents the quality standards at which water is to be supplied. The values of $\mathbf{L}^*$, $\mathbf{T}^*$, and $\mathbf{Q}^*$ may be constant or they may change. The vector $\mathbf{T}^*$ in particular may vary, especially when dealing with an increasing demand.

The ascertainment of the matrix $\mathbf{S}$ involves ordinarily a great deal of research and investigation in natural sciences: geology, hydrology, meteorology, oceanography, and others. On the other hand, the matrix $\mathbf{S}^*$ requires for its evaluation research and analysis in economics, sociology, and other social sciences.

The transformation of matrix $S$ into $S^*$ is achieved by

$$S^* = \theta S. \tag{3.7}$$

The transforming matrix $\theta$ is in fact the system that enables the development, utilization, and control of the resource so that the objectives of the development project are achieved. The matrix $\theta$ is usually divided into two major submatrices: $\theta_1$, which is composed of the design parameters of the physical components of the system ("hardware"); and $\theta_2$, which contains the operational aspects of the system ("software"). Thus

$$\theta = (\theta_1, \theta_2). \tag{3.8}$$

The analysis and solution of equation (3.7) is the realm of water resources engineering.

## 2. Engineering Problems

As already mentioned, three kinds of problems have to be solved from an engineering point of view when planning the development of water resources: (i) the determination of the optimal dimensions of the various components of the system; (ii) the optimization of the scale of development, that is, of target outputs, or the extent of the area serviced by the system; (iii) the establishment of optimal operating policies for the system.

Denoting by $X_1, X_2, X_3$, the solutions of these problems, respectively, and the benefit connected with these solutions by $B$, then

$$B = f(X_1, X_2, X_3). \tag{3.9}$$

In engineering terms, the problem of development of water resources is to maximize $B$ subject to a number of technological, natural, economical, and other constraints. However, in addition to $X_i$, which represent those aspects of the situation that we can (or hope to) control, there are environmental factors $Y_j$, which are uncontrollable. Thus a more complete representation of the engineering problems in water resources development is [3]

$$B = f(X_i, Y_j). \tag{3.10}$$

Many different problems in water resources engineering were recently discussed in literature [4, 5]. However, some of the most pressing problems will be mentioned briefly below.

(i) *The Hydrological Process.* Since water resources engineering deals with the development and utilization of a renewable natural resource, it is of paramount importance to have a complete understanding of the natural cyclical process involved. Even though some significant advances were made in this direction [6], fundamental physical processes in meteorology are yet to be elucidated. A thorough knowledge of conditions affecting the formation of droplets in clouds may afford important tools for the control and inducement of precipitation.

Both surface and subsurface hydrology are in need of further study. Research in stream hydrology has adapted a number of modern techniques to the analysis of surface hydrological problems [7], and groundwater investigations have relied considerably on geology [8]. Nevertheless, much remains to be done in this direction. The recent establishment of a committee on mathematical models in hydrology within the International Association of Scientific Hydrology, with its working groups on stochastic and parametric hydrology, holds considerable promise for the future.

(ii) *Hydraulic Engineering.* Until recently, dams and other structures were built at the best sites with the most favorable foundation conditions, and used the most suitable materials. It is needed to expand the research in the fields of engineering geology, soil mechanics, and construction materials.

(iii) *Urban Hydrology.* The rapid urbanization of many regions of the world signals the necessity of understanding the changes in the hydrological process due to the extensive areas with paved roads and having collection systems for rainwater. The influence of urbanization on hydrology is apparent on surface flows as well as on aquifer response, such as in the coastal plain of Israel.

(iv) *Evaporation and Transpiration.* Of the water reaching the soil as precipitation, about 10% is lost, on the average, through evapotranspiration. The problems in this group are manifold: development of plant varieties necessitating reduced amounts of moisture; improved control and management of the moisture regime in the root zone of the soil (irrigation and drainage); evaporation reduction of free water surfaces.

(v) *Water Desalination.* As the conventional sources of water are being developed and as demand increases, attention is focused on nonconventional sources [9]. The main engineering problems in this group are those of increased efficiency from the point of view of energy input, and improved engineering design for lower investment and reduced running costs.

(vi) *Oceanography.* No list of engineering problems in water resources engineering would be complete without mentioning the oceans, the most important link in the hydrological cycle. Oceanographic research is only beginning now, but it opens continuously new possibilities in the development and beneficial utilization of oceans.

## 3. Economic Problems

Economic problems are intimately connected with the engineering aspects of all stages of water resources development. The feasibility of an engineering design is a function mostly of the objectives to be attained, the rate of interest on capital, the conditions of repayment, and social values as reflected by welfare economics. Some of the main problems are as follows.

(i) *The Optimizing Criterion*. Whether the goals of development are set by the elected representatives of the people under strong executive leadership, or through a bargaining process among various pressure groups, the decision-making echelon must specify the optimizing criterion. This may be expressed as maximum economic efficiency [10], maintenance of full employment in a given region, maximum return per cubic meter of water developed, and so on. In any case, many subsidiary problems arise right at the outset in the development of water resources, mainly because of insufficient data. It is the responsibility of the water resources engineer to gather, process, present, and interpret all available information so as to enable the decision-making body to define the optimizing criterion.

(ii) *Evaluation of Benefits*. In general, benefits can be classified as *tangible* (direct or indirect) or *intangible*. Even the evaluation of direct benefits present problems. Consider, for example, flood control, or inland navigation. Population growth and urban and industrial development in a river basin require that water resources development projects be planned also with respect to the mitigation of flood damages or for the improvement and maintenance of river navigation. More studies are needed to develop methods for better evaluation of the effects of these activities [11].

Much more acute is the problem of evaluating intangible benefits, such as recreation [12]. Increasing population, leisure, incomes, mobility, and urbanization create an increasing demand for recreation. It is only recently that recreation has been recognized as a water derivative, similar to flood control, hydro power, and navigation. The absence of a market (in the traditional sense) for recreation presents some specific problems in the economics of water resources development and utilization, which have not yet been investigated beyond an exploratory stage.

(iii) *Water Reallocation and Transfer*. In planning regional development, the role of water resources in the overall production process is analyzed often with the aid of an input–output matrix of the Leontieff type. This analysis brings out the regional economic interdependencies existing between water and various sectors of economic activity. For example, it is desirable to increase the irrigation water supply to a certain area in a region. One of the alternatives could be the transfer of certain amounts of water from other areas within the region. This transfer has not only a direct bearing on production processes in the areas in question, but also requires the investment of other regional resources (capital, labor, building materials, etc.) in order to effectuate it. The Leontieff matrix is only a partially satisfactory tool for the analysis of these situations. Its main shortcoming resides in the fact that it is almost incapable of dealing with dynamic situations or with stochastic processes.

(iv) *Waste Disposal Problems*. It appears that water quality will shortly become one of the major water resource problems in Israel. Elsewhere, it is already approaching critical dimensions, causing a great deal of concern [11]. The analysis of this problem necessitates the identification and evaluation of various means of quality control. The various alternatives have to be balanced among themselves and against damages caused by low quality water.

## 4. Management Problems

Sound development of water resources cannot ignore the management aspect, after the system is designed and built. Management is not synonymous with operation: whereas operation is related primarily to changes induced in the "hardware" components of the system in order to attain a certain objective, "management" implies also the social setting or organization within which operation takes place. Some of the management problems needing attention are discussed briefly below.

(i) *River Forecasting for Water Resources Management*. As more structures are constructed for more purposes, the need for improved river and reservoir forecasting methods is being felt. This need becomes more acute as the number of agencies in the management of flow and storage increase. But even in countries such as Israel, where water resources are managed with a high degree of interinstitutional coordination, forecasting methods need refinement. For this purpose, more complex and realistic hydrological models have to be developed.

(ii) *Flood Damage Management*. Human use of flood plains carries within itself the risk of damages. The problem of flood damage management has been recently reviewed [13], with special emphasis on the questions still outstanding. First of all, it is very important to collect data on flood losses. In this way, the range of mean annual values can be determined more accurately. Next, the relationship between flood characteristics and flood losses should be investigated. Finally, these studies should lead to the development of better methods of comparing the feasibility of different land uses within the same flood plain. These problems of flood damage management have to be investigated in both urban and rural reaches.

(iii) *Institutional Problems*. Comprehensive water resources development within a hydrological basin very often involves decisions to be taken by several agencies. For example, water supply planners, a regional drainage district, and a waste water disposal system may be active in the same basin. The problem is, then, what mechanism should be evolved by which these different decision makers (some of which may be public, others private) can be induced to undertake such measures as will lead to the overall optimal solution?

(iv) *Policy Problems*. Policy issues in water resources development have been studied intensively in the last two decades. Problems that seem to have major significance in the future were examined recently [14]. The most significant are (1) how to achieve a rational public understanding of water resource use problems and opportunities; (2) how to achieve a reasonable approximation of a social optimum through a public decision-making process; (3) how to change a policy to accord with the changing environment within which water resources activities are undertaken.

We point out that solutions of these problems involve a large infusion of value judgments. For this reason, research in this area should be encouraged to the same extent as in the purely engineering technological field: the more the issues about which such judgments must be made are illuminated by accurate data, the better such judgments will tend to be.

## B. DESIGN PROBLEMS

### 1. Comprehensive Water Resources Planning

During the last decade, a striking development occurred in the design of water resources systems: concepts and techniques of operations research and systems analysis were adapted and applied to the design process. The major significance of this fact is that the use of these concepts and techniques requires the contributions of many disciplines from the physical and social sciences. As a result, the problems of design have a very distinct interdisciplinary quality and their analysis has to be carried out in a systems context.

It seems then that comprehensive water resources planning focuses on the processes used by man to control and adapt the water resources for his use [15]. These processes are (1) collection and analysis of basic data; (2) planning; (3) construction and development; and (4) management. The problems, which require a substantial research effort for their satisfactory solution, are presented in accordance with the major steps of the planning process: (1) establishment of the design objectives; (2) translation of the objectives into design criteria; and (3) use of the design criteria for the maximum realization of the objectives.

(i) *Establishing Objectives of Design.* Important problems in need of research concern the ability of the governmental process to arrive at the required decisions on objectives. Although the main disciplines involved are political science and economics, the statement of the objectives has an important effect on the technological aspect of the detailed design of individual projects in a comprehensive plan.

(ii) *Transforming Objectives into Design Criteria.* The two main problems relating to criteria requiring further research are (1) the use of alternative costs as a substitute for benefits in plan formulation; and (2) the relation of water resources planning to planning for urban and suburban land use, highways, recreation, and so forth.

(iii) *Preparation of the Regional Water Resource Plan.* This step of the planning process encompasses the full range of the systems analysis activity, as described in Chapter 2. Some of the more pressing problems are reviewed briefly below.

First, techniques for regional economic projections have to be investigated. These include regional input–output models, water uses by major industries, alternative water pricing, and analysis of the relative sensitivity of water demands to changes in levels of economic activity by sectors as compared to changes in technology, water pricing, and management.

Second, further research is needed on the derivation of water resource benefit functions, especially for nonmarketable effects, such as flood-control measures and recreation.

Third, much has to be done toward a more accurate derivation of the technological function. Synthetic streamflow generation has to be adapted to many different types of streams and to different patterns of water resource development. Also urgently needed is the development of operational flow models based on relatively abundant meteorological data, instead of scarce hydrological information.

Fourth, methods applicable to preliminary screening of system alternatives must be improved and refined. These methods must necessarily take into account the physical and economic-social linkages between individual system units. Specifically, simulation and optimization method (e.g., linear and dynamic programming) should be emphasized.

Fifth, suitable techniques have to be developed for detailed studies leading to optimization. We must not only devise more complex simulation techniques, but also develop analytical approaches.

Finally, the system design process as a whole has to be advanced so as to keep in step with the increasing complexity of planning for comprehensive water resources development.

Some advanced thinking on comprehensive water resources planning was recently formulated and published [16].

## 2. Basic Data for Design

In addition to the general problem of the *amount* of basic data necessary for design that has to be gathered in the field, three important aspects require investigation in depth [4]:

(i) *Uncertainty*. Uncertainty is primarily of two kinds: (a) that connected with the randomness of the hydrological process itself, and (b) that which stems from difficulties in estimating future demands for water, future technological developments, or future political decisions. The procedures developed for dealing with consequences of hydrological uncertainty—specifically, synthetic hydrology—will be touched upon later. As for the other aspects of uncertainty, a very important problem is that of incorporating flexibility in water resources systems. Whether flexibility is achieved by stage construction, by modifications of original facilities, or by changing operating procedures, criteria have to be formulated for optimizing flexibility.

(ii) *Relative Accuracy of Data*. The importance of this aspect of basic design data cannot be overemphasized. No matter how refined the analytical methods used in systems design, the outcome cannot be more precise than the data involved. Hence studies are needed regarding the relative accuracy of data required for various types of water resources systems. In this way, a better allocation of the resources available for planning can be made. Also, more rational decisions can be made with respect to the degree of refinement of the overall planning effort.

(iii) *Synthetic Hydrology*. The analysis and evaluation of streamflow data for the purpose of designing water resource systems made extensive use of the calculus of probabilities. However, averages and variances of hydrological data were hardly sufficient for this purpose: the pattern (or sequence) of flows also had to be evaluated. A particular field hydrological trace was thus considered to be a sample of size one (taken from an infinite population), and efforts were made to estimate additional items from this population. This activity became known as "synthetic streamflow data generation" or, in short, synthetic hydrology. Later, it was suggested [17] that the term "operational hydrology" would be more appropriate. Although synthetic (operational) hydrology can be useful in both analytical and simulation models, it has been used almost exclusively in the latter [18]. The main problem in synthetic hydrology is, therefore, its incorporation in analytical models. The solution of this problem will make a substantial contribution toward the improvement of rational design of water resource systems.

## 3. Stochastic Problems in the Design of Reservoirs

A storage reservoir is one of the most important elements in a water resource systems. The design of reservoirs must take into account the stochastic aspect of the inflows. The design of a water-storing reservoir is not unlike that of an inventory system [19]. The main difference between the two is that in an inventory system the input is controllable and the output is random, whereas in a water storage reservoir the converse obtains: inflows are stochastic and discharges are made, generally, following an operating rule.

This situation is bound to affect significantly the design of reservoirs, and for this reason the problem of water storage behind dams was investigated in considerable theoretical detail [20].

Storage reservoirs can be classified into two groups: independent and dependent reservoirs [21]. An independent reservoir is a storage facility operated independently of any other reservoir. A dependent reservoir is a storage facility designed and operated in conjunction with other reservoirs.

Three distinct cases can be defined in the latter category: (a) the inflow into the reservoir depends partly or entirely on the regulated outflow of upstream reservoirs; (b) the dependent reservoir is operated in conjunction with downstream reservoirs; (c) the releases from the dependent reservoir are conditioned upon the operation of reservoirs in an adjacent river basin.

Much of the theoretical analysis was done with regard to independent reservoirs. When stochastic elements were considered, the flow regulation by the reservoir was often assumed to be a linear relationship between inflow and outflow [22]. However, the linear assumption is seldom tenable, and it is necessary to investigate the design of reservoirs when nonlinear relations are assumed between the stochastic inflow and the regulated outflow.

Of more practical interest is, of course, the case of dependent reservoirs. The design of multistructure (and multipurpose) systems consisting of several interrelated reservoirs is one of the cardinal problems today in water resources engineering. The analysis of such systems with inclusion of stochastic elements has hardly been attempted. A relatively simple case is now under investigation [23]. In this case, a watershed in the semiarid climatic zone has streams that are dry in summer. It is desired to utilize the winter flows as sources of water supplies. The simplifying assumption—quite tenable—is that the reservoirs on the main stream and/or on the tributaries do not have to provide for overyear storage. Obviously, the problem becomes much more complex when perennial streams are involved.

## 4. Water Resources Planning in Metropolitan Areas

A basic problem in designing water resource systems in urban areas is that of the interrelationships between spatial patterns of land utilization on one hand, and water supply and waste disposal facilities on the other [4]. This is a complex problem, giving rise to a number of questions. For example, does extensive urban development generate increased costs in water supply and waste disposal? In other words, is there an optimal size of metropolitan area with regard to water supply and waste disposal costs? Also, is there any price mechanism for the reduction of peak demands in water systems? Some of these questions and others connected with the planning the development of an urban area *ab initio* were considered recently [24].

A specific problem related to water resources planning in metropolitan areas is currently under study in Israel [25]. Sand dune areas of the coastal plain are prospective sites for urban development. At the same time, they can be used successfully as spreading grounds for the recharge of the underlying Pleistocene aquifer. The water used for aquifer replenishment is that from winter floods carried by streams crossing the area. Settling basins and spreading grounds are important components of systems utilizing flood waters for groundwater recharge. If these components happen to be in areas zoned for urban development, they can be integrated within the metropolitan planning as recreational facilities, mostly as "blue spots" in public parks. If so, two important problems arise: (a) considering the relatively high price of urban land, what is the optimal size of these facilities? (b) If these blue spots have to be maintained as long as possible through the long dry summer of the semiarid zone, how should they be operated? Here, as in many other problems in water resources engineering, the design aspect is hardly separable from the operating policy.

## C. OPERATIONAL PROBLEMS

### 1. General Comments

As has already been mentioned in this chapter, the optimal development of water resources is conditional also on the establishment of appropriate operating policies. By *operating policy* we understand a time schedule of releases from reservoirs, of pumpages from aquifers and/or reservoirs, and of aquifer recharge operations. It is clear that not all water resource systems will necessitate the three kinds of operations. At any rate, the establishment of such schedules, which indicate quantities of water to be affected through the action of the manager at defined points in time, is an important problem in water resources engineering. The problem is, of course, the selection of the operating procedure that will best achieve the stated objective(s) of the development scheme.

It was customary for a long time to establish operating rules on the basis of personal judgment alone [26]. No alternative procedures were tested. The rules were, generally, simple: (1) store all inflow unless needed to meet a target output; (2) when available, release water from storage to fulfill immediate needs; (3) study all damaging floods on record in the flood control analysis. As water resource systems became more complex, however, it became apparent that operating procedures consist of three (and possibly four) kinds of decisions [27]. Storage and release of water must be apportioned among (1) reservoirs; (2) purposes; (3) time periods; and possibly (4) depth layers from a reservoir to provide water of required quality. Furthermore, it was recognized that operating procedures are sequential decision problems and have to be treated as such [28]. These problems take account of the fact that a decision is likely to have consequences that extend over a considerable period of time. A decision regarding the release of water from a reservoir, for example, is of this nature. The consequences of such a decision are not the single yield of that release, but also the yields from a sequence of releases following the first one. These yields are not exactly predictable, each being a variable with a probability distribution that depends also on the original decision.

The analysis of operating procedures is performed with the help of certain methods of applied mathematics, such as inventory theory, queuing theory, and dynamic programming. There is a pressing need to adapt these and other analytical techniques to operational problems in water resources engineering, and to improve and refine methods already adapted. A review and evaluation of several analytical techniques used in water resources engineering is presented in the next chapter.

It would be impossible to discuss operational problems without mentioning flexibility. Once an operating rule has been established and adopted, some degree of flexibility must be allowed. We should remember that a policy is a sequence of decisions, and that these decisions are made in face of uncertainty: hydrological uncertainty, or economic uncertainty, or both. Better methods for decision making under uncertainty have to be developed.

Operational problems have been discussed in detail at a seminar on river basin planning held in the United States [16].

## 2. Operating Rules

The establishment of guideposts for the operation of storage facilities is one of the crucial problems to be solved in water resources engineering. It is, in fact, an effort to overcome the discrepancy so often observed between the desirable amounts of water at a certain point in time and the naturally available quantities at the same point. The operating rules then become indicators for the decisions connected with keeping water in storage or releasing it.

Clearly, these decisions are made in the face of uncertainty. Attempts were made to provide confidence limits for the operation of storage facilities [29]. The active storage in a reservoir was divided into three regions (see Figure 3.1): the upper region (region I), within which water has to be abstracted from the reservoir at the full capacity of the abstracting facilities

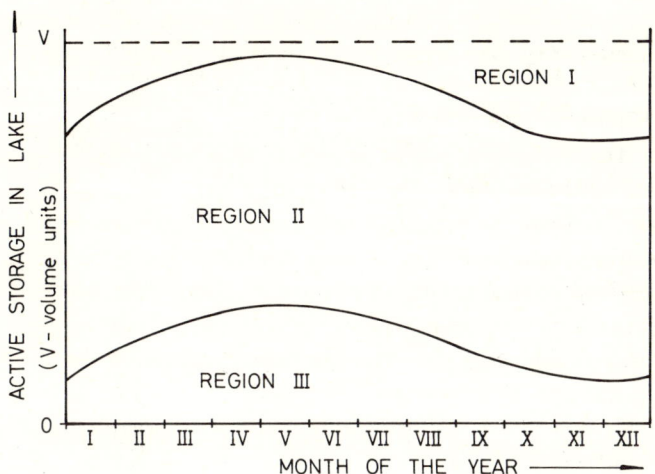

FIGURE 3.1. Control chart for Lake Kinneret.

in order to minimize the likelihood of loss of water through spills from this reservoir; the middle region (region II), within which water can be pumped from the reservoir in a most economic manner for the satisfaction of current needs; the lower region (region III), within which pumping has to be discontinued, to minimize the likelihood of shortages of water. The lines dividing these regions represent given probabilities of spills or of shortages. Obviously, this is only a first try for the analytical derivation of storage control limits, and much further work is necessary.

If in the case mentioned above the criteria for the establishment of operating rules were defined in relatively simple terms (minimize likelihood of spills, or of shortage), a more complex situation obtains when reservoirs have to be operated in connection with more heavily industrialized regions. There, it is necessary to take into account the water quality downstream from the point of storage, as affected by the industrial wastes discharged into the stream [4]. In such cases, storage reservoirs are also operated for what is known as "low flow augmentation." The low flow augmentation is nothing more than water quality improvement under the conditions sketchily described earlier. Within this context, it is necessary to develop water quality improvement benefit functions that will become criteria for operating policies. These functions should be related to various water quality parameters (chlorides, alkalinity, hardness, total dissolved solids, heat, turbidity, etc.) of importance to various uses: agricultural, industrial, municipal, and recreation.

A special kind of operating rules are those connected with hydro power production. It is clear that the objective of operating a hydro system is the maximization of net benefits. The complication arises from the fact that the same commodity (power) is sold at two prices, dependent upon time: firm power, which commands a higher price and which has to be supplied in quantities defined contractually; and dump power, which has a lower price. The problem is almost always considered in deterministic terms [30], firm power being a fixed number. It should be realized, however, that firm power is, in fact, a probabilistic quantity. True, the probability of delivering it is very high (perhaps 0.95, or better), yet this aspect has not been fully analyzed.

The most complex operating rules are those connected with multipurpose reservoirs. In simple terms, we can state that the objective of operating such systems is to manipulate supply so as to reduce competition among demands and to increase complementarity among them [31]. The principal demands are irrigation, electrical power production, flood prevention, municipal and industrial water supply, navigation, waste carrying, and recreation. This is a field within which much still remains to be investigated, analyzed, and improved, whether considering deterministic situations or introducing stochastic elements.

## 3. Optimizing Techniques

In order to derive an optimal procedure for the operation of a water resource system, usually three avenues are open: (a) application of analytical techniques; (b) use of simulation; (c) a combination of these two methods.

The analytical techniques can be classified in a number of ways. For convenience, these would be classified into linear programming algorithms and dynamic programming algorithms. Mention should be made also of the possibility of combining linear and dynamic programming in order to analyze large and complex systems.

Fairly complex linear programming algorithms were used to analyze operational problems of reservoirs, where the analysis was based on the theory of probability. Simpler formulations of the problem considered only the serial correlation between inflows [32], while more sophisticated approaches considered also the Markovian process linking the amounts stored and quantities released from reservoirs during two adjacent periods of time [33]. Although linear programming contributed substantially toward the development of optimal operating policies, it did not solve the basic problem of the operation of water resource systems. By the nature of things, the operation of such systems is a process in which decisions are taken at discrete points in time (sometimes, also in space), not only in the face of uncertainty but also as a response to changing conditions. Since many linear programming algorithms exist in other fields, it would be profitable to continue the effort in investigating them with the view of adaptation to water resources engineering.

The applications of dynamic programming to water resources development were reviewed elsewhere [2]. The dynamic programming algorithms are of several types [34]. For the deterministic approach, we can (i) recursively work forward in time from the start, or (ii) work backward from a given end and condition to the start [35, 36].

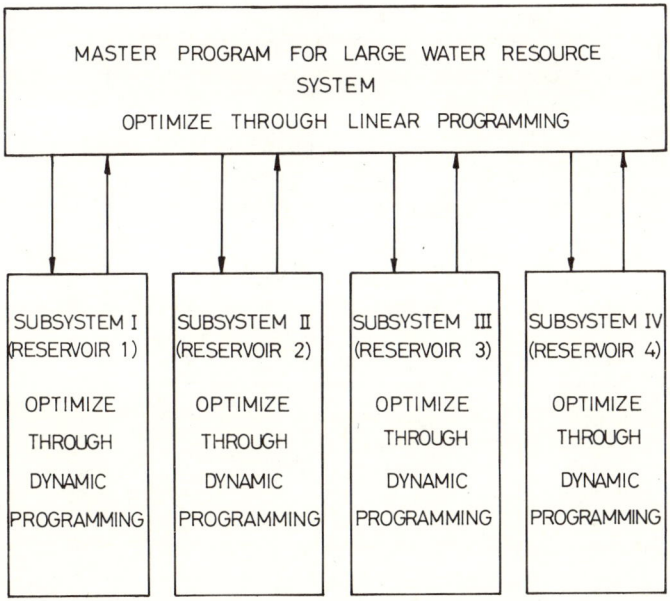

FIGURE 3.2. Schematic representation of a large water resource system optimized through linear and dynamic programming and applying the decomposition principle.

In the stochastic version, we can assume a discrete probability distribution for the inflows and also (iii) work forward as in (i) [37]; or (iv) work backward as in (ii) [38]. Dynamic programming shows much promise in the analysis and solution of operational problems.

Interesting attempts were made in combining linear and dynamic programming, for the purpose of deriving optimal operating rules for complex water systems [39]. A system under consideration is the California Water Project. In a simplified version, four major reservoirs were to be operated so as to

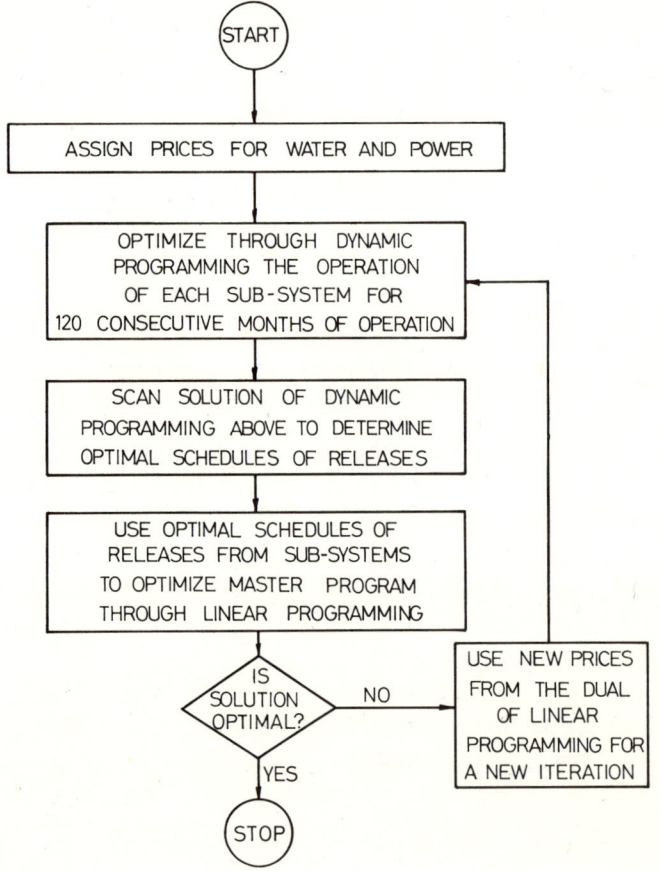

FIGURE 3.3. Flow chart for optimization of large water resource system.

supply water to a demand region and to generate hydro power. Two questions had to be answered: (1) Given a hydrological record of 10 consecutive years (the worst in a 35-year trace), what is the maximum firm power and class I water that can be produced? (2) Having established the firm power and class I water, how should the system be operated in order to maximize net revenues? The analysis applied the decomposition principle postulated by Dantzig [40], which is applicable to situations in which the management of large industrial enterprises has to maximize overall profits from a number of quasi-independent plants. The general structure of the problem, as formulated through a combination of linear and dynamic programming, is shown schematically in Figure 3.2. A generalized flow chart for computation is shown in Figure 3.3. Some progress was made in the computational aspect of this approach [41]. Much, however, remains to be done in perfecting the analysis and solution of such large-scale complex problems.

A technique that finds increased use in the analysis of water resource problems is simulation. Simulation in itself is not optimization, but it can be used effectively to search out local optima in given situations [42]. Some techniques have already been adapted for the design of water resource systems [18], others are being currently investigated for the selection of near-optimum (or quasi-optimum) operating rules for complex systems [43]. This area is still largely unexplored and has many possibilities for developing simulation models of systems too complex for a compressed mathematical formulation, or for which analytical methods may not exist.

A combination of analysis and simulation was successfully tried recently [34]. An optimal operating rule was derived analytically for a reservoir, based on a simulated hydrological record. Simulation and analysis can well support one another in dealing with complex water resource systems. So far, only a small beginning has been made, with much more to come if such systems are to be operated at or near optimum.

## D. RECAPITULATION

Water resources engineering has been developed to cope with complex systems, in which technology and economics, physical sciences and social sciences, affect their design and operation. The function of water resources engineering is to make available (in time, space, and quality) a water resource of given properties (as occurrence in time, space, and quality). Referring to equation (3.7), we could define availability $A$ as the ratio of $\mathbf{S}^*$ to $\mathbf{S}$:

$$A = \frac{S^*}{S}. \qquad (3.10)$$

Problems encountered in water resources engineering can be divided into three groups: (a) problems connected with the planning process; (b) those connected with the design of water resource systems; and (c) problems arising out of the operation of the systems. Some of these problems were analyzed and satisfactory practical solutions offered; many more remain to be formulated, analyzed, and solved.

The problems connected with the planning process are related to the variable $X_2$ in equation (3.9). The question here is to what extent should one plan the development of the regional water resources? This is a rather difficult question, which has, as a rule, engineering, economic, and management aspects.

The design problems relate to variable $X_1$ in equation (3.9). The question of determining the optimal dimensions of the various components of a water resource system has to be answered in the general context of comprehensive water resources planning. Three particular aspects have been emphasized: (a) how much data (and how accurate) are necessary for the various types of water resource systems; (b) the stochastic problems arising in the design of storage facilities; (c) the particular problems generated by the rapid urbanization of a region.

Operational problems correspond to the variable $X_3$ in equation (3.9). Roughly put, the question is as follows. Assuming that the optimal dimensions of the various components of the system have been established and that the target outputs have been optimized, how is the system to be operated (manipulated, utilized) such that a given criterion will have an optimum value? Here we may detect two major aspects: (a) the establishment of an optimal policy for the operation of the system; (b) the optimization technique applicable to the specific problem.

This list of problems in water resources engineering is far from being exhaustive. It only serves to highlight some of the main questions that arise in most cases of planning and designing a water resource system. The current practice, whether in Israel, California [44], or the Indus Valley, bears witness to this.

**REFERENCES**

1 B. T. Bower, "Symposium: Water Resources Research: Introduction," *Natura Resources J.* **5**(1965), No. 2, 218.

## Problems in Water Resources Engineering

2  N. Buras, "Dynamic Programming and Water Resources Development," *Advan. Hydroscience* **3**(1966), 372–412.
3  R. L. Ackoff, S. K. Gupta, and J. S. Minas, *Scientific Method: Optimizing Applied Research Decisions*. Wiley, New York, 1962.
4  B. T. Bower, "Some Important Research Problems in the Water Resources Field," *Natural Resources J*. **5**(1965), No. 2, 286.
5  W. C. Ackerman, "Main Research Problems in Hydrology and Engineering," in *Water Research* (A. V. Kneese and S. C. Smith, eds.), pp. 495–501. Johns Hopkins Press, Baltimore, Maryland, 1966.
6  N. H. Crawford, "Some Observations on Rainfall and Runoff," in *Water Research* (A. V. Kneese and S. C. Smith, eds.), pp. 343–353. Johns Hopkins Press, Baltimore, Maryland, 1966.
7  J. A. Harder, "Analog Models for Stream Hydrology," in *Water Research* (A. V. Kneese and S. C. Smith, eds.), pp. 413–422. Johns Hopkins Press, Baltimore, Maryland, 1966.
8  R. J. M. De Wiest, *Geohydrology*. Wiley, New York, 1965.
9  J. W. McCutchan and W. M. Pollit, "Sea Water Conversion: Its Potential and Problems," in *Water Research* (A. V. Kneese and S. C. Smith, eds.), pp. 423–437. Johns Hopkins Press, Baltimore, Maryland, 1966.
10  J. V. Krutilla and O. Eckstein, *Multiple Purpose River Development*. Johns Hopkins Press, Baltimore, Maryland, 1958.
11  A. V. Kneese, "Economic and Related Problems in Contemporary Water Resources Management," *Natural Resources J*. **5**(1965), No. 2, 236.
12  J. L. Knetch and R. K. Davis, "Comparisons of Methods for Recreation Evaluation," in *Water Research* (A. V. Kneese and S. C. Smith, eds.), pp. 125–142. Johns Hopkins Press, Baltimore, Maryland, 1966.
13  G. F. White, "Optimal Flood Damage Management: Retrospect and Prospect," in *Water Research* (A. V. Kneese and S. C. Smith, eds.), pp. 251–269. Johns Hopkins Press, Baltimore, Maryland, 1966.
14  I. K. Fox, "Policy Problems in the Field of Water Resources," in *Water Research* (A. V. Kneese and S. C. Smith, eds.), pp. 271–289. Johns Hopkins Press, Baltimore, Maryland, 1966.
15  M. M. Hufschmidt, "Research on Comprehensive Planning of Water-Resource Systems," *Natural Resources J*. **5**(1965), No. 2, 223.
16  C. E. Kindswater, ed., *Organization and Methodology for River Basin Planning*. Georgia Institute of Technology, Atlanta, Georgia, 1964.
17  M. B. Fiering, "Synthetic Hydrology: An Assessment," in *Water Research* (A. V. Kneese and S. C. Smith, eds.), pp. 331=341. Johns Hopkins Press, Baltimore, Maryland, 1966.
18  M. M. Hufschmidt and M. B. Fiering, *Simulation Techniques for Water-Resource Systems*. Harvard University Press, Cambridge, Massachusetts, 1966.
19  G. Hadley and T. M. Whitin, *Analysis of Inventory Systems*. Prentice-Hall, Englewood Cliffs, New Jersey, 1963.
20  P. A. P. Moran, *The Theory of Storage*. Methuen, London, 1959.
21  V. M. Yevdjevich, "Stochastic Problems in Design of Reservoirs," in *Water Research*

(A. V. Kneese and S. C. Smith, eds.), pp. 375–411. Johns Hopkins Press, Baltimore, Maryland, 1966.
22. M. J. Melentijevich, "Storage Equations for Linear Flow Regulation," *J. Hydrology* **4**(1966), No. 3, 201.
23. S. Meyers, *Mathematical Models for Optimal Water Development in Small Agricultural Watersheds*, M. S. thesis, Technion, Haifa, 1969.
24. D. K. Todd, ed., *Impact of Water on Land*, Report No. 9, Water Resources Center, University of California, Los Angeles, 1966.
25. J. Cahana, *The Interrelation between Urbanization and Water Resources Development in a Dune Area of the Coastal Plain in Israel*, Ph. D. thesis, The Hebrew University, Jerusalem, 1969 (in preparation).
26. W. W. Reedy, "Conventional Methods of Analysis," in *Design of Water-Resource Systems* (A. Maass *et al.*, principal authors), pp. 299–323. Harvard University Press, Cambridge, Massachusetts, 1962.
27. B. T. Bower, M. M. Hufschmidt, and W. W. Reedy, "Operating Procedures: Their Role in the Design of Water-Resource Systems by Simulation Analyses," in *Design of Water-Resource Systems* (A. Maass *et al.*, principal authors), pp. 443–458. Harvard University Press, Cambridge, Massachusetts, 1962.
28. R. Dorfman, "Basic Economic and Technologic Concepts: A General Statement," in *Design of Water-Resource Systems* (A. Maass *et al.*, principal authors), pp. 88–158. Harvard University Press, Cambridge, Massachusetts, 1962.
29. B. V. Dean and N. Buras, *Effective Control and Economic Scheduling of Lake Kinneret Pumping Operations*, Tahal Report No. 282, Tel Aviv, 1963.
30. E. Kuiper, *Water Resources Development*. Butterworth, London, 1965.
31. E. A. Ackerman and G. O. G. Löf, *Technology in American Water Development*. Johns Hopkins Press, Baltimore, Maryland, 1959.
32. E. H. Lloyd, "A Probability Theory of Reservoirs with Serially Correlated Inputs," *J. Hydrology* **1**(1963), No. 1, 99.
33. J. Bernier, *La Gestion des Réservoirs à Buts Multiples*, Report HYD-66/No. 11, Electricité de France, 1966.
34. G. K. Young, Jr., *Techniques for Finding Reservoir Operating Rules*, Ph. D. thesis, Harvard University, Cambridge, Massachusetts, 1966.
35. W. A. Hall, "Aqueduct Capacity under an Optimum Benefit Policy," *Proc. Amer. Soc. Civil Engineers* **87**(1961), No. IR3, paper No. 2923.
36. W. A. Hall, "Optimum Design of Multiple-Purpose Reservoir," *Proc. Amer. Soc. Civil Engineers* **90**(1964), No. HY4, 141.
37. N. Buras, "Conjunctive Operation of Dams and Aquifers," *Proc. Amer. Soc. Civil Engineers* **89**(1963), No. HY6, 111.
38. J. D. C. Little, "The Use of Storage Water in a Hydroelectric System," *J. Operations Research Soc. Amer.* **3**(1955), 187.
39. N. Buras, *The Optimization of Large Scale Water Resource Systems: Operational Aspects*, Report to Water Resources Center, University of California, Los Angeles, 1965.
40. G. B. Dantzig, *Linear Programming and Extensions*. Princeton University Press, Princeton, New Jersey, 1963.

41 S. C. Parikh, *Linear Dynamic Decomposition Programming of Optimal Long Range Operation of a Multiple Multi-Purpose Reservoir System*, Operations Research Center Report ORC 66-28, University of California, Berkeley, **1966**.
42 R. R. Berman, "Simulation as a Problem-Solving Technique," *Proc. Amer. Soc. Civil Engineers* **93**(1967), No. PL1, 21–45.
43 Tahal, Water Planning for Israel, Ltd., Tel Aviv, private communication, 1967.
44 J. S. Bain, *Northern California Water Industry*. Johns Hopkins Press, Baltimore, Maryland, 1966.

Chapter 4

# SOME PROBABILISTIC METHODS APPLIED IN WATER RESOURCES

## A. STATISTICAL APPLICATIONS

A distinguishing feature of water resource system design is the stochastic or random nature of streamflow, groundwater natural recharge, and precipitation. In addition, the smaller the time unit considered, the greater the serial correlation between the magnitudes of sequential events. Is is possible that random fluctuations occur relative to some definite trend or periodicity over long periods. Seasonal periodicity is a natural occurrence, hence the use of the Rippl diagram or mass curve [1] for reservoir analysis is a gross simplification of reality. The chances of streamflow exhibiting a similar sequence of discharges in the future as in the recorded past is small indeed. There is a slim chance that the reservoir size chosen on the basis of the Rippl analysis will provide maximum regulation of streamflow. Furthermore, the extension of the analysis to more than one structure in a series is doubtful indeed. Neither is this analysis suited to problems involving overyear storage, nor the determination of flexible operating procedures dependent on current reservoir contents. Hence the attempts to formulate statistical approaches to this problem.

A first attempt at statistical analysis was made by Hazen [2], who constructed Rippl diagrams for each year's streamflow record, thus deriving a probability distribution of required storage. Problems deriving from the mass curve in the form of the maximum range of streamflows were investigated by Hurst [3], Feller [4], and Anis and Lloyd [5]. The range $R$ is defined as the accumulated differences between the maximum and minimum values of a residual mass curve of a stream for a given period of $N$ years. This is equivalent to the capacity of a never-fail reservoir, which would never have spilled nor run dry during the $N$ years of record, having provided a constant draft equal to the mean annual streamflow. In general, the long-term average $E(R)$ was found to be

## Some Probabilistic Methods Applied in Water Resources

$$E(R) = As\sqrt{N} \tag{4.1}$$

where $A$ is a constant, $s$ the sample standard deviation of the annual discharge, and $N$ the length of record.

Actual measurements indicated that $N^{3/4}$ rather than $N^{1/2}$ fit the field data. Perhaps this is due to the correlation between annual streamflows. Sophisticated statistical analyses of the range concept have been made, and its relation to hydrological problems has been shown [6, 7]. The utility of this approach is that of defining an upper limit for the reservoir size, subject to the dependability of available data.

It may be shown, however, that the means of groups of streamflows that include a nonrandom assortment of individual events will have a greater spread or deviation than if the group consisted of random events alone [8]. The effect of persistence greatly affects the upper limit of storage capacity. Due to this effect, a much longer record is needed to estimate the range of storage required for water supply [9]. It was shown that due to the variability of means, complete regulation yielding the mean annual flow of a stream is impossible to achieve. Indeed, successive increments to reservoir capacity add increasingly smaller increments to regulated streamflow. Furthermore, the existence of losses, such as evaporation, make increases in reservoir capacity futile, as regulation is hardly improved above a certain point. Such considerations are of paramount importance when optimum designs, in the economic and physical sense, are sought: there is a limit to the practical size of reservoirs.

An application of some of the foregoing concepts [10] was used for a reservoir whose annual inflow distribution could be approximated by the form

$$X = \bar{X} + K_\alpha \sigma, \tag{4.2}$$

its discharge rule being of the form

$$D = a + kS. \tag{4.3}$$

Here $X$ is the magnitude of annual inflow; $\bar{X}$ the mean annual value of inflow; $K_\alpha$ a frequency factor giving the probability $\alpha$ that streamflow is $\geqslant X$ (this is the standard normal deviate $t$ in the case when inflows are normally distributed); $\sigma$ the standard deviation of inflows; $D$ the annual discharge from the reservoir; $S$ the reservoir storage at the end of the year; and $a$ and $k$ constants.

When no serial correlation exists, the storage capacity $S_1$ required for a given probability of spillage $\alpha$ is

$$S_1 = K_\alpha \left[ \frac{\sigma^2 - \sigma_{d_1}^2}{\sigma_{d_1}} \right] \qquad (4.4)$$

where the standard deviation of annual discharges

$$\sigma_{d_1} = \sigma \left( \frac{k}{2+k} \right)^{1/2}. \qquad (4.5)$$

If the serial correlation between annual inflows can be described by the simple model

$$r_n = r a^{n-1} \qquad (4.6)$$

where $r_n$ is the serial correlation coefficient of lag $n$, $a$ a constant, and $r$ the serial correlation coefficient of lag 1, then the storage required is

$$S_2 = K_\alpha \left[ \frac{c^2 \sigma^2 - \sigma_{d_2}^2}{\sigma_{d_2}} \right] \qquad (4.7)$$

where

$$\sigma_{d_2} = \sigma \left( \frac{k}{2+k} \right)^{1/2} \left[ 1 + \frac{2r}{(1+k-a)} \right]^{1/2} \qquad (4.8)$$

and

$$c = \left[ 1 + \frac{2r}{(1+k-a)} \right]^{1/2}. \qquad (4.9)$$

Due to the nonrepresentativeness of historical mass curves, a methodology combining mass curves and frequency curves has been used for estimating storage requirements [11–13]. The results are presented in the form of curves that show how much gross yield can be sustained in Kansas rivers with varying sizes of reservoirs for several selected probabilities of deficiency. These graphs also make possible the analysis of operating these reservoirs for flood control.

Low flow frequency curves were used to compute mass diagrams on a probability basis. From these diagrams, which are nonsequential mass curves, outflow was computed for various storage values on a specified risk basis. The methodology consists of deriving low flow frequency curves having durations of 6, 12, 24, 48, and 96 months as parameters. Choosing any selected probability, a mass curve is constructed using the corresponding duration and low flow values. The mass curve is then analyzed using various constant draft values to yield a curve of sustained gross yield versus maximum storage requirements. The procedure may be repeated for all critical recurrence intervals and covers low flow periods of up to 8 years. The same procedure was used to find storage needed to regulate floods with frequency curves for durations up to 6 months. In both cases, results were extended on a regional basis. A graphical procedure [13] was developed to allow for evaporation losses in estimating required storage for low flow periods.

A similar methodology has been used and extended for the analysis of low streamflow sequences and reservoir design in Illinois [14]. It was shown how, for a given reservoir size, the safe draft rate is determined for given frequencies and durations, thus determining how long the reservoir would be subject to drawdown. Evaporation losses were accounted for by considering the variability of evaporation and rainfall for various periods, ranging from 1 to 60 months. Maximum net evaporation was computed by subtracting minimum precipitation (for each period) from maximum pan evaporation during the same interval, both values having the same recurrence interval. It was assumed that evaporation and rainfall values were closely correlated under drought conditions. The results were subsequently used to derive the net draft rate and its duration sustainable for any reservoir capacity. Net yield frequency curves were integrated so as to determine the risk level connected with a given reservoir size and mean draft. Mean recurrence intervals (MRI) were converted to the design period $n$ by means of the relation

$$n = \frac{\log P_n}{\log[1 - (1/\text{MRI})]} \qquad (4.10)$$

where $P_n$ is the probability of not exceeding an event having a mean recurrence interval of (MRI) in $n$ years. The curve was used to derive a net yield having an acceptable risk of failure, thus greatly improving the engineer's choice of a dam size and of an operating procedure for the drought period.

## B. STOCHASTIC PROCESSES AND WATER STORAGE

The methods just discussed have several limitations. The low flow sequences, unless derived synthetically, do not represent all possible combinations of the streamflow regime. The longer the record used, the greater appears to be the variation in the volume of storage required for streamflow regulation [15]. Furthermore, the methodology assumes that dams are full when a low flow sequence begins, or empty before a flood period occurs. This may not necessarily be always true and depends on past management of the reservoir. More comprehensive data on the performance of reservoir systems are required, especially if draft must be varied to suit monthly fluctuations in streamflow and demand.

The points of interest in practical storage problems are usually (a) probability distribution of water volumes stored in a reservoir at given times, for given conditions; (b) probabilities that a given volume of water in storage is not exceeded in a given time; (c) probability that the volume in storage reaches a maximum (or a minimum) in a given period; (d) probability that the reservoir remains full or empty for a given time; (e) the stationary probabilities of storage volumes for given operating rules. These probabilities may be derived using a Markov process analogy or queuing models [16–18]. Although some notable practical applications can be pointed out [19–22], this analytical approach stemmed largely from an interest in the formidable mathematical and probabilistic problems involved [10].

The basic model, based on an analogy with inventory problems and Markov processes, requires that a continuous inflow having a fixed probability distribution be fed into a reservoir of fixed finite capacity, from which a continuous constant draft is removed. Equations are set up for determining the probability distribution of reservoir contents. In the simpler models a random inflow is assumed: the quantity flowing into the dam in any interval of length $t$ has the same probability distribution as, but is independent of, the quantity flowing in during any other nonoverlapping interval of the same duration. An important point is to relate the reservoir contents at any given time to its contents in the succeeding interval, taking into account the inflow and outflow during the interval and allowing for the possibility of zero draft when the reservoir is empty and/or for spillage. Computationally, the integral equations formed by the continuous model are not readily tractable, so that practical considerations of finding a numerical solution require the use of discrete intervals and of quantities leading to a system of difference equations. These are solved by matrix inversion: the accuracy of the solution, or size of matrix, depends solely on the capability of the electronic computer used.

It may be shown [17] that the assumption of independent inflows leads to a sequence of mutually independent variables; that is, the time sequence of values of reservoir contents form a Markov Chain of the form

$$P\{X_r = x_r | X_{r-1} = x_{r-1}\}. \qquad (4.11)$$

This means that the probability $(P)$ of an event $X_r$ having a magnitude $x_r$ in the $r$th interval depends only on the magnitude of the event in the preceding interval; that is, $X_{r-1} = x_{r-1}$. Thus, if the reservoir contents at the beginning and end of the $t$th interval are denoted by $Z_t$ and $Z_{t+1}$, respectively, a transformation of reservoir content (state) must satisfy the relation

$$Z_{t+1} = Z_t + X_t - D_t \qquad (4.12)$$

where $X_t$ is the inflow into the reservoir during period $t$ and $D_t$ is the discharge from it during the same period. Care must be taken to allow for boundary effects (i.e., when the dam is full or empty). A concise method of displaying the relationship between $Z_t$ and $Z_{t+1}$ for various values of $X_t$ would be to carry out the computations for given $Z_t$ and $D_t$, then use the results to form a matrix with columns labeled by values of $Z_t$, rows by $Z_{t+1}$, and entries consisting of the corresponding values of $X_t$.

The operating equations may be written in the form $Z_{t+1} = Z_t + Y_t$, where $Y_t$ is the net accepted input (positive) or net delivered output (negative) [16]. Since $Z_t$ itself depends on $X_{t-1}$ and the only value affecting $Y_t$ is $X_t$, it is clear that $Z_t$ is independent of $Y_t$; whence

$$\begin{aligned} P\{Z_{t+1} = r\} &= P\{Z_t + Y_t = r\} \\ &= \sum_s P\{Z_t = s\} P\{Y_t = r - s\} \\ &= \sum_s a_{rs} P\{Z_t = s\}. \end{aligned} \qquad (4.13)$$

Now $Y_t = r - s$ precisely when $Z_t = s$ and $Z_{t+1} = r$, that is, when $X_t$ has the value (or set of values) entered in the column labeled $Z_t = s$ and the row labeled $Z_{t+1} = r$. The value of $a_{rs} = P\{Y_t = r - s\}$ is therefore given by the probability that $X_t$ has the corresponding value. In practical analysis, the values of $X_t$ in the matrix are replaced by the corresponding transition probabilities $a_{rs}$. If the state of the reservoir at $t = 0$ ($Z_{t=0} = r$) is known and the initial state probability vector is

$$\mathbf{P}_0 = \begin{bmatrix} P\{Z_{t=0} = 0\} = 0 \\ P\{Z_{t=0} = 1\} = 0 \\ \vdots \\ P\{Z_{t=0} = r\} = 1 \\ \vdots \\ P\{Z_{t=0} = n\} = 0 \end{bmatrix}; \qquad (4.14)$$

and if the $n \times n$ transition matrix (where $n$ is the number of states of $Z_t$ and $Z_{t+1}$) is represented by $\mathbf{Q}$, then

$$\mathbf{P}_1 = \mathbf{Q} \cdot \mathbf{P}_0. \tag{4.15}$$

Here $\mathbf{P}_1$ is the probability vector of admissible states of given $\mathbf{P}_0$. Similarly

$$\mathbf{P}_{t+1} = \mathbf{Q} \cdot \mathbf{P}_t = \mathbf{Q}^2 \cdot \mathbf{P}_{t-1} = \mathbf{Q}^3 \cdot \mathbf{P}_{t-2} \cdots = \mathbf{Q}^t \cdot \mathbf{P}_0. \tag{4.16}$$

Continuing in this manner, the distribution of $P\{Z_t = r\}$ can be found.

Although it is not obvious, it may be shown [17] that, ultimately, for sufficiently large values of $t$, the value of $\mathbf{P}_{t+1}$ differs by a negligible amount from $\mathbf{P}_t$; that is, the solution converges to a limiting form such that

$$\mathbf{P}_{t+1} \cong \mathbf{P}_t. \tag{4.17}$$

This solution represents a set of stationary probabilities that are not affected by the initial state of the reservoir.

The foregoing method has been demonstrated using analytical solutions [21–24], and the solution offers information as to the long-term operation of a reservoir. In some cases convergence may be reached within the economic life of the reservoir; in others, convergence takes a longer time. Hence the necessity of studying the transient nature of the Markov process represented by the reservoir model. This is of particular importance if the operation of a reservoir is to be studied during a low flow sequence when the initial state (or probabilities thereof) is known.

The transient behavior may be studied by a generating function or a $z$ transform [25]. If

$$\mathbf{P}_{t+1} = \mathbf{Q} \cdot \mathbf{P}_t = \mathbf{Q}^t \cdot \mathbf{P}_0 \tag{4.18}$$

and if the $z$ transform of the vector $\mathbf{P}_t$ is represented by the symbol $\pi(\mathbf{z})$, then equation (4.18) becomes

$$z^{-1}[\pi(\mathbf{z}) - \mathbf{P}_0] = \mathbf{Q} \cdot \pi(\mathbf{z}). \tag{4.19}$$

Through rearrangement, equation (4.19) becomes

$$\pi(\mathbf{z}) = (\mathbf{I} - z\mathbf{Q})^{-1} \cdot \mathbf{P}_0 \tag{4.20}$$

where $\mathbf{I}$ is the identity matrix. The solution of all transient problems is contained in the matrix $(\mathbf{I} - z\mathbf{Q})^{-1}$. For a complete solution of any transient problem, the rows of $(\mathbf{I} - z\mathbf{Q})^{-1}$ must be weighted by the initial state probabilities, summed, and then an inverse transform taken of each element in the resulting matrix. Therefore, if the matrix $\mathbf{H}_t$ is the inverse transform of $(\mathbf{I} - z\mathbf{Q})^{-1}$ such that $\mathbf{H}_t = \mathbf{Q}^t$, then

$$\mathbf{P}_t = \mathbf{H}_t \cdot \mathbf{P}_0. \tag{4.21}$$

The matrix $\mathbf{H}_t$ is a response matrix made up of a stochastic submatrix $\mathbf{S}$, whose rows are identical with those of the stationary state probability vector, and a transient submatrix $\mathbf{T}_t$, which is a function of $t$, so that

$$\mathbf{H}_t = \mathbf{S} + \mathbf{T}_t. \tag{4.22}$$

As $t$ becomes larger, $\mathbf{T}_t \to 0$ and the elements of $\mathbf{S}$ are the stationary probabilities required. It should be noted that the $ij$th element of $\mathbf{H}_t$ represents the probability that the system will occupy state $j$ at time $t$, given that it occupied state $i$ at $t = 0$.

The foregoing method contains no internal optimizing procedure, so that the optimal size of the structure and its operating policy must be chosen beforehand. The choice of the optimal draft and reservoir size is often based on a subjective judgment concerning the probability of spills or emptiness. A constant draft is not essential, so that a policy of releases depending on $Z_t$, $X_t$, or $Z_t + X_t$ can be stipulated [19]. In this case the probability distribution of $Z_t$ determines that of $D_t$ [10], so the expected discharge can be determined.

A practical example using the foregoing reservoir model incorporates an operating rule that is a function of available water in storage [20]. The choice between alternative dam sizes depends on maximum release and on the recurrence interval of a "lean year" (less than maximum demanded draft released). In addition, evaporation losses are included, which are a function of storage. The choice of an optimal dam size and release rule is made from a table of possible reservoir sizes (net of evaporation losses), maximum releases, mean storage, mean draft, and mean recurrence interval of lean years. It was shown that regardless of dam size chosen, the mean draft remained constant. Increasing the reservoir size gave rise to an increase in mean storage, while mean draft remained the same: the advantage of increasing the dam size (with a particular maximum release) is solely to lengthen the expected period of return of the lean year.

If economic data are available, the present value of benefits may be calculated. In the transient case, an expected value for each time period is calculated from the distribution of $Z_t$ and brought to the present value. However, the expected present value of net benefits does not yield any information about the variability of net benefits that might be expected during the economic life of the structure [26]. The probability distribution of discharges may be used to calculate the standard deviation of discharges. The latter are used to plot indifference curves for the purpose of choosing the optimal design [26].

Problems related to flood damage or inability to supply water during low flow periods are analogous to an insurance situation [26, 27]. A method of overcoming risks associated with uncertainty has been suggested in the form of cost of uncertainty, which must be included in the costs of the project. It is assumed that an equalization fund is established when the structure is completed: this fund makes up the deficit between expected benefits and real income during lean years, while the surplus above expected benefits is used to replenish the fund during "good years." However, it is unwise to set up a fund equal to the cost of the project if insurance is sought against the worst imaginable sequence of "bad years"; for this purpose the chance that the fund be exhausted is set at an arbitrary confidence level. When the size of the fund has been computed for each alternative design, it can be added to costs, so that the design having the largest present value of net benefits may be chosen. The expression derived for the size $F$ of the fund is given [26] by

$$F = \frac{t_\alpha \sigma}{\sqrt{2r}} \qquad (4.23)$$

where $t_\alpha$ is the normal deviate with probability $\alpha$ of being exceeded; $\sigma$ the standard deviation of the single-year outcome distribution; and $r$ the rate of interest earned by the equalization fund. This method has been used for predicting uncertainties of flood damage when designing flood-proofing measures in an urban flood plain [28].

A disadvantage of the cost of uncertainty concept as outlined above lies in the assumption of a normal distribution of damages. This distribution is not necessarily true, especially in the case of rare occurrences, such as floods, which tend to assume an exponential or gamma distribution. A method of deriving the cost of uncertainty depending on skew distributions has been demonstrated for flood damage [27]. The general method relies on the use of the risk concept [27, 29]. A generalization of the Poisson process yields the total damage over the economic life of the project when spills or shortages of water cause varying amounts of damage. It may be shown [27, 15] that the probability $F(D_m, T)$ that the total damage will not exceed a critical value $D_m$ in a given period $T$ is given by

$$F(D_m, T) = \sum_{n=0}^{\infty} \frac{(\lambda T)^n}{n!} \int_0^{D_m} [f(D)]^{n^*} dD \qquad (4.24)$$

where $\lambda$ is the probability of a spill or draft below the required amount in any single unit time period and $[f(D)]^{n^*}$ the probability that $n^*$ exceedances together cause damage $D$. Solutions of $[f(D)]^{n^*}$ are available [27] for various damage distributions. If the average and standard deviation of damage are known, equation (4.24) forms a useful method for evaluating alternative designs. By a trial-and-error procedure, a value of $D_m$ can be found such that $F(D_m, T) = \alpha$, where $\alpha$ is an arbitrarily set confidence limit. Then an equalization fund equal to the expected total damage (or costs) $D_m$ during the period $T$ will be sufficient in all periods of length $T$, with probability $1 - \alpha$.

It may be seen that, provided that the number of alternatives is not too large and if computation is feasible by available computers, reasonable methods for choosing alternative designs exist. Fairly realistic models of reservoir design and operation are available, so that reasonable choices can be made. Although the inflow probability distributions used as input need not be known with a high degree of certainty, it is important to differentiate between flow regimes during different seasons or months in a given water year. This is particularly obvious in semiarid regions, where entirely different release policies may be required for different times of the year. If a two-season model is assumed (summer and winter), the probability distribution of admissible states at the end of one season becomes the initial state distribution of the following one [30].

In order to derive the stationary input distribution for $t$ summers $\mathbf{P}_t^{(1)}$, equation (4.16) yields

$$\mathbf{P}_t^{(1)} = \mathbf{Q}_1 \mathbf{P}_{t-1}^{(1)}, \qquad (4.25)$$

where $\mathbf{Q}_1$ is the transition matrix for the summer season. Hence

$$\mathbf{P}_t^{(1)} = \mathbf{Q}_1^t \mathbf{P}_0^{(1)} = \mathbf{B}_1 \mathbf{P}_0^{(1)}. \qquad (4.26)$$

For the winter season

$$\mathbf{P}_t^{(2)} = \mathbf{Q}_2^t \mathbf{P}_0^{(2)} = \mathbf{Q}_2^t \mathbf{P}_t^{(1)} = \mathbf{B}_2 \mathbf{P}_t^{(1)}. \qquad (4.27)$$

Substituting equation (4.26) in (4.27) yields

$$\mathbf{P}_t^{(2)} = \mathbf{B}_2 \mathbf{B}_1 \mathbf{P}_0^{(1)}. \qquad (4.28)$$

Given a water year of $s$ seasons,

$$\mathbf{P}_t^{(s)} = \mathbf{B}_s \mathbf{B}_{s-1} \cdots \mathbf{B}_1 \mathbf{P}_0^{(1)} = \mathbf{C} \mathbf{P}_0^{(1)}. \tag{4.29}$$

The foregoing method was applied in practice for comparing pump capacities and probability of emptiness using various drafts for an off-channel reservoir [31]. The multiseason concept may also be extended to models in which the seasons are of unequal length [31, 32]. In a specific case [31], where the serial correlation was low and negligible, the model allowed fewer state variables, reducing the matrix from $11 \times 11$ to $6 \times 6$. Frequently distributions were derived on the basis of increments and decrements of storage obtained from a residual mass diagram. The method is of importance, as most rivers do not exhibit seasonal variations beginning on a specific date. A decision criterion used in these models was probability of emptiness.

When using seasonal models, the assumption of independence of streamflow during adjacent seasons is not valid in many cases. Serial correlation and persistence become less negligible as unit time intervals are decreased. If the serial structure of inflows is such that it can be reasonably approximated by a Markov chain [33], a natural extension of the probability routing method results in a sequence of reservoir content distributions having Markovian properties. The degree of accuracy of the results using discrete distributions depends on the computing facilities available. A model having independent inflows requires $n + 1$ equations for a solution if reservoir volume is approximated by $n$ admissible states. If the serial structure results in an inflow distribution having $a$ values, the Markovian input model requires the solution of $(n + 1)a$ equations.

The general theory of Markovian inputs was applied to storage problems in a simple model having a three-valued input distribution [34, 35]. The essential requirement is that the model be set up in terms of a joint distribution of reservoir contents $Z_t$ and inflow $X_t$ at time $t$. For each $t$, $X_t$ is influenced by $X_{t-1}$, and $Z_t$ by both $Z_{t-1}$ and $X_{t-1}$, $X_t$ being the input in the ensuing interval $(t, t + 1)$. The bivariate process is Markovian with the probability

$$P\{Z_{t+1} = r, X_{t+1} = r'\}$$
$$= \sum_{s,s'} P\{Z_{t+1} = r, X_t = r' | Z_t = s, X_t = s'\} P\{Z_t = s, X_t = s'\} \tag{4.30}$$

where $P\{Z_{t+1} = r, X_{t+1} = r' | Z_t = s, X_t = s'\}$ is an element of the transition matrix. The stationary distribution $P\{Z_t = s, X_t = s'\}$ of $Z_t$ and $X_t$ is found by solving a matrix equation having the form of (4.16). Allowance for

## Some Probabilistic Methods Applied in Water Resources

flexible release policies and seasonal inflow characteristics follows the same path as outlined above for the independent input model.

Difficulties of dimensionality encountered in the use of the foregoing method arise from the fact that a general matrix for an $m$-valued inflow distribution would require the estimation of $(m-1)^2$ parameters from the data, which are usually sparse. It has been suggested [35] that a simple autoregression structure based on the bivariate normal distribution be used, if the inflow data can be satisfactorily fitted to a normal distribution. The method has been applied to a practical problem involving a two-season model [36] of the operation of an off-channel reservoir. An analysis was made of the effect of the correlation coefficient on the probability of emptiness: the results indicated that increasing serial correlation tended to greatly increase the probability of failure compared to that calculated for an independent inflow case. It was considered that in practical cases a serial correlation coefficient of less than about 0.25 did not significantly affect results.

Another limitation of storage models, from the computational point of view, becomes apparent when analyzing systems of several dams in series. In this case, the output from one dam becomes the input into the following

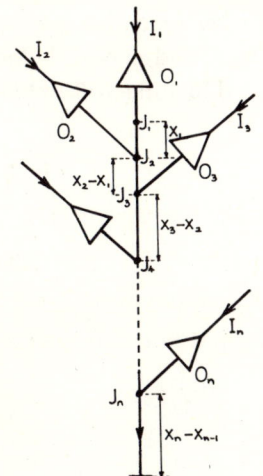

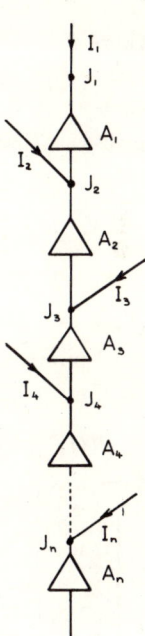

FIGURE 4.1. Multireservoir system with dams situated above confluences of streams.

FIGURE 4.2. Multireservoir system with dams situated below confluences of streams.

one downstream. The solution of such problems is extremely complicated when stochastic inputs are used. A problem of this type has been solved [37] using Markov chain methods. Probabilities of flooding were derived on the assumption that the inputs were dependent random variables forming a nonhomogeneous Markov chain. In the problems analyzed distinction was made between dams situated upstream or downstream from confluences in a river system (see Figures 4.1 and 4.2). The river system consists of a number of tributaries providing inputs of $I_1(t), I_2(t), \ldots, I_n(t)$ units of volume at time $t$ at the confluences $J_1, J_2, \ldots, J_n$, respectively. It is assumed that the velocity of flow is not related to discharge: hence the time taken by the flood wave to reach junctions $J_2, J_3, \ldots, J_{n+1}$, respectively, remains $\tau_1, \tau_2, \ldots, \tau_n$. Furthermore, each inflow $I_r$ is assumed to take on a range of discrete values $0, 1, \ldots, s$, while a monotonically increasing function $F(x)$ indicates volumes of flow along the length of the river $x$ such that flooding occurs only when these are exceeded. At distances $0, x_1, x_2, \ldots, x_{n-1}$ along the river, measured from a common origin, the inputs $I_1(t), I_2(t + \tau_1), I_3(t + \tau_1 + \tau_2), \ldots, I_n(t + \sum_{i=1}^{n-1} \tau_i)$ are introduced into the system. If, for example,

$$I_1(t) + \cdots + I_j(t + \tau_1 + \tau_2 + \cdots + \tau_{j-1}) > F_j \tag{4.31}$$

where $F_j = F(x_j)$, then flooding will occur along the river reach $(x_{j+1} - x_j)$ during the time interval starting at $t + \tau_1 + \cdots + \tau_{j-1}$ and ending before $t + \tau_1 + \cdots + \tau_j$, downstream from the junction $J_j$. Flooding will extend until the first point $x$ is reached for which

$$F(x) > I(t) + \cdots + I_j(t + \tau_1 + \cdots + \tau_{j-1}). \tag{4.32}$$

It was assumed that $I_1$ has a distribution given by the row vector

$$\mathbf{P}_1(t) = \{p_0(t), p_1(t), \ldots, p_s(t)\} \tag{4.33}$$

where this distribution may be thought of as periodic in time $t$ with a period of 12 months. The random variables $I_1, I_2, \ldots, I_n$ form a nonhomogeneous Markov chain defined by the matrices

$$P\{(I_{i+1}(t + \tau_i) = v | I_1(t) = u)\} = \mathbf{P}_{i+1}(t + \tau_i)$$

$$= \begin{bmatrix} p_{00}^{(i+1)}(t + \tau_i) & p_{01}^{(i+1)}(t + \tau_i) & \cdots & p_{0s}^{(i+1)}(t + \tau_i) \\ p_{10}^{(i+1)}(t + \tau_i) & p_{11}^{(i+1)}(t + \tau_i) & \cdots & p_{1s}^{(i+1)}(t + \tau_i) \\ \vdots & & & \\ p_{s0}^{(i+1)}(t + \tau_i) & p_{s1}^{(i+1)}(t + \tau_i) & \cdots & p_{ss}^{(i+1)}(t + \tau_i) \end{bmatrix} \quad (i = 1, \ldots, n - 1). \tag{4.34}$$

It follows that the distribution of the sum of inputs

$$0 \leqslant I_1(t) + \cdots + I_r(t + \tau_1 + \cdots + \tau_{r-1}) \leqslant rs \qquad (4.35)$$

flowing past the point $J_r$ ($r = 1, 2, \ldots, n$) at time $t + \tau_1 + \tau_2 + \cdots + \tau_{r-1}$ is

$$P^{(r)}(t + \tau_1 + \cdots + \tau_{r-1})$$
$$= \mathbf{P}_1(t) * \cdots * \mathbf{P}_{r-1}(t + \tau_1 + \cdots + \tau_{r-2}) * \mathbf{P}_r(t + \tau_1 + \cdots + \tau_{r-1})$$
$$= \{P_0^{(r)}(t + \tau_1 + \cdots + \tau_{r-1}), \ldots, P_{rs}^{(r)}(t + \tau_1 + \cdots + \tau_{r-1})\}. \qquad (4.36)$$

Here the dependence of the $P_i^{(r)}(t + \tau_1 + \cdots + \tau_{r-1})$ on the individual intervals $\tau_1, \ldots, \tau_{r-1}$ needs to be expressed explicitly. The symbol $*$ represents a shift operation [38] which precedes the matrix multiplication. Hence the probabilities of flooding below the junctions $J_1, \ldots, J_n$ at times $t, t + \tau_1$, $t + \tau_1 + \tau_2, \ldots, t + \tau_1 + \cdots + \tau_{n-1}$, respectively, are

$$P_r\{I_1(t) > F_1\} = 1 - \sum_{i=0}^{[F_1]} P_i^{(1)}(t) = q_1(t)$$

$$P_r\{I_1(t) + I_2(t + \tau_1) > F_2\} = 1 - \sum_{i=0}^{[F_2]} P_i^{(2)}(t + \tau_1) = q_2(t + \tau_1)$$

$$\vdots$$

$$P_r\{I_1(t) + \cdots + I_n(t + \tau_1 + \cdots + \tau_{n-1})\} > F_n$$
$$= 1 - \sum_{i=0}^{[F_n]} P_i^{(n)}(t + \tau_1 + \cdots + \tau_{n-1}) = q_n(t + \tau_1 + \cdots + \tau_{n-1}), \qquad (4.37)$$

where $[F_j]$ represents the integral part of $F_j$.

If a number of dams are built on the tributaries as shown in Figure 4.1, the following release rule is assumed to regulate the outputs $O_1$.

$$O_i = I_i \qquad \text{if} \quad 0 \leqslant I_i \leqslant M_i,$$
$$O_i = M_i \qquad \text{if} \quad M_i < I_i \leqslant K_i,$$
$$O_i = I_i - (K_i - M_i) \qquad \text{if} \quad K_i < I_i \leqslant s, \qquad (4.38)$$

where $M_i$ represents some suitable value for the tributary input, $K_i$ is the maximum flow that can be contained by dam $i$ when release $M_i$ is allowed, and $I_i - (K_i - M_i)$ is the total release including the overflow $I_i - K_i$ that occurs when $I_i > K_i$. The release rule may be represented by the input–output transition matrix $\mathbf{Q}_i$ of the form

$\mathbf{Q}_i = \{P_r(O_i = v | I_i = u)\}$

$$= \begin{array}{c|c|c|c|} & 0\ 1\ 2\ \cdots\ M_i & M_{i+1}\ M_{i+2}\ \cdots\ s-(K_i-M_i) & s-(K_i-M_i-1)\ \cdots\ s \\ \hline 0 & 1 & & \\ 1 & \phantom{0}1 & & \\ 2 & \phantom{00}1 & & \\ \vdots & \phantom{000}\ddots & & \\ M_i & \phantom{0000}1 & & \\ \hline M_{i+1} & & 1 & \\ M_{i+2} & & \phantom{0}1 & \\ \vdots & & \phantom{00}\vdots & \\ K_i & & \phantom{000}1 & \\ \hline K_{i+1} & & \phantom{0}1 & \\ K_{i+2} & & \phantom{00}1 & \\ \vdots & & \phantom{000}\ddots & \\ s & & \phantom{0000}1 & 0\ \cdots\ 0 \\ \end{array}$$

(4.39)

Thus the transition matrix for the output $O_i$ given the input $I_{i-1}$ is

$$\{P_r(O_i = v | I_{i-1} = u)\} = \mathbf{P}_i \mathbf{Q}_i \qquad (4.40)$$

where $\mathbf{P}_i$ is a matrix analogous to expression (4.34). It follows that the distribution of the sum of outputs

$$0 \leqslant O_1 + \cdots + O_r \leqslant rs - \sum_{i=1}^{r}(K_i - M_i) \qquad (4.41)$$

flowing past the junction $J_r$, $r = 1, \ldots, n$, at time $t + \tau_1 + \cdots + \tau_{n-1}$ is given by

$$\mathbf{P}_1(\mathbf{Q}_1 * \cdots * (\mathbf{Q}_{r-2} * \mathbf{P}_{r-1}(\mathbf{Q}_{r-1} * \mathbf{P}_r \mathbf{Q}_r)) \cdots)$$

$$= \left\{ \pi_0^{(r)}, \ldots, \pi_{rs - \sum_{i=1}^{r}(K_i - M_i)}^{(r)} \right\}. \qquad (4.42)$$

It can therefore be shown that for $F_i > \sum_{r=1}^{i} M_r$, $i = 1, 2, \ldots, n$, and for matrices $\mathbf{P}_i$ similar to expression (4.34) with the nonzero elements $p_{uv}^{(i)}$, the distributions of the sums of outputs are given by

## Some Probabilistic Methods Applied in Water Resources

$$P_r\{O_1 > F_1\} = 1 - \sum_{i=0}^{[F_1]} \pi_i < q_1$$

$$P_r\{O_1 + O_2 > F_2\} = 1 - \sum_{i=0}^{[F_2]} \pi_i^{(2)} < q_2$$

$$\vdots \qquad\qquad \vdots$$

$$P_r\{O_1 + \cdots + O_n > F_n\} = 1 - \sum_{i=0}^{[F_n]} \pi_i^{(n)} < q_n \qquad (4.43)$$

at times $t, t + \tau_1 + \cdots + \tau_{n-1}$, respectively. This technique can also be used for dams downstream from the junctions $J_r$.

A similar model has been used for the analysis of pollutant transport in streams, but using relatively simpler Markov chain theory [15]. Here two interdependent stochastic variates, water and pollutant, are "queued" simultaneously. The model uses a stochastic formulation of hydrology with a serial correlation of lag one between inflows, as well as between pollutants. A decay mechanism for organic wastes, thermal wastes, and radioactive wastes is included. The objective of the model is to predict the quality and quantity of water at different control points along a river, given the pattern of flow, temperature, solar radiation, shape of channel, and dam location, as well as the pollutant loading pattern. The river is divided into a finite number of reaches having similar hydrological and physical characteristics. The basic model is represented schematically in Figures 4.3 and 4.4.

The model considers four levels of inflow represented by a transition matrix for unit time intervals. The outflow through any river reach is represented as a function of river reach storage and inflow by

$$q_B = \tfrac{2}{3}(q_A + S_A), \qquad (4.44)$$

where $q_A$ is the inflow into reach A, $q_B$ the inflow into reach B, $S_A$ the storage

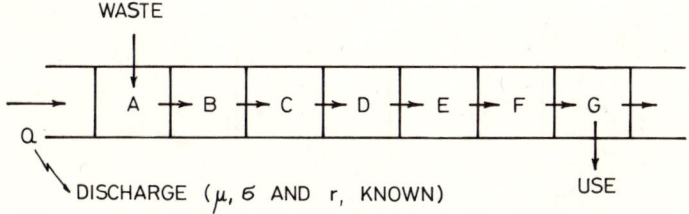

FIGURE 4.3. Schematic flow of water and waste through reaches $A$ to $G$ of a river. The concentration of pollutant known from storage in each reach.

in reach A, and reach B is downstream from reach A. Assuming constant velocities and perfect mixing of the pollutant, the flow ($q$) and storage ($S$) values are incorporated into a conditional probability matrix whose element positioning is determined by the values of

$$S_{A,t} + q_{A,t} = S_{A,t+1} + q_{B,t+1} + \text{(an operating rule)}. \tag{4.45}$$

The matrix yields the stationary probability distribution for flow and storage in any reach. The joint probability of two given flow events following each other is

$$P\{q_{B,t} = 0, q_{B,t+1} = 0\} = \sum_{j=1}^{m}\sum_{i=1}^{n} P_i(q_{B,t} = 0)(q_{B,t+1} = 0 | q_{B,t} = 0). \tag{4.46}$$

Routing of the pollutant is more complicated because pollutant transport is dependent on hydrology and there is no theoretical upper bound for the level of storage of pollutant in any reach. There is also no upper bound for the flow of pollutant from reach to reach. In addition, pollutants decay,

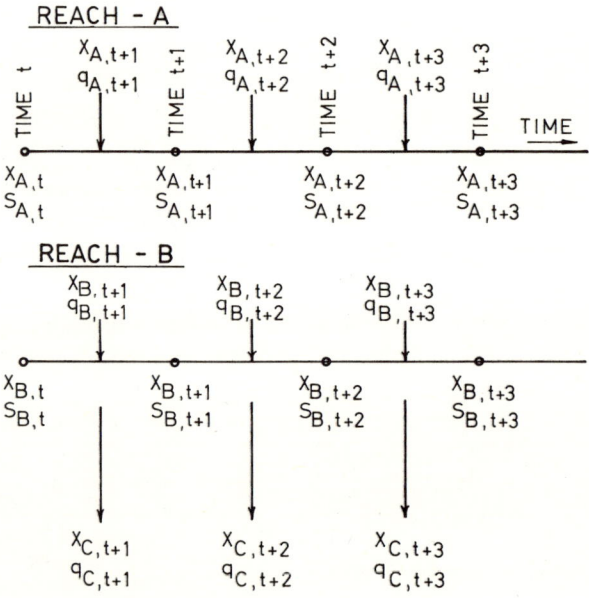

FIGURE 4.4. Schematic representation of multiperiod routing of water and waste. $X_{N,t}$ = waste content of reach $N$ at time $t$; $S_{N,t}$ = storage in reach $N$ at time $t$.

as opposed to water quantities, which remain constant. The routing of pollutants as a function of discharge is solved by matrix multiplications, the decay process being incorporated into the structure of the transition matrices.

In many instances, it is necessary to choose the size of waste treatment plants needed at fixed locations along a river course. The foregoing model may be used to derive stationary distributions of discharge and quality between key points where such plants may be needed. It should be remembered, however, that input of wastes is also a stochastic variable. Periods of low stream flow of long duration and the resulting damages are of importance when choosing the plant size. The decision will have to be based on frequency of damage as opposed to the higher costs of larger treatment plants. Several models have been derived to treat this problem [39, 40]. A relatively simpler model assumes that for each discrete daily stream and sewage flow there exists one set of parameters (such as temperature, the initial biological oxygen demand (BOD), and dissolved oxygen concentrations) that determine, along with sewage effluent, the minimum dissolved oxygen concentrations in the stream. Therefore, given the volume of stream and sewage flow, other parameters are assumed known. Streamflow and sewage are denoted by the vectors $\mathbf{S}_i$, $i = 1, 2, \ldots, m$, and $\mathbf{W}_k$, $k = 1, 2, \ldots, n$, respectively. Serial correlation is disregarded in this simple model. The probability that any one combination of streamflow and waste flow results in a minimum dissolved oxygen concentration $DO_{\min}$ less than a specified level $DO_L$ is given by

$$P\{DO_{\min} < DO_L\} = \sum_{i=1}^{m} P\{\mathbf{S}_i(t)\} \sum_{k \in V_i} P\{\mathbf{W}_k(t)\}. \qquad (4.47)$$

Here $P\{\mathbf{S}_i(t)\}$ is the probability that the streamflow at time $t$ is $\mathbf{S}_i$; $P\{\mathbf{W}_k(t)\}$ the probability that the sewage flow at time $t$ is $\mathbf{W}_k$; $V_i$ the set of sewage flows that result in $DO_{\min} < DO_L$ for streamflow $i$ where $0 \leqslant V_i \leqslant n$; and $k \in V_i$ all sewage flows $k$ that are contained in the set $V_i$. The probability of violating the specified concentration $DO_L$ for periods of various length during a season of low flows is estimated on the basis of transition probabilities. For any two-day period,

$$P\{DO_{\min} < DO_L\} = \sum_{i=1}^{m} P\{\mathbf{S}_i(t)\} \sum_{k \in V_i} P\{\mathbf{W}_k(t)\} \cdot \sum_{j=1}^{m} M_{ij} \sum_{l \in V_j} P\{\mathbf{W}_l(t+1)\}$$

$$(4.48)$$

where $M_{ij} = P\{S_j(t+1)|S_i(t)\}$ is the probability of being in the state $j$ at time $(t+1)$ given state $i$ at time $t$. Here "state" is, in fact, "streamflow."

This model may be extended for periods of any length by the multiplication of transitional matrices for each day, as shown for the case of a multiseason reservoir model in equations (4.25) through (4.29). Similar conditions may be assumed, except that for each sewage flow there is a probability distribution $P\{B_k[\mathbf{W}_k(t)]\}$ of possible BOD concentrations. If $U_{ik}$ denotes a set of BOD concentrations that result in $DO_{\min} < DO_L$ for streamflow $i$ and for sewage flow $k$, then for any consecutive two-day period

$$P\{DO_{\min} < DO_L\} = \sum_{i=1}^{m} P\{\mathbf{S}_i(t)\} \cdot \sum_{k=1}^{n} P\{\mathbf{W}_k(t)\} \cdot \sum_{b \in U_{ik}} P\{B_b|\mathbf{W}_k(t)\}$$

$$\cdot \sum_{j=1}^{m} M_{ij} \cdot \sum_{l=1}^{n} P\{\mathbf{W}_l(t+1)\} \sum_{c \in kjl} P\{B_c|\mathbf{W}_l(t+1)\}. \quad (4.49)$$

In the event that streamflows and waste discharges are correlated and if serial correlation of the sewage flows exists, the foregoing model may be extended provided that to each streamflow corresponds only one BOD concentration. The state of the system is then described by a two-dimensional vector of sewage and streamflows: the sewage flow on any day depends on that day's streamflow as well as the previous day's sewage flow. The state transition probabilities are now joint transition probabilities, each being the probability of streamflow $j$ and sewage flow $i$ at time $t+1$, given streamflow $k$ and sewage flow $l$ at time $t$. Each joint transition probability is the product of the streamflow transition probability and the conditional probability of the sewage flow, given the preceding sewage flow and present streamflow. Thus given the state of the system, the minimum dissolved oxygen concentration can be determined within each reach of the stream. For any two-day period

$$P\{DO_{\min} > DO_L\} = \sum_{i \in Z} P\{\mathbf{S}_i(t)\} \sum_{j \in Z} M_{ij} \quad (4.50)$$

where $Z$ is the set of states in which $DO_{\min} < DO_L$.

The foregoing model can be extended to allow for several possible BOD concentrations for each sewage and streamflow, if the stream and sewage BOD concentrations are independent. At any time

$$P\{DO_{\min} < DO_L\} = \sum_{i=1}^{m} P\{\mathbf{S}_i(t)\} \cdot \sum_{k=1}^{r_i} P\{SB_k|\mathbf{S}_i\} \sum_{l \in U_{ik}} P\{WB_l|\mathbf{S}_i\} \quad (4.51)$$

where

$P\{SB_k|S_i\}$ = probability of the $k$th initial BOD concentration in the streamflow associated with the $i$th state;

$P\{WB_l|S_i\}$ = probability of the $l$th BOD concentration in the sewage flow associated with the $i$th state;

$U_{ik}$ = a set of all sewage flow BOD concentrations that result in $DO_{min} < DO_L$, given the $i$th state and $k$th initial streamflow BOD concentration;

$r_i$ = the total number of initial BOD concentrations associated with the streamflow in the $i$th state.

It has been suggested [40] that the probabilities of having less than any specified dissolved oxygen concentration downstream from a waste water treatment plant during any period can be used in a simple control model. Operating costs may be reduced by storing temporarily a portion of the treated effluent at times when its release into the stream would result in a dissolved oxygen concentration less than specified. The stored effluent would be released later when the stream's conditions permit, or when the concentration of waste in the plant effluent has decreased. The basic partial control offered by storage facilities would result in a decrease in plant efficiency in terms of waste removal. The simple control model described above (see Figure 4.5) allows a least-cost combination of treatment plant

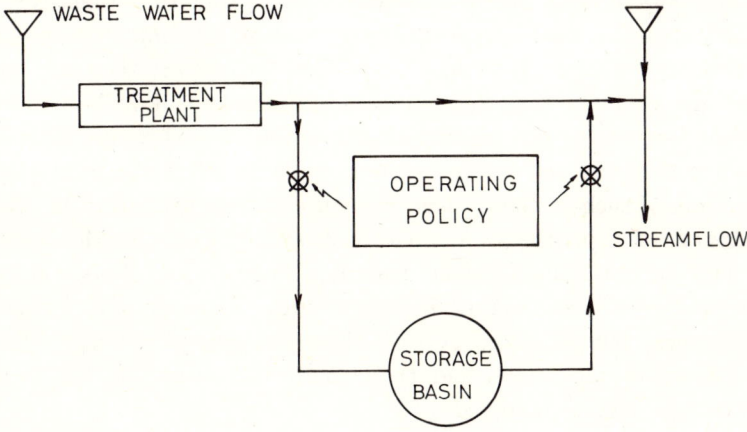

FIGURE 4.5. Waste water treatment system.

efficiency and storage capacity that will satisfy a deterministic or probabilistic stream standard. The chosen operating policy is used to determine the state transition matrices. Several solutions may yield the least-cost combination of plant efficiency and storage capacity such that the stream standard criterion is maintained.

## C. STORAGE CONTROL PROBLEMS

Probabilistic concepts have also been used for effective control and scheduling of pumping operations from a lake [41] when used conjunctively with a large aquifer system. The problem was that of integrating a major pipeline that would permit the utilization of nearly all of the available fresh water in Israel [42]. The pipeline system connected a major surface reservoir in the northern part of the country (Lake Kinneret) with a complex of subsurface water resources (aquifers) in the central and southern regions of Israel. Regional water supply schemes, delivering irrigation, domestic, and industrial water to consumers, are connected with the main pipeline system.

Because the available fresh water is limited and less than sufficient to meet the envisioned total agricultural, industrial, and domestic needs of Israel, it was necessary to develop policies that reduce the amount of available water not delivered to consumers to the smallest quantity possible. Thus, one objective of the problem was to apply control procedures that reduce to a minimum the losses due to uncontrolled spills from the surface reservoir. A second objective was to operate the system at a minimum total annual cost, and at the same time meet established consumer demand, by the efficient use of Lake Kinneret pumping stations and of wells in different regions of Israel. A third pipeline design objective was to analyze various alternative pumping and storage systems so as to select the most effective combination of such systems. The procedures developed had to be *adaptive* and capable of adjusting to a range of inputs of water, so that pumping rates could be optimally adjusted according to levels and flows. They also had to be *dynamic*, so that as the water levels, demands, and forecasts of inflow change, the pumping rates could be changed accordingly. Finally, a *feasible* set of procedures had to be derived, considering the technical and economic factors involved.

The system under study was considered as one represented by a single supply, a single delivery channel (pipeline), and a single demand point (see

## Some Probabilistic Methods Applied in Water Resources

Figure 4.6). The values of inflows were given by a probability distribution, where the distribution function and parameter values (average and standard deviation) were estimated from historical values. The amounts in lake and aquifer storage, $L$ and $S$, respectively, are state variables, known to the pipeline operator at the time pumping decisions are made. The control variables are pumpage quantities from the lake and from groundwater, $X$ and $Y$, each restricted by the maximum values of the corresponding installed pumping capacities. Monthly values of the demand $D$ of consumers $C$ are known in advance. Of course, the sum of $X$ and $Y$ is not to be less than $D$ and the difference between this sum and $D$ is the amount of water recharged into the aquifer during a month.

As indicated, it is necessary to control the levels of Lake Kinneret so as to assure that the national water system utilizes the available water to the

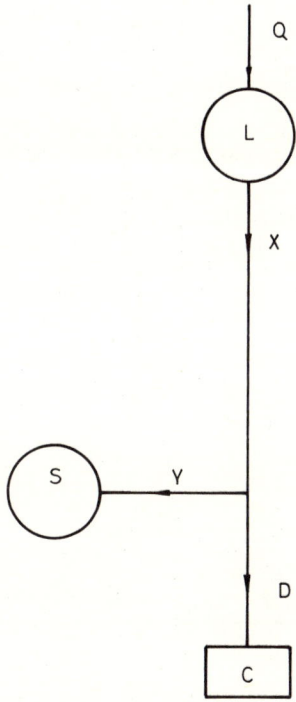

FIGURE 4.6. Simplified representation of Israel water scheme.

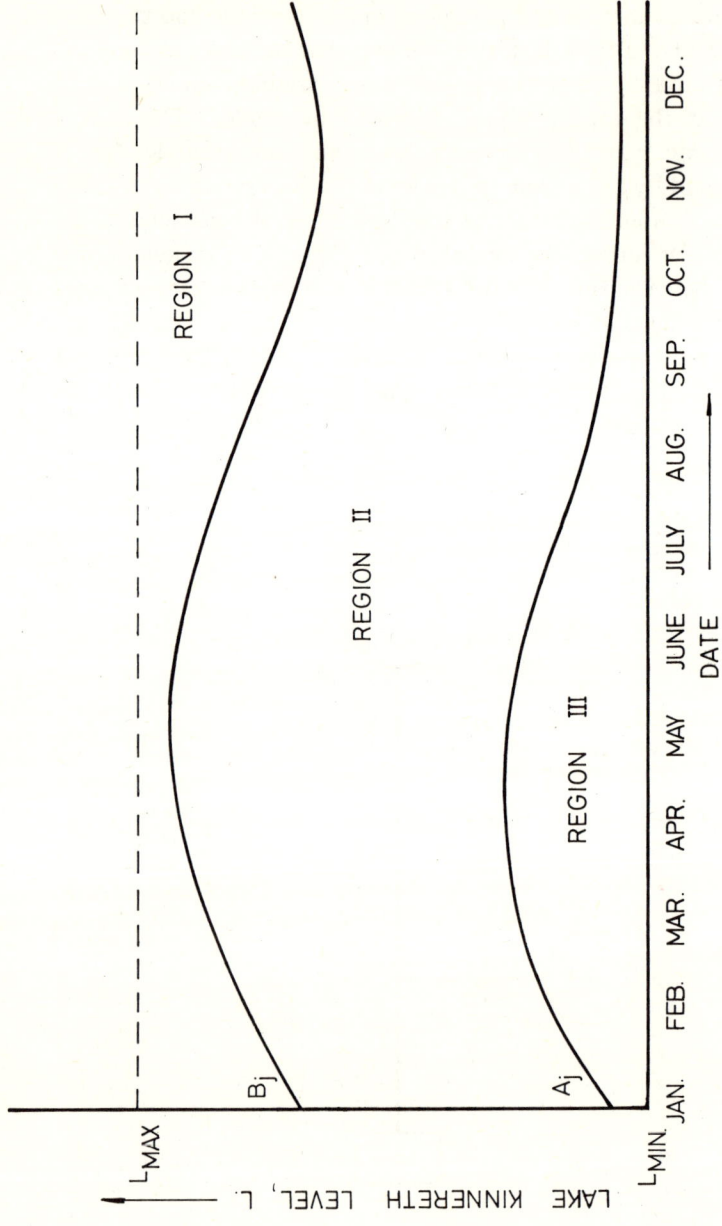

FIGURE 4.7. Control curves in the storage (volume)–time continuum.

greatest extent. However, acceptable levels of Lake Kinneret will be different for different time periods, or months of the year. Thus there are two parameter values that describe the state of the lake: the month of the year $j = 1, 2, \ldots, 12$; and the level of the lake at month $j$, $L_j$. Thus the level of the lake at any time ought to be between two levels

$$A_j \leqslant L_j \leqslant B_j, \qquad j = 1, 2, \ldots, 12, \tag{4.52}$$

where the minimum and maximum levels $A_j$ and $B_j$ are to be determined. The variables $A_j$ and $B_j$ are continuous functions of time, which divide the continuum lake–time into three regions as shown in Figure 4.7.

In region I, the level of the lake is considered to be too high, and there is a high probability that spills will occur in the near future (within one or two years); and to avoid spills it is necessary to pump water from Lake Kinneret at a maximum rate.

In region III, the level of the lake is considered to be too low, and there is a significant chance (greater than 1 in 20) that evaporation in the summer months will reduce the useful storage level of the lake below the safety level $L_{\min}$ and that the system will be unable to deliver the required quantity of water. In this region it is necessary to reduce the rate of pumping from Lake Kinneret and to use groundwater for meeting the demand.

In the intermediate region, region II, there is no foreseeable risk of either not utilizing the available water or incurring shortages. In this region, it is necessary that the operation of the major pipeline be efficient, that is, the costs of pumping be minimized.

For the upper control limit, we seek a time-dependent function of lake levels such that, for any installed pumping capacity, the level of the lake for each month is determined to prevent uncontrolled spills with a specified probability. Let $i = 1, 2, \ldots, 12$ represent the months of May, June, July, ..., March, April. We consider the month of May as the first month of the hydrological year because the prevention of spills from Lake Kinneret during winter months must consider pumping policies during the previous summer months. Let $L$ be the maximum useful storage capacity of Lake Kinneret; $L_i$ the level of Lake Kinneret at beginning of month $i$, $0 \leqslant L_i \leqslant L$; $Q_i$ the flow of water into Lake Kinneret during month $i$; $x_i$ the sum of flows into Lake Kinneret from month $i$ to the end of the period, $= \sum_{j=i}^{12} Q_j$; $P$ the maximum monthly carrying capacity of the pipeline.

In order to prevent spills during the year, the following inequalities must be satisfied.

## Scientific Allocation of Water Resources

$$Q_{12} + L_{12} - P \leqslant L$$

$$Q_{11} + Q_{12} + L_{11} - 2P \leqslant L$$

$$Q_{10} + Q_{11} + Q_{12} + L_{10} - 3P \leqslant L$$

$$\dots\dots\dots\dots\dots\dots\dots\dots$$

$$Q_1 + Q_2 + \cdots + Q_{12} + L_1 - 12P \leqslant L, \tag{4.53}$$

or

$$x_{12} + L_{12} - P \leqslant L$$

$$x_{11} + L_{11} - 2P \leqslant L$$

$$\dots\dots\dots\dots\dots$$

$$x_1 + L_1 - 12P \leqslant L. \tag{4.54}$$

In short,

$$x_j + L_j - (13 - j)P \leqslant L, \qquad j = 1, 2, \ldots, 12. \tag{4.55}$$

Hence the maximal value of inflow that results in no spills, $A_j$, is when

$$x_j \leqslant L - L_j + (13 - j)P = A_j, \qquad j = 1, 2, \ldots, 12 \tag{4.56}$$

and we have

$$L_j = L + (13 - j)P - A_j, \qquad j = 1, 2, \ldots, 12. \tag{4.57}$$

Equation (4.57) determines the lake levels $L_j$ for values of $L$, $P$, and $A_j$. Now, $L$ and $P$ are system parameters, determined by the system storage and pumping constraints. However, $A_j$ is a decision variable, determined by system management, and represents the risk of spills to be tolerated. It can be determined for different confidence levels of no spills $a$ from a table of normal variates and substituted in the following equation.

$$A_j = \mu_j + \alpha(a)\sigma_j, \qquad j = 1, 2, \ldots, 12. \tag{4.58}$$

Here $A_j$ is assumed to be normally distributed with mean $\mu_j$ and variance $\sigma_j^2$.

In estimating the expected losses of water due to uncontrolled spills from Lake Kinneret, we should consider only the winter season (November 1 to April 30), since no such losses occur during the summer months. We introduce the following notation.

$L =$ maximum useful storage capacity of Lake Kinneret;

$j = 1, 2, \ldots, 6$, month of the year (November, December, ..., April);

$L_j$ = level of the lake at the beginning of the $j$th month, $0 \leq L_j \leq L$;
$P$ = maximum monthly pumping capacity of the system;
$P_j = (7-j)P$ = cumulative maximum amount pumped out in months $j, j = 1, \ldots, 6$;
$x_j$ = cumulative inflow into Lake Kinneret from the $j$th month through the end of the winter season (April 30);
$p(x_j)$ = probability density function for lake inflow from $j$th month to end of the winter season (April 30);
$f(j, L_j, P)$ = expected losses due to spills if at the beginning of the $j$th month the lake level is $L_j$ and the system has a maximum monthly pumping capacity $P$.

We assume that $p(x_j)$ is normally distributed with mean $\mu_j$ and standard deviation $\sigma_j$.

Now suppose that the lake is at a level $t$, an amount $x$ flows into the lake, and an amount $p$ is pumped out at a constant rate. If $s$ denotes the amount of spill, then

$$s = \begin{cases} 0 & \text{if } t+x-p \leq L \\ t+x-p-L & \text{if } t+x-p \geq L. \end{cases} \quad (4.59)$$

Therefore, spills will occur if

$$x \geq L - (t-p). \quad (4.60)$$

The expected loss of water is the mean spill averaged over the values of the probability distribution, such that

$$x_j \geq L - [L_j - (7-j)P] = L - (L_j - P_j). \quad (4.61)$$

Thus

$$f(j, L_j, P) = \int_{L-(L_j-P_j)}^{\infty} (x_j + L_j - P_j - L)p(x_j)\, dx_j. \quad (4.62)$$

Specifically

$$f(j, L_j, P) = \frac{1}{\sqrt{2\pi}\,\sigma_j} \int_{T_j}^{\infty} (x_j - T_j) \exp\left[-\frac{(x_j - \mu_j)^2}{2\sigma_j^2}\right] dx_j \quad (4.63)$$

where

$$T_j = L - (L_j - P_j). \quad (4.64)$$

Using the transformation

$$\frac{x_j - \mu_j}{\sigma_j} = y, \qquad (4.65)$$

we get

$$x_j - T_j = \mu_j + \sigma_j y - T_j, \qquad (4.66)$$

$$f(j, L_j, P) = \frac{1}{\sqrt{2\pi}} \int_{(T_j - \mu_j)/\sigma_j}^{\infty} (\mu_j + \sigma_j y - T_j) \exp\left(-\frac{y^2}{2}\right) dy. \qquad (4.67)$$

Letting

$$G(j, L_j, P) = \frac{1}{\sqrt{2\pi}} \int_{(T_j - \mu_j)/\sigma_j}^{\infty} \exp\left(-\frac{y^2}{2}\right) dy \qquad (4.68)$$

and since

$$\int_A^{\infty} y \exp\left(-\frac{y^2}{2}\right) dy = \left[-\exp\left(-\frac{y^2}{2}\right)\right]_A^{\infty} = \exp\left(-\frac{A^2}{2}\right), \qquad (4.69)$$

we have that

$$f(j, L_j, P) = (\mu_j - T_j) G(j, L_j, P) + \frac{\sigma_j}{\sqrt{2\pi}} \exp\left[-\frac{(T_j - \mu_j)^2}{2\sigma_j^2}\right]. \qquad (4.70)$$

The function $G(j, L_j, P)$ given in equation (4.68) is tabulated in normal distribution tables, while the second member on the right-hand side of equation (4.70) is an exponential function, also tabulated in standard mathematical handbooks. Equation (4.70) is the *expected loss function*.

For the lower control limit, we seek a time-dependent function of the level of Lake Kinneret such that for any time of the year, for any pumping capacity of the well fields connected with the system, for any storage level in aquifers, and for a given probability of not falling below the minimum useful storage level of the lake, a minimum level of the lake is specified. If the lake is below this level, then there ought to be no further pumping until the lake rises above the minimum level curve. The following notation is introduced.

$j = 1, 2, \ldots, 12$, the months of the year, starting with November;
$L_j$ = level of Lake Kinneret at the beginning of month $j$;

$x_j =$ cumulative inflow from the beginning of the $j$th month to the end of the hydrological year (October 31);
$P =$ maximum monthly pumping capacity of wells;
$P_j = (13 - j)P =$ maximum cumulative pumping capacity of wells to end of hydrological year (October 31);
$d_j =$ cumulative consumer demand from the beginning of the $j$th month to the end of the hydrological year (October 31);
$y_j =$ cumulative inflow into aquifers from the beginning of the $j$th month to the end of the hydrological year;
$S_j =$ useful storage in aquifers at the beginning of the $j$th month.

The following restrictions or inequalities must be satisfied. Regarding

lake level $\qquad x_j + L_j \geqslant 0;$ \hfill (4.71)

total volume $\qquad x_j + L_j + y_j + S_j \geqslant d_j;$ \hfill (4.72)

pumping capacity $\qquad x_j + L_j \geqslant d_j - P_j.$ \hfill (4.73)

These conditions can be written as common inequalities on $x_j$:

$$x_j \geqslant -L_j, \quad x_j \geqslant -L_j + d_j - y_j - S_j, \quad x_j \geqslant -L_j + d_j - P_j; \quad (4.74)$$

and combining them, we obtain

$$x_j \geqslant -L_j + \max\{0, d_j - y_j - S_j, d_j - P_j\}. \quad (4.75)$$

Assuming that the aquifer capacity and storage quantities are such that $P_j \leqslant y_j + S_j$, then

$$x_j \geqslant -L_j + \max\{0, d_j - P_j\} = B_j. \quad (4.76)$$

The probability that $x_j \geqslant B_j$ is given by $P(x_j \geqslant B_j)$ where

$$P(x_j \geqslant B_j) = \frac{1}{\sqrt{2\pi}\,\sigma_j} \int_{B_j}^{\infty} \exp\left[-\frac{(x_j - \mu_j)^2}{2\sigma_j^2}\right] dx_j. \quad (4.77)$$

Again, $x_j$ is assumed to be normally distributed with parameters $\mu_j$ and $\sigma_j$. Let $a$ be the probability such that $P(x_j \geqslant B_j)$. If $K_\alpha$ is such that

$$P(x_j \geqslant K_\alpha) = a, \quad (4.78)$$

then

$$K_\alpha = B_j = \mu_j - \alpha(a)\sigma_j. \quad (4.79)$$

Here $\alpha(a)$ is obtained from a table of normal distribution. Therefore

$$L_i = \alpha(a)\sigma_j - \mu_j + \max\{0, d_j - P_j\}. \qquad (4.80)$$

This is the lower control limit function for a probability of $a$ of no shortage.

Inventory theory has been used to solve a minimum-cost problem of operating a system of two reservoirs [22], a smaller one being needed to store excess water that would have otherwise spilled from the larger. The water thus saved is returned to the larger reservoir in summer. The problem posed was to find that combination of the size of the downstream reservoir and the pumping capacity that will utilize a certain quantity of water at minimum cost, for any feasible quantity of the water to be used. The inflow into the larger reservoir was assumed to be a negative binomial distribution, so that the expected value of the amount of water $u$ pumped per time period, $E(u)$, is given by

$$E(u) = \frac{1}{\lambda}\left\{1 - \frac{\exp[-\lambda(u+1)y]}{\sum_{i=0}^{n}(-1)^i[(n-i+1)\lambda y\exp(-\lambda y)]^i/i!}\right\} \qquad (4.81)$$

where $y$ is the maximum amount that can be pumped into the smaller reservoir per time period, $\lambda$ the expected inflow into the larger reservoir, and $n$ the number of time periods needed to empty a full reservoir at zero input.

As the equation above is not suitable for analytical treatment, the pumping capacity is defined in units of expected flow per time period $\theta = \lambda y$. Similarly, $w$ is the average amount pumped per time period

$$w = \lambda E(u), \qquad (4.82)$$

so that

$$w = \left\{1 - \frac{\exp[-(n+1)\theta]}{\sum_{i=0}^{n}(-1)^i[(n-i+1)\theta\exp(-\theta)]^i/i!}\right\}. \qquad (4.83)$$

Optimization is based on graphs of $w$ versus $\theta$ for various values of $n$, and on cost functions of reservoir size $R_1(Q)$ and of pumping capacity $R_2(y)$. The total annual cost per unit volume of water pumped is given by

$$C = a + b\frac{R_1(Q)}{E(u)} + c\frac{R_2(y)}{E(u)} \qquad (4.84)$$

where $a$, $b$, $c$ are constants and $Q$ is reservoir size. Using various combinations of $Q$, $n$, and $y$, a least-cost solution may be obtained. The expected amount pumped $E(u)$ is found in terms of expected inflow. Results showed that increasing the reservoir size above $3y$ did not significantly increase $w$, the average amount pumped per time period. A larger pumping capacity requires a smaller reservoir and vice versa.

It should be noted that the optimization in this example is a graphical process limited to two or three dimensions. A definite relation between variables is necessary and multiperiod problems are not tractable.

This example, as well as the others presented in this chapter, shows that probability methods are most useful when analyzing field data. In this way, the information contained in the data can be evaluated and used as a basis for various programming techniques.

**REFERENCES**

1 W. Rippl, "The Capacity of Storage Reservoirs for Water Supply," *Proc. Inst. Civil Engineers* **71**(1883), 270.
2 A. Hazen, "Storage to be Provided in Impounding Reservoirs for Municipal Water Supply," *Trans. Amer. Soc. Civil Engineers* **77**(1914), 1539.
3 H. E. Hurst, "Long-Term Storage Capacity of Reservoirs," *Trans. Amer. Soc. Civil Engineers* **116**(1951), 770.
4 W. Feller, "The Asymptotic Distribution of the Range of Series of Independent Random Variables," *Ann. Math. Statist.* **22**(1951), 427.
5 A. A. Anis and E. H. Lloyd, "On the Range of Partial Sums of a Finite Number of Independent Normal Variates," *Biometrika* **40**(1953), 35.
6 V. M. Yevdjevich, *The Application of Surplus, Deficit and Range in Hydrology*, Hydrology Paper No. 10, Colorado State University, Fort Collins, Colorado, 1965.
7 M. J. Melentijevich, *The Analysis of Range with Output Linearly Dependent upon Storage*, Hydrology Paper No. 11, Colorado State University, Fort Collins, Colorado, 1965.
8 N. C. Matalas and W. B. Langbein, "Information Content of the Mean," *J. Geophys. Research* **67**(1962), No. 9.
9 L. B. Leopold, *Probability Analysis Applied to a Water Supply Problem*, U.S. Geological Survey Circular No. 410, 1959.
10 W. B. Langbein, "Queuing Theory and Water Storage," *Proc. Amer. Soc. Civil Engineers* **84**(1958), No. HY5.
11 L. W. Furness, *Kansas Streamflow Characteristics, Part 4: Storage Requirements to Sustain Gross Reservoir Outflow*, Kansas Water Resources Board Technical Report No. 4, 1962.
12 L. W. Furness, *Kansas Streamflow Characteristics, Part 5: Storage Requirements to Control High Flow*, Kansas Water Resources Board Technical Report No. 5, 1964.
13 M. E. Kubik, *Probability Concepts Applied to Reservoir Yields*, American Society of Agricultural Engineers Paper No. 64-704, 1964.
14 J. B. Stall, *Low Flows of Illinois Streams for Impounding Reservoir Design*, Bulletin No. 51, Illinois State Water Survey, 1964.

15 H. A. Thomas, Jr., and R. P. Burden, *Operations Research in Water Quality Management*, Final Report of Contract PH-86-62-140, Harvard Water Program, 1963.
16 E. H. Lloyd, "A Critical Review of Some Probability Methods in the Simple Reservoir Design Problem," *Proc. Reservoir Yield Symposium*, Water Research Association, Marlow, Bucks, U.K., 1965.
17 P. A. P. Moran, *The Theory of Storage*. Methuen, London, 1959.
18 N. U. Prabhu, "Time Dependent Results in Storage Theory," *J. Appl. Probability* 1(1964), No. 1.
19 D. Nir, *The Operation of Lake Kinneret as a Principal Reservoir in the National Water Scheme*, D. Sc. thesis, Technion–Israel Institute of Technology, Haifa, 1962 (in Hebrew).
20 C. L. Jarvis, "An Application of Moran's Theory of Dams to the Ord River Project, Western Australia," *J. Hydrology* 2(1964), 232.
21 R. A. Morris, *Matrix Methods Applied to the Calculation of Pumped Storage from the River Leam*, Technical Memorandum No. 14, Water Research Association, Marlow, Bucks, U.K., 1963.
22 B. Avi-Itzchak and S. Ben-Tuvia, "A Problem of Optimizing a Collecting Reservoir System," *J. Operations Research Soc. Amer.* 4(1963), No. 1.
23 W. B. Langbein, "Reservoir Storage, General Solution of a Queue Model," *Geological Research* 298(1961).
24 R. A. Morris, "Probability of Reservoir Failure Using Moran's Steady State Probability Method and Gould's Probability Routing Method," *J. Inst. Water Engineers* 19(1965), No. 4.
25 R. A. Howard, *Dynamic Programming and Markov Processes*. Wiley, New York, 1960.
26 A. Maass, N. M. Hufschmidt, R. Dorfman, S. A. Marglin, H. A. Thomas, Jr., and G. M. Fair, *Design of Water-Resources Systems*. Harvard University Press, Cambridge, Massachusetts, 1962.
27 E. H. Wiser, "Stochastic Models in Hydrology," *Amer. Soc. Agricultural Engineers* Paper 65-595, 1965.
28 V. S. Bhavnagri and G. Bugliarello, "Mathematical Representation of an Urban Flood Plain," *Proc. Amer. Soc. Civil Engineers* 91(1965), No. HY1.
29 L. E. Borgman, "Risk Criteria," *Proc. Amer. Soc. Civil Engineers* 89(1963), No. WW3.
30 E. H. Lloyd and S. Odoom, "A Probability Theory of Reservoirs with Seasonal Input," *J. Hydrology* 2(1964), No. 1, 1.
31 R. A. Harris and J. A. Cole, *Computing the Yield of an Off-Channel Reservoir*, Technical Paper No. 44, Water Research Association, Marlow, Bucks, U.K., 1965.
32 J. B. White, "Fixed and Variable Season Matrices," *Proc. Reservoir Yield Symposium*, Water Research Association, Marlow, Bucks, U.K., 1965.
33 N. Chorafas, *Systems and Simulation*. Academic Press, New York, 1965.
34 E. H. Lloyd, "Reservoirs with Serially Correlated Inflows," *Technometrics* 5(1963), No. 1.
35 E. H. Lloyd, "A Probability Theory of Reservoirs with Serially Correlated Inputs," *J. Hydrology* 1(1963), No. 2.
36 R. A. Harris and J. A. Cole, *Serially Correlated Inflows and Subsequent Attainment*

    *of Steady State Probabilities*, Technical Paper No. 45, Water Research Association, Marlow, Bucks, U.K., 1965.
37 J. Gani, *Flooding Models*, Research Report 4/JG3, University of Sheffield, England, 1965.
38 S. Conover, "The Distribution of $\sum f(y_t)$ where $(y_0, y_1, \ldots)$ is a Realization of a Non-Homogeneous Finite State Markov Chain," *Biometrika* **52**(1965), No. 1.
39 D. P. Loucks and W. R. Lynn, "Probabilistic Models for Predicting Stream Quality," *Water Resources Research* **2**(1966), No. 3.
40 D. P. Loucks, *Wastewater Treatment Systems Analysis*, Amer. Soc. Civil Engineers, Conference Reprint No. 368, 1966.
41 B. V. Dean and N. Buras, *Effective Control and Economic Scheduling of Lake Kinneret Pumping Operations*, Water Planning for Israel, Ltd., Tel Aviv, Publication No. 282, 1963.
42 A. Wiener and A. Wolman, "Formulation of a National Water Resources Policy in Israel," *J. Amer. Water Works Assoc.* **54**(1962), No. 3, 257.

# Chapter 5

# APPLICATIONS OF LINEAR PROGRAMMING

## A. GENERAL

Problems that seek to maximize (minimize) a numerical function of a number of variables (or functions), with the variables (functions) subject to certain constraints, form a general class that may be called *optimization problems*. A separate class of optimization problems have been referred to as programming problems: these deal with the determination of optimal allocations of limited resources to meet given objectives. More specifically, they refer to situations where a number of available resources, such as manpower, materials, machines, water, land, and capital, are to be combined to yield one or more products. Usually restrictions exist as to the amount of resource available and its required quality. Despite these constraints, many feasible combinations of the resources and their allocation exist: usually it is required to find some combination that maximizes or minimizes a numerical quantity such as profit or cost.

Linear programming is concerned with solving a special type of problem: one in which all relations among the variables are linear, both in the constraints and in the function to be optimized. The general problem may be described as follows [1]: given a set of $n$ linear inequalities or equations in $r$ variables, nonnegative values of these variables must be determined, which satisfy the constraints and maximize some linear function of the variables. This may be expressed mathematically in the form: optimize

$$z = c_1 x_1 + c_2 x_2 + \cdots + c_n x_n \qquad (5.1a)$$

subject to

$$a_{i1} x_1 + a_{i2} x_2 + \cdots + a_{in} x_n \{\geqslant, =, \leqslant\} b_i. \qquad (5.1b)$$

For each constraint, one, and only one, of the signs $\leqslant$, $=$, $\geqslant$ holds, but the sign may vary from one constraint to another. Values of the variables $x_j$

*Applications of Linear Programming*

are sought to satisfy the conditions (5.1b) for

$$x_j \geqslant 0, \qquad j = 1, 2, \ldots, n. \tag{5.2}$$

The $a_{ij}$, $b_i$, and $c_j$ are known constants. Provided that the variables $x_j$ form a convex set and are not integers, there will be an infinite number of feasible solutions to a linear programming problem. The *simplex* technique is used to find the one that optimizes the objective function. Linear programming has been extended in different directions, such as parametric programming, integer programming, convex programming, stochastic linear programming, and multistage linear programming [2, 3].

## B. WATER QUALITY MANAGEMENT

The linear programming technique has found extensive application in planning waste water treatment plants, when it was assumed that the planning problems were of a single stage and deterministic in nature [4]. It has been shown that the types of problems arising in the management of the quality of natural water systems have linear features, and the possibility of solving them with linear programming is enhanced when marginal cost functions are available [5]. The planning of sewage treatment systems involves the selection of a satisfactory method of treatment at minimum cost, given that the removal efficiency of the plants depends upon their size and loading. The treatment process is defined as one that offers some removal efficiency at a distinct cost associated with each unit of impurity applied to the process. The process has a structure that is a specialized case of the general "network" models [2] solved by linear programming. The treatment is considered as a series of links $(i, j)$ $(i, j = 1, 2, \ldots, n-1, n)$ connecting the nodes $i$ and $j$ [4]. Each node is a treatment plant. The following symbols are defined.

$x_{ij}$ = pounds of BOD that flow from processes $i$ to $j$;
$x_{Ij}$ = pounds of BOD transmitted from input $I$ to any treatment process $j$;
$A$ = BOD input into the system;
$x_{iE}$ = pounds of BOD received from output of treatment process $i$;
$\alpha_j$ = removal efficiency associated with the $j$th treatment process $(\alpha_j \leqslant 1)$;
$\varepsilon_j$ = process factor $(1 - \alpha_j)$ equal to volume of BOD remaining;
$\varepsilon_j x_j$ = pounds of BOD remaining in the system after being treated by the $j$th process;

$c_j$ = cost of the $j$th process, in monetary units (MU) per unit of BOD applied;
$B$ = amount of BOD tolerated in the effluent;
$C$ = total cost of treatment system, given $A$.

As each process node consists of a receptor $j$ and transmitter ($j'$), it is required that

$$\varepsilon_{jj'} \sum_{i,j} x_{ij} - \sum_{k,j} x_{j,k} = 0 \qquad (i \neq j, k \neq j). \tag{5.3}$$

The problem is the minimization of

$$C = \sum_j c_{jj'} x_{jj'} \tag{5.4}$$

subject to

$$\sum_j x_{ij} = A, \tag{5.5}$$

$$\sum_i x_{iE} \leqslant B, \tag{5.6}$$

$$\sum_{i \neq j} x_{ij} - x_{jj'} = 0, \tag{5.7}$$

$$\varepsilon_{jj} x_{jj'} - \sum_{k \neq j} x_{jk} = 0, \tag{5.8}$$

$$x_{ij} \geqslant 0. \tag{5.9}$$

An example of the solution is illustrated in [4].

A more complex application is that of the determination of the degree of water treatment to be demanded from each waste contributor along a stream, given that the volume and characteristics of the pollutant are known. The following symbols are used.

$P_j$ = amount of BOD in population equivalents from city $j$;
$q_j$ = volume of waste (cubic feet per second) from city $j$;
$x_j$ = BOD removal ratio of treatment plant $j$ ($0 \leqslant x_j \leqslant y_j$);
$y_j$ = BOD discharge ratio ($y_j = 1 - x_j$);
$u_j$ = upper bound of treatment plant $j$'s efficiency ($u_j \leqslant 1.0$);
$P_j x_j$ = amount of BOD (in population equivalents) removed at treatment plant $j$;
$P_j y_j$ = amount of BOD discharged to river at point $j$;
$p_{jk}$ = decomposition ratio, fraction of $j$th waste still present at location $k$ ($0 \leqslant p_{jk} \leqslant 1.0$);

## Applications of Linear Programming

$Q_j$ = streamflow at point $j$ (ft³/sec) and in reach downstream to $j + 1$, excluding waste;

$B_j$ = maximum allowable loading at point $j$ (population equivalents/ft³/sec);

$C_j = f_j(x_j)$ = costs of $j$th treatment plant having a removal efficiency of $x_j$.

Figure 5.1 represents a sketch of the river together with an identification of the variables and parameters of the problem.

The general expression for the quality constraint along the $n$ reaches is

$$\frac{\sum_{j=1}^{n} p_{jn} P_j x_j}{(Q_n + \sum_{j=1}^{n} q_j)} \geqslant \frac{\sum_{j=1}^{n} p_{jn} P_j}{(Q_n + \sum_{j=1}^{n} q_j)} - B_n \qquad (5.10)$$

where $p_{jj} = 1$; $j = 1, 2, \ldots, n$. The first term on the right-hand side of expression (5.10) represents the amount of pollution in population equivalents per cubic foot per second that would be present at point $n$ if there were no

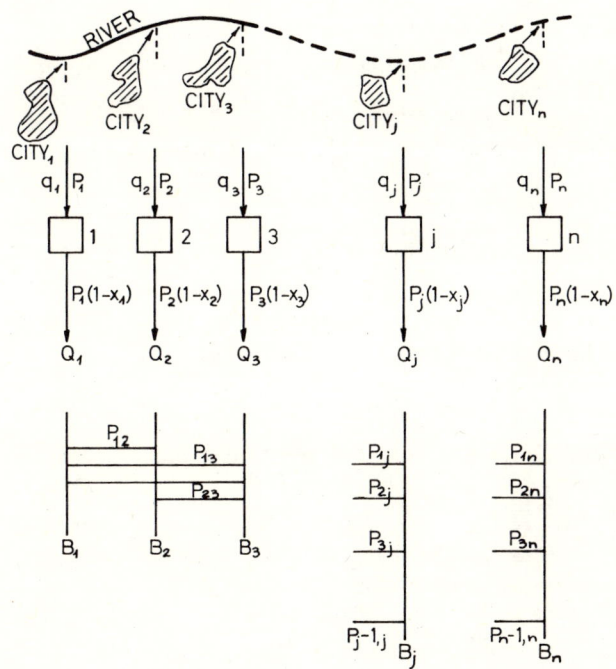

FIGURE 5.1. Schematic diagram of pollution control system along a large river.

treatment of wastes. The second term $B_n$ is the maximum allowable pollution load in reach $n$. Consequently, the left-hand side represents the amount of pollution that must be removed. For simplicity of notation, the constraints may written in the form

$$
\begin{aligned}
a_{11}x_1 &\geqslant b_1 \\
a_{21}x_1 + a_{22}x_2 &\geqslant b_2 \\
a_{31}x_1 + a_{32}x_2 + a_{33}x_3 &\geqslant b_3 \\
&\vdots \\
a_{n1}x_1 + a_{n2}x_2 + a_{n3}x_3 + \cdots + a_{nn}x_n &\geqslant b_n
\end{aligned} \qquad (5.11)
$$

where

$$b_k = \frac{\sum_{j=1}^{k} p_{jk} P_j}{(Q_k + \sum_{j=1}^{n} q_j)} - B_k, \qquad k = 1, 2, \ldots, n, \qquad (5.12)$$

and

$$
\begin{aligned}
a_{ij} &= \frac{p_{ji}P_j}{(Q_i + \sum_{j=1}^{i} q_j)} && \text{if } i \geqslant j, \\
&= 0 && \text{if } i \leqslant j.
\end{aligned} \qquad (5.13)
$$

In matrix form, expressions (5.11) can be written as

$$\mathbf{A}\mathbf{x} \geqslant \mathbf{b} \qquad (5.14)$$

where $\mathbf{A}$ is an $n \times n$ matrix of coefficients, $\mathbf{x}$ and $\mathbf{b}$ are $n$-dimensional column vectors.

A second set of constraints originates from the fact that the degree of treatment is limited to a given maximal value

$$0 \leqslant x_j \leqslant u_j, \qquad j = 1, 2, \ldots, n. \qquad (5.15)$$

The total costs of a system of $n$ treatment plants are

$$
\begin{aligned}
Z &= C_1 + C_2 + C_3 + \cdots + C_n \\
&= f_1(x_1) + f_2(x_2) + f_3(x_3) + \cdots + f_n(x_n) \\
&= \sum_{j=1}^{n} f_j(x_j).
\end{aligned} \qquad (5.16)
$$

Several solutions of the problem are possible, depending on the prevailing institutional and legal conditions: (i) each polluter must provide the same degree of removal; (ii) each polluter may discharge as much waste as possible without violating the stream standard $B_n$ (valid, perhaps, for upper reaches only); (iii) an overall least-cost solution.

Solution (ii) is not admissible, while solution (i) is given by finding the constraint $k$ among those of expressions (5.11), where

$$\frac{b_k}{\sum_{j=1}^{k} a_{ij}} = \max_{i} \left\{ \frac{b_i}{\sum_{j=1}^{i} a_{ij}} \right\}. \tag{5.17}$$

The required degree of treatment at each plant is then

$$\bar{x} = \frac{b_k}{\sum_{j=1}^{k} a_{ij}} \tag{5.18}$$

and the costs are

$$\sum_{j=1}^{n} f_j(\bar{x}_j). \tag{5.19}$$

Solution (iii) is not a pure linear programming problem, due to the technological constraints associated with the problem. Most treatment plants are primary plants, full treatment plants, or of some intermediate type. The cost function associated with this type of problem is a discontinuous function and requires that the problem be formulated rather in terms of integer programming. If the costs of waste treatment increase approximately linearly with the degree of treatment, then for the $j$th plant the cost function is

$$0.30 c_j \hat{x}_j, \qquad 0 \leqslant \hat{x}_j \leqslant 3 \hat{x}_j = \text{integer}, \tag{5.20}$$

where $c_j$ is a constant for the $j$th plant. This formulation ensures that the values taken on by $\hat{x}_j$ are either 0, 0.3, 0.6, or 0.9. The original linear programming problem is replaced by an integer programming problem: minimize

$$0.30 \sum_j c_j \hat{x}_j \tag{5.21}$$

subject to

$$0.30 \sum_i a_{ij} \hat{x}_j \geqslant b_j, \qquad i = 1, 2, \ldots, m; \tag{5.22}$$

$$\hat{x}_j \leqslant 3, \qquad j = 1, 2, \ldots, n; \tag{5.23}$$

and $\hat{x}_j = $ integer.

At least one numerical example of a solution of the foregoing problem can be found in the literature [6]. The possibility of adding additional parameters, such as a minimum dissolved oxygen level, was shown and the necessity to deal with variable streamflow as well as with the dynamic aspects of development were pointed out.

An attempt has been made to program investments in regional water quality improvement in the Delaware River Basin by means of various mathematical models based on linear and nonlinear programming techniques [7, 8]. The general problem of improvement at minimum cost is presented as follows [7]. Let a water resource be composed of a finite number $m$ of interconnected segments where $c_i$ ($i = 1, 2, \ldots, m$) is the dissolved oxygen (DO) improvement sought in segment $i$. The target improvements, described by the vector $\mathbf{C} = (c_i)$, are attained through any one of a convex set of alternative changes to the inputs of the water resource. Let $x_j$ be the decrease of the rate at which its effluent ultimately depletes oxygen from the system at input $j$, $j = 1, 2, \ldots, n$. The vector $\mathbf{x} = (x_j)$ generates DO improvements through a dynamic linear system which consists of a transformation function responding to outputs from the previous upstream segment. Let $a_{ij}$ be the DO improvement in segment $i$ per unit of $x_j$; then $\mathbf{A}$ will be an $m \times n$ matrix of coefficients so that $\mathbf{Ax}$ is the vector of DO changes resulting from $\mathbf{x}$. Thus if $u_j$ is the present rate at which the $j$th effluent ultimately depletes oxygen from the system, and $\mathbf{U}_j = (u_j)$ is the vector of oxygen demand, the constraints are

$$\mathbf{Ax} \geqslant 0, \qquad (5.24)$$

$$\mathbf{x} \leqslant \mathbf{U}, \qquad (5.25)$$

$$\mathbf{x} \geqslant 0. \qquad (5.26)$$

If the relevant cost functions are convex and may be assumed to be composed of linear segments, the objective function is

$$\text{minimize} \quad \mathbf{dx} \qquad (5.27)$$

where $\mathbf{d} = (d_j)$ is a row vector with $d_j$ being the unit cost of $x_j$.

The problem may be extended to deal with a "uniform treatment policy," that is, to specify the minimum proportion of the influent's oxygen demand that is removed by all the treatment plants. This proportion is set at the lowest possible value from which an acceptable stream quality will result in all its reaches. The choice is made by a sensitivity analysis in the form of parametric linear programming where the criterion is least cost. The following symbols are defined in addition to the notation used above.

$B_j$ = rate at which the influent into the $j$th waste source would deplete oxygen if discharged untreated;

$q_j = u_j/B_j$ = proportion of $B_j$ present in the $j$th effluent;

$s_j = u_j - x_j$ = oxygen demand of $j$th effluent after instituting program element $x_j$;

$\hat{q}_j = s_j/B_j$ = proportion of $B_j$ present in the $j$th effluent after instituting program element $x_j$, $j = 1, 2, \ldots, n$.

The linear programming formulation seeks to minimize the cost of the constrained improvements, subject to the additional set of constraints that the $\hat{q}_j$ be identical. The latter constraint minimizes the proportion of influent wastes removed, as cost is an increasing function of the $x_j$. The problem is formulated, therefore, as follows.

Minimize

$$\mathbf{dx} \tag{5.28}$$

subject to

$$\mathbf{x} \geqslant 0, \tag{5.29}$$

$$\mathbf{Ax} \geqslant \mathbf{c}, \tag{5.30}$$

$$\mathbf{x} \leqslant \mathbf{U}, \tag{5.31}$$

$$\frac{x_j}{B_j} - \frac{x_{j+1}}{B_{j+1}} = q_j - q_{j+1}, \tag{5.32}$$

where $\mathbf{c}$ is a predetermined standard.

It has been shown [7] that the foregoing formulation is not acceptable for a case in which a certain proportion greater than some $q_j$ exists such that $\mathbf{Ax} \geqslant \mathbf{c}$. This difficulty can be overcome by a mixed integer linear programming formulation. It is also shown how the problem may be solved on the basis of maximizing a benefit–cost ratio using the theory of fractional linear programming problems.

In reality, the design efficiency of a waste treatment plant may be considered as the mean value of a probability distribution function from which the operating efficiency is a random sample [7]. Most of the variance of the DO time series is a direct result of fluctuations in air and water temperatures as well as of tributary inflows and lateral outflows. These exogenous parameters not only determine the value of $\mathbf{A} = (a_{ij})$, but also that of $\mathbf{c} = (c_i)$. It may be assumed that for a finite number of possible environmental conditions stationary probabilities are known. If not, they may be found by using queuing models [9]. If the streamflow is divided into a range of $K$ values, the stochastic analog to equations (5.28)–(5.32) is minimize

$$\mathbf{dx} \tag{5.33}$$

subject to

$$0 \leqslant \mathbf{x} \leqslant \mathbf{U} \tag{5.34}$$

and

$$\sum_{k=1}^{K} p_k \mathbf{A}^k \mathbf{x} \geqslant \sum_{k=1}^{K} p_k \mathbf{c}^k, \tag{5.35}$$

where

$$p_k = P[(\mathbf{A}, \mathbf{c}) = (\mathbf{A}^k, \mathbf{c}^k)], \quad k = 1, 2, \ldots, K. \tag{5.36}$$

Here $\mathbf{c}$ is a random vector and $\mathbf{A}$ is a random matrix, both being functions of the environment. Every feasible program of the stochastic formulation results in a vector of expected DO increases, at least as great as the expectation of $\mathbf{c}$.

In some cases, it is necessary to design the waste water reclamation facilities on the basis of a minimal variance in the DO time series, due to damage resulting from several days of sustained low concentrations. The feasible programs are then determined by the constraints

$$0 \leqslant \mathbf{x} \leqslant \mathbf{U}, \tag{5.37}$$

$$\mathbf{dx} \leqslant \mathbf{M}, \tag{5.38}$$

and

$$\sum_{k=1}^{K} p_k \mathbf{A}^k \mathbf{x} \geqslant \sum_{k=1}^{K} p_k \mathbf{c}^k \tag{5.39}$$

where $\mathbf{M} = (M_j)$ is a row vector in which the elements are budgetary constraints on $d_j x_j$, $j = 1, 2, \ldots, n$. The optimality criterion (to be minimized) is

$$\sum_{i=1}^{m} \text{(variance of DO improvement in segment } i \text{ of the river)}.$$

This leads to a quadratic programming problem, which can be written as

$$\sum_{i=1}^{m} \left[ \sum_{k=1}^{K} p_k \left( \sum_{j=1}^{n} a_{ij}^k x_j \right)^2 - \left( \sum_{k=1}^{K} p_k \sum_{j=1}^{n} a_{ij}^k x_j \right)^2 \right]. \tag{5.40}$$

*Applications of Linear Programming*

## C. DESIGN AND OPERATION OF RESERVOIRS

Linearized models of water supply systems have been used with limited success in order to solve problems involving the choice of dam capacities, their scales of development, and their operating policies [10–13]. Although the technique can cope with simultaneous optimization of many variables, it becomes unsuitable when multiperiod multistructure problems with overyear storage are formulated as having a stochastic hydrology with serial correlation between inflows. An additional computational complication in multivariable problems of this type is the introduction of discounting factors, when expected present value of net benefits must be determined to evaluate the feasibility of water resource development projects. Three versions of a multistructure model of increasing complexity have been published [10], each requiring a different set of simplifying assumptions. The necessity of such assumptions was even more evident when treating single-dam stochastic models [12, 13] which do not optimize all three aspects of dam design simultaneously, that is, the size, the allocation of storage to various water derivatives, and the operating policy. In these cases linear programming loses some of its advantage arising from its inherent ability to treat multivariable problems.

The simplest multistructure model treated by linear programming assumes that the hydrology is composed of a succession of identical river flows, having a value equal to that of some critical year, or the long-term average discharge. In this case the model yields optimal structure sizes, an optimal set of outputs that can be obtained with the given flows and structures, as well as an optimal operating procedure for achieving these outputs. This was done by treating both structure sizes and target outputs for various water derivatives as variables that must be chosen in order to yield a maximum value of an economic objective function while satisfying given hydrological and technological constraints. An important aspect of the model was that although some terms of the objective function representing capital costs of structures and marginal benefits from various water derivatives were not linear, it was shown how the linear programming algorithm could be used. This required the approximation of such functions by linear segments. The severest limitation of the model lies in the deterministic assumption of the hydrological process, which precludes the provision of overyear storage.

The configuration of this simple river basin system is shown in Figure 5.2. In this diagram, the top figure in each hydrological reach represents the wet-season flow, while the bottom figure is the dry-season flow, both in $10^6$ acre-ft. $Y$ is active capacity of reservoir $B$, $Z$ is active capacity of reservoir $C$, and $I$ is annual irrigation supply, all also in $10^6$ acre-ft. The problem may be stated as: determine

$$\max \pi = B_1(E) + B_2(I) - K_1(Y) - K_2(Z) - K_3(E) - K_4(I) \quad (5.41)$$

subject to

$$33 - Y \geqslant 0, \quad (5.42)$$

$$39 - Y - 0.425I \geqslant 0, \quad (5.43)$$

$$1.8 + Y - 0.575I \geqslant 0, \quad (5.44)$$

$$39 - Y - Z - 0.275I \geqslant 0, \quad (5.45)$$

$$Y + Z + 0.275I + 3.47E \leqslant 6.9, \quad (5.46)$$

and

$$-Y - Z + 0.25I + 3.47E \leqslant 3.9, \quad (5.47)$$

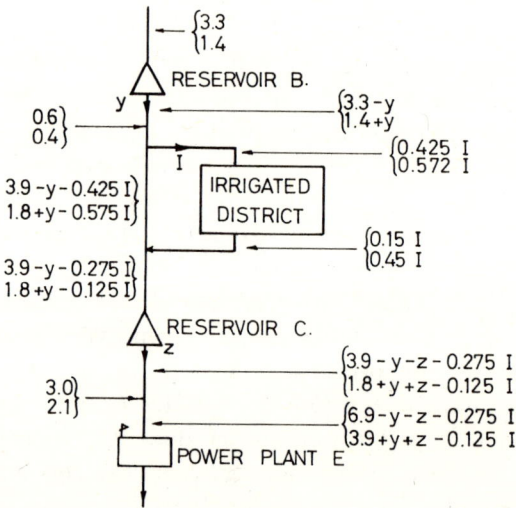

FIGURE 5.2. Schematic diagram of a multipurpose water resource development project. (Reprinted by permission of the publishers, from Arthur Maass *et al.*, *Design of water-resource systems*, Harvard University Press, Cambridge, Massachusetts, copyright 1962 by the President and Fellows of Harvard College.)

## Applications of Linear Programming

where

$B_1(E)$ is the present value of power sold, in $10^6$ dollars;
$B_2(I)$ is the present value of water sold for irrigation, in $10^6$ dollars;
$K_1(Y)$ is the capital cost of building reservoir $B$ to capacity $Y$ ($10^6$ acre-ft) in $10^6$ dollars;
$K_2(Z)$ is the capital cost of building reservoir $C$ to capacity $Z$ ($10^6$ acre-ft) in $10^6$ dollars;
$K_3(E)$ is the capital cost of building the power plant to capacity $E$ in $10^9$ kwh/year, in $10^6$ dollars;
$K_4(I)$ is the capital cost of building the irrigation system to capacity $I$ in $10^6$ acre-ft/year, in $10^6$ dollars.

The first three cost functions are simple nonlinear functions:

$$K_1(Y) = \frac{43Y}{(1 + 0.2Y)}, \qquad (5.48)$$

$$K_2(Z) = \frac{47Z}{(1 + 0.3Z)}, \qquad (5.49)$$

$$K_3(E) = 20.6E - E^2. \qquad (5.50)$$

Regarding $K_4(I)$, in order to supply more than $3 \times 10^6$ acre-ft of irrigation water, pumping capacity is needed. Hence, the capital cost function is divided into two parts: $I_1$ denoting the nonpumped portion and $I_2$ the pumped portion. Then the capital cost function for the irrigation project is

$$K_4(I) = 44I_1 + 64I_2 + 4.5I_1{}^+ + 0.5I_2{}^+ \qquad (5.51)$$

where $I_1 + I_2 = I$, $I_1 \leqslant 3$, and $I^+$ is a function that takes on the value of unity when $I > 0$, and otherwise equals zero. The objective function, equation (5.41), is explicitly expressed in terms of the design variables as

$$\pi = 229.4E + E^2 + 1.4I_1 - 48.7I_2 + 1045 \log_{10}(1 + 0.2I)$$

$$- 4.5I_1{}^+ - 0.5I_2{}^+ - \frac{43Y}{(1 + 0.2Y)} - \frac{47Z}{(1 + 0.3Z)}. \qquad (5.52)$$

Due to the nonlinearity of the objective function, equation (5.52), the problem is solved by introducing a new set of variables, which approximate it by a sequence of linear segments. To carry out this ingenious approximation, the original variables $Y$, $Z$, $E$, and $I$ are expressed as functions of sets of five weights:

$$Y = \sum_{i=1}^{5} i\alpha_i, \tag{5.53}$$

$$Z = \sum_{j=0}^{5} j\beta_j, \tag{5.54}$$

$$E = \sum_{k=0}^{5} k\gamma_k, \tag{5.55}$$

$$I = \sum_{l=0}^{5} l\delta_l. \tag{5.56}$$

All weights are nonnegative, each set of weights totals unity, no more than two weights in any set are permitted to be positive, and those two must be adjacent. All the original variables must be replaced by their equivalents in the constraints and the objective function. Although the format of the problem formulated in equations (5.41)–(5.47) and expressed in terms of the new variables is that of a linear programming problem, there is no guarantee that a solution will satisfy also the restrictions verbally described above as to the nature of the transformed variables. The algorithm has to be solved several times, deleting some of the new variables ($\alpha_i$, $\beta_j$, $\gamma_k$, $\delta_l$) by setting them equal to zero in each iteration. The solution is achieved when not more than two weights are positive and adjacent for each variable $Y$, $I$, $Z$, and $E$.

The success of the computational technique depended on the fact that, while not linear, the objective function was separable into a series of components containing one variable only. This characteristic of the objective function was exploited when each of its components was replaced by a chordal approximation employing linear interpolation of a single variable. If the objective function is not separable, as is demonstrated in an extension of the model, the linearization procedure is substantially more involved. It is shown that if the constraints are nonlinear functions of two variables and are representable by plane surfaces, linear approximations of these functions are possible by constructing grids. The functions are evaluated at each of the nodal points of the grids. Then the linear approximation is a weighted average of the values of the function at the interaction points, where the weights satisfy the following rules. (a) They are nonnegative; (b) their sum equals unity; (c) no more than three are positive; (d) all the points with positive weights are corners of the same square of the grid. For example, if the weights are denoted by $\Delta_{ij}$, the approximation takes the form

*Applications of Linear Programming*

$$f(Y, a) = \sum_i \sum_j \Delta_{ij} f(i, j) \tag{5.57}$$

where $f(i, j)$ is the value of the function being approximated at the point $Y = i, a = j$. Although functions of more than two variables can be linearized in this manner, the number of auxiliary variables that must be introduced increases rapidly with the dimensionality of the function.

The problem of computational restrictions becomes very important in limiting the number of variables to be optimized when complex problems are attempted. If a total of 250 constraints is a practical limit to the magnitude of a programming problem of the foregoing type and if the annual water cycle is divided into 12 monthly periods, only 20 constraints are available for each month. This number will allow the optimization of a system of a very moderate number of elements. In addition, the difficulty of solution increases as the third power of the number of equations. As soon as streamflow with a high degree of interannual variability is considered, overyear storage is required. An estimation of optimal reservoir size requires the consideration of the long-term operation of the system. In other words, optimization of a 5-year sequence of monthly flows in a drought period includes 600 periods. This formulation is certain to include more than the permissible number of constraints. If such a sequence is derivable from residual mass curves, then the solution to the multistructure multiperiod problem is useful in estimating the amounts necessary for overyear storage.

Retaining the possibility of treating nonlinear functions, a simple model is presented for the solution of a four-season problem by use of the "decomposition principle" [2] of linear programming. The simplified system is presented in Figure 5.3. The following symbols are used.

$f_1(t)$ = inflow to reservoir $B$, which has an active storage capacity of $Y$ units, during time period (season) $t$, $t = 1, 2, 3, 4$;

$S(t)$ = amount of water stored in reservoir $B$ at the beginning of time period $t$;

$a(t)$ = amount of water released from reservoir $B$ during time period $t$;

$f_2(t), f_3(t)$ = inflows from tributaries (2) and (3) into the main stream during time period $t$;

$I$ = annual irrigation demand;

$K_t$ = proportion of total irrigation demand in time period $t$, $0 \leqslant K_t \leqslant 1$,

$$\sum_{t=1}^{4} K_t = 1; \tag{5.58}$$

## Scientific Allocation of Water Resources

$K_t'$ = irrigation return flow coefficient for time period $t$, $0 \leqslant K_t' \leqslant 1$,

$$\sum_{t=1}^{4} K_t' \leqslant 1; \tag{5.59}$$

$E_t$ = power generated during time period $t$.

The problem can be formulated mathematically as follows. Maximize

$$\pi = 221E - 32Y \tag{5.60}$$

subject to

$$a(t) + f_2(t) \geqslant K_t I, \qquad t = 1, 2, 3, 4, \tag{5.61}$$

$$a(t) \leqslant S(t) + f_1(t), \tag{5.62}$$

$$S(t) \leqslant S(t-1) + f_1(t-1) - a(t-1), \tag{5.63}$$

$$S(t) + f_1(t) - a(t) \leqslant Y, \tag{5.64}$$

$$a(t) + f_2(t) - (K_t - K_t')I + f_3(t) \geqslant 6.95 E_t, \tag{5.65}$$

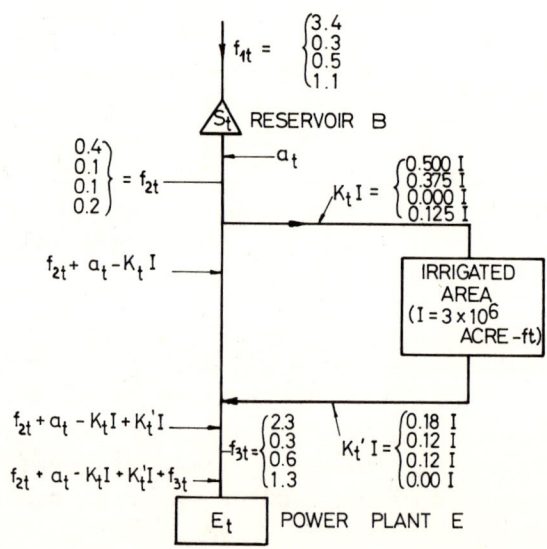

FIGURE 5.3. Configuration of a four-period deterministic water resource model. (Reprinted by permission of the publisher, from Arthur Maass *et al.*, *Design of water-resource systems*, Harvard University Press, Cambridge, Massachusetts, copyright 1962 by the President and Fellows of Harvard College.)

and
$$E_t \geqslant C_t E, \qquad (5.66)$$

where $E$ is the annual energy output and $C_t$ is a specified seasonal proportion of it.

In this formulation we have a problem with 14 decision variables (4 each of $S(t)$, $a(t)$, $E(t)$) constrained by 24 conditions (each of the six expressions (5.61) through (5.66) are in fact 4 conditions). Observe that constraints (5.61), (5.62), and (5.65) contain decision variables related only to one time period; that constraint (5.63) has decision variables that link two consecutive time periods; and constraints (5.64) and (5.66) contain the variables $Y$ and $E$ common to all periods.

All the constraints relating to the first period may be replaced by a single constraint only. The same is possible for the remaining three periods. This is done by solving a linear programming subproblem for each period, the subproblem including all the constraints that relate exclusively to that period: three, in this example. When this has been done, a master problem is solved which contains all constraints relating to more than one period, plus a supplementary constraint for each period. The result of this decomposition technique is that in the case of this example the 24 constraints are replaced by a set of problems having up to 3 constraints each and one additional problem that has 16 constraints. In general, the reduction in problem size is equal to the number of periods multiplied by one less than the number of constraints in each period.

The inherent limitations of the foregoing models become apparent when applications to real-life systems are made. These shortcomings are more stringent when treating problems having stochastic streamflows. The simplest model of this kind deals with a single reservoir, a single season, and a single use. It is assumed that the inflow can take on 5 possible values $f_i$ each having a probability $p_i$. Let $I$ denote the guaranteed annual quantity of irrigation water; $K$ the reservoir capacity; $y_i$ the quantity of water that will be supplied if inflow $f_i$ is realized; and $S$ the quantity of water in storage at the beginning of the season (year).

The expected value of annual net benefits will be

$$B = 15I - 1.5K - 30 \sum p_i (I - y_i)^+, \qquad (5.67)$$

where the constants represent dollars per acre-foot (or in general, monetary units per unit volume). Note that $30 \sum p_i (I - y_i)^+$ is an expected loss function that is positive if $I - y_i > 0$.

The constraints are

$$y_i \leq S + f_i, \qquad i = 1, 2, 3, 4, 5, \tag{5.68}$$

and

$$\sum p_i(S + f_i - y_i) \geq S, \tag{5.69}$$

which simplifies to

$$\sum p_i y_i \leq \sum p_i f_i = 3.5. \tag{5.70}$$

Equation (5.70) represents a modification of $S$: this has become a decision variable equivalent to a target level for initial storage. Since equation (5.67) is not linear (because of the expression $(I - y_i)^+$), the auxiliary variables $u_i$, $i = 1, 2, 3, 4, 5$, are introduced ($u$ stands for undersupply). These variables satisfy

$$u_i \geq I - y_i, \tag{5.71}$$

$$u_i \geq 0. \tag{5.72}$$

The benefit function then becomes

$$B = 15I - 1.5K - 30 \sum p_i u_i \tag{5.73}$$

and the problem may be solved by the simplex method or the decomposition principle.

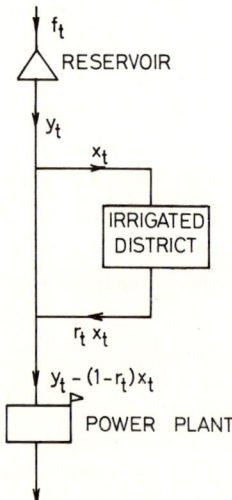

FIGURE 5.4. Configuration of a three-season stochastic model. (Reprinted by permission of the publishers, from Arthur Maass *et al.*, *Design of water-resource systems*, Harvard University Press, Cambridge, Massachusetts, copyright 1962 by the President and Fellows of Harvard College.)

## Applications of Linear Programming

A more complex model containing three seasons, two uses of water, and stochastic inflows represents an extension of the foregoing model. Its configuration is shown in Figure 5.4. Four decisions are involved in the design process: the reservoir capacity $(K)$; the target output of irrigation water $(I)$; the generating capacity of the power plant $(G)$; the quantity of firm energy to be provided $(E)$. The annual net benefits (anb), in $10^6$ dollars, are given by

$$\text{anb} = 3.2I + 0.007E - 1.5K - 7.38G + \text{value of dump energy}$$
$$- \text{ irrigation water shortage costs.} \tag{5.74}$$

If amounts of irrigation water of $x_1$ and $x_2$ are needed in the first and second seasons only, then the supply is $0.4I$ and $0.6I$, respectively. If $x_1$ and $x_2$ are actual amounts of irrigation water supplied, irrigation water shortage costs are

$$8(0.4I - x_1) + 10(0.6I - x_2) = 9.2I - 8x_1 - 10x_2. \tag{5.75}$$

If $q_1$, $q_2$, and $q_3$ denote the flow through the turbines in the three seasons, the cost of thermal power necessary to meet demand $E$ under conditions of deficient supply of water is

$$0.0085[(0.4E - 144q_1)^+ + (0.3E - 144q_2)^+ + (0.3E - 144q_3)^+]$$
$$+ 0.0005E - 0.072(q_1 + q_2 + q_3). \tag{5.76}$$

Since the expression in square brackets is composed of three linear segments, new variables $e_1$, $e_2$, and $e_3$ are defined such that

$$e_1, e_2, e_3 \geqslant 0, \tag{5.77}$$

$$e_1 \geqslant 0.4E - 144q_1, \tag{5.78}$$

$$e_2 \geqslant 0.3E - 144q_2, \tag{5.79}$$

$$e_3 \geqslant 0.3E - 144q_3. \tag{5.80}$$

The annual net benefit function then becomes

$$\text{anb} = -6I + 0.0065E - 1.5K - 7.38G + 8x_1 + 10x_2$$
$$+ 0.072(q_1 + q_2 + q_3) - 0.0085(e_1 + e_2 + e_3). \tag{5.81}$$

The physical meaning of $e_t$ is the amount of thermal energy supplied in period $t$, $t = 1, 2, 3$.

The objective function, equation (5.81), cannot be optimized directly, because $x_1$, $x_2$, $q_1$, $q_2$, $q_3$, $e_1$, $e_2$, and $e_3$ depend on the random variable $f_t$, the seasonal inflow. Instead, the expected value of annual net benefits is optimized and the constraints for operation during the first season are derived. These are

$$S_1 + f \geqslant y_{1f}, \tag{5.82}$$

$$S_1 + f - y_{1f} \leqslant K, \tag{5.83}$$

$$S_1 + \sum_{f=3}^{5} p_f f - \sum_{f=3}^{5} p_f y_{1f} \geqslant S_2, \tag{5.84}$$

$$x_{1f} \leqslant y_{1f}, \tag{5.85}$$

$$x_{1f} \leqslant 0.4I, \tag{5.86}$$

$$q_{1f} \leqslant y_{1f} - 0.4x_{1f}, \tag{5.87}$$

$$144 q_{1f} \leqslant 1898G, \tag{5.88}$$

$$e_{1f} \geqslant 0.4E - 144 q_{1f}, \tag{5.89}$$

where

$S_1$ = assumed contents of reservoir at the start of the first season;
$y_{1f}$ = releases made from the reservoir during the first season, given inflow $f$, $f = 3, 4, 5$;
$x_{1f}$ = irrigation water supplied during the first season, given inflow $f$;
$q_{1f}$ = flow through the turbines during the first season, given inflow $f$;
$e_{1f}$ = thermal energy supplied during the first season, given inflow $f$;
$S_2$ = minimum expected content of reservoir at the end of the first season;
144 = conversion factor for power plant in kilowatthours per acre-foot of flow;
1898 = length of season in hours, multiplied by the load factor = 8760/3 × 0.65.

In order to solve the problem, all random variables in the objective function, equation (5.81), must be replaced by their expected values. If $f$ has three possible values, there are three possible values for $x$ having probabilities identical to those of the values of $f$. Therefore

$$\text{expected value of} \quad x_1 = \sum_{f=3}^{5} p_f x_{1f}. \tag{5.90}$$

Similar substitutions yield a problem having a standard linear programming format, which may be solved by standard methods.

It was found that the use of expected values tended to introduce an optimistic bias into the result. It is false to assume that the reservoir has a "normal" content at the beginning of each period. The bias is to be weighted against the fact that if 3 inflow states were possible in each season, 9 contingencies were dealt with instead of 27 possible inflow patterns. Another drawback of the technique is the use of a small number of inflow values: the number of constraints to be handled is roughly proportional to the number of possible values of the basic variables. The computational burden increases considerably when tributaries are added to the main river. Important features of the foregoing stochastic model are the use of loss functions when commitments are not met and the omission of fixed commitments from the constraints.

The rather extreme limitation that storage at the beginning of each season equaled its expected value was overcome by the development of a stochastic sequential model based on linear programming [14]. This model utilizes the probability distribution of initial storage and yields a stochastic storage–yield relationship for a single reservoir capacity in the form of probability distributions of expected draft. These maximize the expected value of the objective function to give an optimal combination of target output and operating procedure for that output, including overyear storage. Finally, by methods of sampling and iteration, a reservoir capacity is chosen such that its optimal outputs and operating procedure confer a maximum value to the objective function.

Assume a multiperiod model of a reservoir of capacity $M$, where subscript $i$ ($i = 1, 2, \ldots, n$) denotes a specific period while subscript $t$ ($t = 1, 2, \ldots, T$) represents the cumulated runoff periods up to a given time. Let $_iX_t$ be the streamflow during period $i$ of a year and period $t$ of the total time series, with the probability $_iP_j$ ($j = 0, 1, \ldots, a$) of having $j$ volume units. Furthermore, let the storage at the start of period $i$ equal $_iR_t$ volume units, and $_iK_r$ ($r = 0, 1, \ldots, M$) be the probability of $_iR_t$ equaling $r$. Then the probability of $_iX_t = j$ and $_iR_t = r$ is $(_iP_j)(_iK_r)$ or $_ig_{j,r}$. If $j + r = K$, where $K = 0, 1, \ldots, (a + M)$, then $_ig_{j,r} = {_ig_{j,K-j}}$. Finally let $_ih_{c,s}$ denote the probability of reservoir storage $_iS_t$ being $s$ after a draft $_iy_t = c$ units occurred during the period where $(c + s) \leqslant (a + M)$. To be in balance, the amount of water available for use at the beginning of a period (inflow plus storage) must equal the draft during the period plus the storage at the end of the period, or $j + r = c + s = K$. Since the probability of storage at the end of a period must equal the probability of the same state at the beginning of the following period,

$$\sum_j {}_ig_{j,k-j} = \sum_c {}_ih_{c,k-c}. \tag{5.91}$$

An optimal operating policy is defined as the value of the draft ${}_iy_t$ given ${}_iX_t + {}_iR_t$, so that a set of ${}_ih_{c,s}$ values (that add up to unity) defines an operating procedure. Now

$$\text{Prob}\{{}_iy_t = c|({}_iX_t + {}_iR_t) = k\} = \frac{\text{Prob}\{{}_iy_t = c, ({}_iX_t + {}_iR_t) = k\}}{\text{Prob}\{{}_iX_t + R_t = k\}}$$

$$= \frac{\text{Prob}\{{}_iy_t = c, S_t = (k-c)\}}{\text{Prob}\{{}_iX_t + {}_iR_t = k\}}$$

$$= \frac{{}_ih_{c,k-c}}{\sum_c {}_ih_{c,k-c}}. \tag{5.92}$$

A list of all ${}_ih_{c,k-c}$ values will yield a complete operating policy, while a solution using linear programming will yield optimal values for ${}_ih_{c,k-c}$. It is shown that the storage–yield relationship yields two sets of constraint equations, namely, $n$ equations (one for each value of $i$)

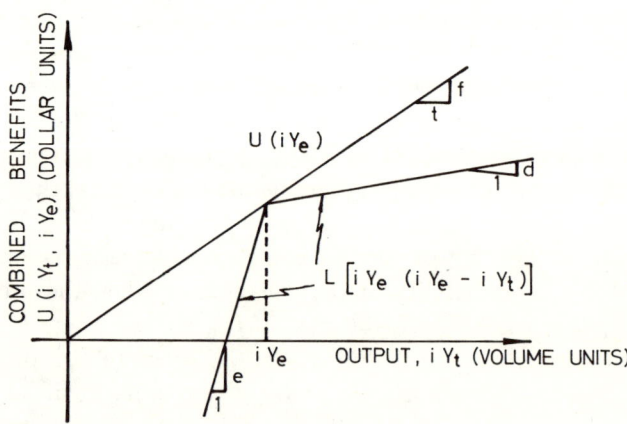

FIGURE 5.5. Function relating combined benefits $u$ to target outputs ${}_iY_e$ and to actual outputs ${}_iY_t$.

## Applications of Linear Programming

$$\sum_{c,s} {}_i h_{c,s} = 1 \tag{5.93}$$

and $(a + M)$ equations of the form

$$\sum_j {}_i P_j \left( \sum_c {}_{i-1} h_{c,r} \right) = \sum_c {}_i h_{c,k-c}. \tag{5.94}$$

Keeping the reservoir capacity and level of development constant allows capital and operation, maintenance and replacement costs to be fixed. If the target output is denoted by ${}_i y_e$, the gross benefit function is given by

$$u({}_i y_t, {}_i y_e) = f({}_i y_e) + d({}_i y_t - {}_i y_e)^+ - e({}_i y_e - {}_i y_t)^+ \tag{5.95}$$

where the subscript $+$ indicates that the bracketed terms are only operative when they are greater than or equal to zero. The function is shown graphically in Figure 5.5. The objective function may then be written as

$$u({}_i y_t, {}_i y_e) = u(c, {}_i y_e) = {}_i u_c \tag{5.96}$$

where $e = 1, 2, \ldots, m$ represent different activities. Since it is required to maximize the expected value of gross benefits $E(u)$, the objective function becomes

$$E(u) = \sum_{i,c,s} ({}_i u_c)({}_i h_{c,s}). \tag{5.97}$$

Using linear programming, an optimal policy may be found for a given value of ${}_i y_e$, while parametric programming finds the values of ${}_i y_e$ that maximize expected net benefits. Trying different reservoir sizes by sampling will yield an ultimate optimal solution for reservoir capacity, target outputs, and operating procedure.

A similar problem has been solved with emphasis on the trade offs between several purposes, such as irrigation, power generation, and flood control [15].

### D. AQUIFER MANAGEMENT

An outstanding example of linearization and use of linear programming computational techniques is that of optimization of an irrigation and drainage project in West Pakistan [16]. Leakage of irrigation canals over a period of over 60 years raised the regional water table, causing waterlogging and salinity problems over an area of approximately 5.6 million acres. About 100,000 acres per year were lost to agriculture. The proposed solution to the problem is a network of tube wells, which are to combat waterlogging and salinization by lowering the water table, as well as to supplement surface water supplies. A sketch of the control system is shown in Figure 5.6. The saline area (of 5.6 million acres) is underlain by groundwater with an average concentration of total dissolved solids of 6000 mg/liter, while the nonsaline area of the same project has groundwater with an average salinity of 700 mg/liter. The saline area is potentially excellent farmland, if reclaimed and if extra water is made available for irrigation and for the maintenance of a favorable salt balance.

The study presents the following solution. In the nonsaline area, the groundwater is to be pumped extensively, in order to recover the infiltrating

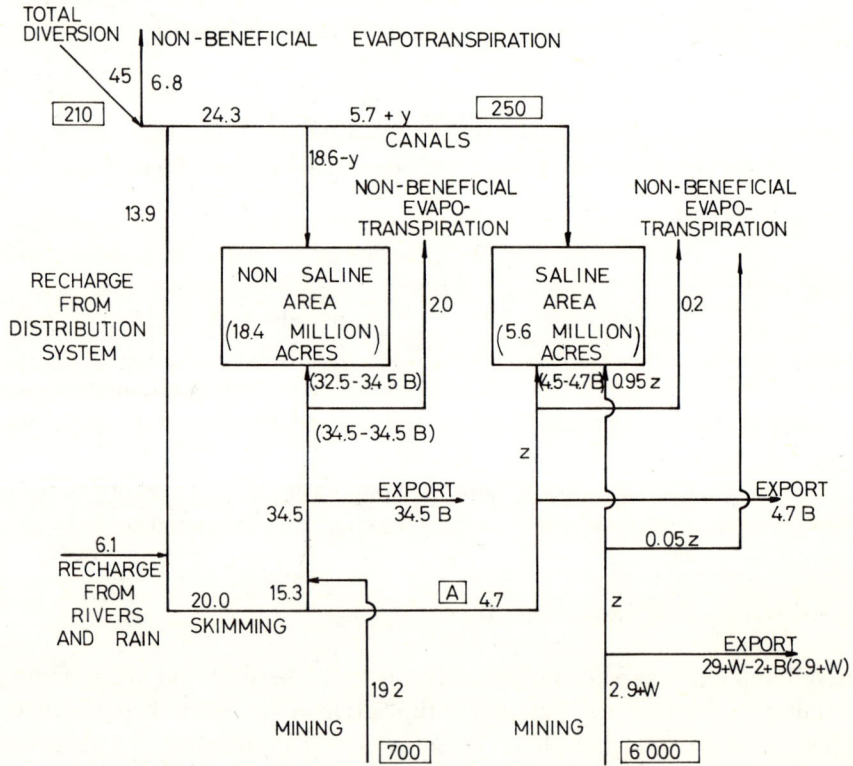

FIGURE 5.6. Flow sheet for the irrigation and drainage problem in West Pakistan (after [16]).

"fresh" water (750–1000 mg/liter) and to "mine" the aquifer at a rate such that after 30 years the water table will be lowered 100 ft. In the saline area, the infiltrating fresh water will be recovered by shallower ("skimming") wells. The aquifer will be mined by a set of deep wells on order to achieve two important results: (i) to reduce the general hydraulic gradient in the direction of the nonsaline area; and (ii) to provide additional water, which is to be diluted with higher quality canal water, for irrigation in the area. Although this solution means that a larger proportion of available surface water will be directed to the saline area, pumped fresh water will be exported from that area. It was shown that, on the basis of previous studies, a certain proportion of all tube-well effluent must be exported in order to prevent salt accumulation in this hydroagronomic system.

Given an upper limit of water salinity with respect to crop salt tolerance, it was necessary to determine what amount of mined water from the saline area might be economically used for irrigation so as to maximize the benefits resulting from the project. This entailed finding optimum values for three decision variables: (i) the flow of canal water diverted to the saline area to dilute saline tube-well effluent ($Y$); (ii) the amount ($0.95Z$) of saline groundwater to be diluted with the surface water and applied to crops in the saline area; (iii) the rate of mining ($W$) in the saline area in excess of 2.9 million acre-ft/year required to prevent the movement of saline groundwater into the nonsaline area. Any solution must satisfy the following constraints.

1. If one third of the tube wells have an effluent with excessive salinity and/or high sodium adsorption ratio (SAR) [17], then the ratio of surface water to one third of the tube-well water in the nonsaline area must be equal to or greater than one:

$$\frac{18.6 - Y}{\frac{1}{3}[32.5 - 34.5B]} \geq 1, \tag{5.98}$$

where $B$ is the fraction of tube-well water to be exported to prevent salt accumulation.

2. The salinity of applied irrigation water in the saline area must be less than some specified upper limit $C_{max}$. In other words,

$$(4.5 - 4.7B)A + 0.95Z(6000) + (5.7 + Y)250$$
$$\leq [5.7 + Y + 0.95Z + (4.5 - 4.7B) + R]C_{max} \tag{5.99}$$

where $A$ = concentration of recharge water in the saline area and $R$ = the effective rainfall.

3. The ratio of surface water to half the tube-well water in the saline area must equal at least two, due to the excessive SAR of the latter:

$$\frac{5.7 + Y}{\frac{1}{2}[4.5 - 4.7B + 0.95Z]} \geqslant 2. \tag{5.100}$$

4. The export of mined water from the saline area must equal at least the fraction $B$ of the pumped water:

$$2.9 + W - Z \geqslant B(2.9 + W). \tag{5.101}$$

5. The total annual amount of irrigation water in the nonsaline area must be at most equal to the product of the total area (18.4 million acres) and the average annual irrigation application $\varDelta$:

$$(18.6 - Y) + (32.5 - 34.5B) \leqslant 18.4\varDelta. \tag{5.102}$$

6. The total amount of irrigation water applied annually to the saline area must be less than the product of the total area (5.6 million acres) and the average rate of irrigation $K\varDelta$:

$$(5.7 + Y) + (4.5 - 4.7B) + 0.95Z \leqslant 5.6(K\varDelta) \tag{5.103}$$

where $K$ is the additional amount of water required for leaching ($K > 1$). The annual net benefits from the total irrigated area will then be

$$N = b_A \left[ \frac{51.1 - 34.5B - Y}{\varDelta} + \frac{10.2 - 4.7B + 0.95Z + Y}{K\varDelta} \right]$$
$$- C_w(20.0 + 19.2 + 2.9 + W) - C_m Y - C_e(34.5B)$$
$$- C_e(4.7B) - C_e(2.9 + W - Z) \tag{5.104}$$

where $b_A$ = annual benefits per million acres; $C_w$ = annual unit cost of tube-well water; $C_m$ = annual unit cost of increasing canal capacity to the saline area; $C_e$ = annual unit cost of exporting saline water from the irrigated area. Each term in equation (5.104) may be divided by $C_w$, forming a relative net benefit function

$$\mathrm{nb} = \left[ \frac{L}{3.5}\left(\frac{1}{K} - 1\right) - M \right] Y + \left[ \frac{0.95L}{3.5K} + F \right] Z - (F + 1)W$$
$$+ \left[ -42.1 + 13.6L + \frac{2.78L}{K} - 6.82F \right] \tag{5.105}$$

where

$$\text{nb} = \frac{N}{C_w}, \tag{5.106}$$

$$L = \frac{b_A}{C_w}, \tag{5.107}$$

$$M = \frac{C_m}{C_w}, \tag{5.108}$$

and

$$F = \frac{C_e}{C_w}. \tag{5.109}$$

In equation (5.105) also the values $B = 0.01$ and $\Delta = 3.5$ ft/year were substituted.

In the objective function, equation (5.105), $K$ is a function of the concentration of the applied irrigation water in the saline area $C$, which is, in turn, a function of $Y$ and $Z$: $K = f[C(Y, Z)]$. However, if $K$ is considered constant, the nonlinear terms in the objective function are linearized.

The problem may now be stated generally as

$$\max\{F(\mathbf{X}) | \mathbf{a}_i^T \mathbf{X} \leqslant b_i\}, \qquad i = 1, 2, \ldots, m; \quad \mathbf{X} \geqslant 0, \tag{5.110}$$

where $\mathbf{a}_i^T \mathbf{X} \leqslant b_i$, $i = 1, 2, \ldots, m$, is a set of technological (linear) constraints; $\mathbf{X}$ is a vector of decision variables having components $x_1, x_2, \ldots, x_n$; $\mathbf{a}_i^T$ is the transpose of vector $\mathbf{a}_i$.

The method of solution chosen is a "steepest ascent" technique [18], which is based on the principle that if the initial starting point is located in a feasible region, the maximum can be obtained by taking finite steps from one point to another along the gradient. The gradient $\nabla F$ points locally in the direction of the maximum increase of the function $F(X)$, which is the steepest ascent. Expressed mathematically, if one is located at point $X^{(k)}$ on the response surface at the $k$th step, the next point $X^{(k+1)}$ along the route of ascent may be determined from

$$X^{(k+1)} = X^{(k)} + \lambda^{(k+1)} \nabla F \tag{5.111}$$

where $\lambda^{(k+1)}$ is a scalar multiple of the gradient such that the product $\lambda^{(k+1)} \nabla F$ is the $(k + 1)$th step of size $\delta^{(k+1)}$.

In order to solve the problem by linear programming methods, the objective function is linearized in the vicinity of a feasible point $X^{(k)}$ and the decision variables are bounded around $X^{(k)}$ in such a way that a linear subproblem of the original nonlinear problem is created. The subproblem is solved by the simplex method, yielding a new feasible point $X^{(k+1)}$ such that $F[X^{(k+1)}] > F[X^{(k)}]$. This procedure is repeated until

$$F[X^{(k+1)}] - F[X^{(k)}] \leqslant \mathscr{E}, \tag{5.112}$$

where $\mathscr{E}$ is a tolerance limit that can be made arbitrarily small.

At any step $k$, the linear subproblem is of the form

$$\max\{\nabla F^T X | a_i^T X \leqslant b_i\}, \quad i = 1, 2, \ldots, m; \quad \alpha_j \leqslant x_j \leqslant \beta_j;$$
$$j = 1, \ldots, n; \quad X \geqslant 0; \tag{5.113}$$

where $\alpha$ and $\beta$ are the vectors of lower and upper bounds, respectively, on the decision variables $x_j$.

The nonlinear objective function $F = F(x_1 \cdots x_n)$ is approximated by a linear function over a short range, by expressing the total differential of $F(x)$ at point $X^{(k)}$ as

$$dF|x = x^{(k)} = \nabla F^{(k)} dx. \tag{5.114}$$

Then, for a given finite step $\Delta x$,

$$F[X^{(k+1)}] - F[X^{(k)}] = \nabla F^{(k)}[X^{(k+1)} - X^{(k)}] \tag{5.115}$$

so that

$$F[X^{(k+1)}] = \nabla F^{(k)} \cdot X^{(k+1)} - \nabla F^{(k)} \cdot X^{(k)} + F[X^{(k)}], \tag{5.116}$$

where $F[X^{(k)}]$, $\nabla F^{(k)}$, and $X^{(k)}$ are constants in the $(k+1)$th step. The problem is then one of maximizing the quantity

$$F(X) = \nabla F^{(k)} \cdot X + \gamma \tag{5.117}$$

(where $\gamma$ is a constant), subject to (i) a set of technological constraints $a_i^T X \leqslant k_i$ $(i = 1, 2, \ldots, m)$; (ii) a set of bounds on the allowable range of the decision variables $X$ at each step, $\alpha_j \leqslant x_j \leqslant \beta_j$, $j = 1, 2, \ldots, n$. From step to step, the upper and lower bounds on the allowable range of values for the decision variables are allowed to change. The value of the allowable range is determined by a method of finding the optimal step size. The form of the variable constraints

$$\alpha_j \leqslant x_j \leqslant \beta_j \tag{5.118}$$

is such that at each step $\beta_j - \alpha_j$ is equal to the allowable range of the $j$th decision variable. If, at the end of the $k$th step, the $j$th component of the gradient $\nabla F^{(k)}$ is positive, then for the $(k+1)$th step

$$\alpha_j = x_j{}^k - \delta_j{}^{(k+1)} \tag{5.119}$$

and

$$\beta_j = x_j{}^{(k)} + \delta_j{}^{(k+1)} \tag{5.120}$$

where $\delta_j$ is the component of the step size in the $j$th direction. $\delta_j$ is given by an optimal step size procedure, which can be shown to be

$$\delta_j{}^{(k+1)} = \lambda^{(k+1)} \left[ \frac{\partial F(X^{(k)})}{\partial X_j} \right]. \tag{5.121}$$

Here $\lambda$ is a scalar parameter [16].

Solutions exist for different values of $A$, $C_{\max}$, $F$, $L$, $M$, resulting in 72 different combinations. On the basis of a sensitivity analysis and a probable range of values for $L$, $M$, and $F$, a final design is chosen after considering the consequences of an incorrect choice of design.

Parametric linear programming was used in the analysis of a water resource system in which aquifers were major elements [19]. The parametric analysis was performed with respect to economic parameters: cost coefficients, shadow prices, and demand. Three different decision rules were tested and evaluated. The system analyzed (the San Gabriel Valley in Southern California) consisted of five supply sources: local surface water, imported Feather River water, imported Colorado River water, local groundwater, and reclaimed waste water. These sources had to satisfy three types of demand: municipal and industrial, agricultural, and groundwater recharge. Since the period of analysis extended over a sequence of 30 years, the linear programming formulation yielded a matrix of 331 rows and 619 columns. The solution was achieved with the help of data processing facilities in which two computers (IBM 7090 and IBM 7094) were operated under a direct coupling system.

It has been found that this approach enables the analysis of situations in which the objective function consists of a large number of variables. Also, up to 500 constraints can be formulated and handled. The parametric aspects of the analysis provide a fairly good insight into the structure of the solution. Furthermore, shadow prices and marginal productivities can be determined from the dual of the linear programming formulation, so that the actual value of the resources within the formulated problem can be estimated.

The main drawbacks of this approach are the inability to cope adequately with nonlinearities (so frequently encountered in aquifer management problems), and the great difficulties arising in handling stochastic aspects of these problems.

**E. SUMMARY**

Linear programming has been applied to a great variety of problems in water resources engineering: from relatively simple problems of straightforward allocation to very complex situations of operation and management. This programming method found ready acceptance among water resource systems analysts mostly because of its inherent conceptual simplicity and the ease of its graphical representation through geometry.

After some of the simpler problems were analyzed and solved, the major effort of linear programming analysts was concentrated on three aspects of water resources engineering: (a) the important stochastic elements affecting design of such systems; (b) the dynamics involved in their operation; and (c) the nonlinearities that creep up in many places, in both design and operation. Significant advances were made on all three fronts, as illustrated by the discussion in the preceding sections of this chapter. In particular, we should point out the advanced state of analysis through linear programming reached in water quality management and in aquifer utilization. These are complex problems, which cannot be meaningfully isolated from the natural (physical) and economic environment of the region within which they exist.

However, with all the progress made in handling nonlinearities and stochastic elements, linear programming yields only point solutions in the policy space, no matter how many dimensions this space may have. Most situations in which the state of the system changes (in time or in space) and in which decisions have to be taken successively are clearly outside the grasp of linear programming. Such problems and an approach to their analysis are presented in the chapters that follow.

**REFERENCES**

1 G. Hadley, *Linear Programming*. Addison-Wesley, Reading, Massachusetts, 1962.
2 G. B. Dantzig, *Linear Programming and Extensions*. Princeton University Press, Princeton, New Jersey, 1963.

## Applications of Linear Programming

3 R. L. Ackoff, ed., *Progress in Operations Research*, Vol. 1. Wiley, New York, 1961.

4 W. R. Lynn, J. A. Logan, and A. Charnes, "System Analysis for Planning Wastewater Treatment Plants," *J. Water Pollution Control Federation* **34**(1962), No. 6, 565.

5 M. J. Sobel, *On the Management of the Quality of Natural Water Systems*, Twenty-Third National Meeting of Operations Research Society of America, 1963.

6 R. A. Deininger, "Water Quality Management in the Planning of Economically Optimal Pollution Control Systems," *Proc. First Ann. Meeting Amer. Water Resources Assoc.* University of Chicago, 1965.

7 M. J. Sobel, "Water Quality Improvement Programming Problems," *Water Resources Research* **1**(1965), No. 4.

8 R. V. Thomann, "Recent Results from a Mathematical Model of Water Pollution Control in the Delaware Estuary," *Water Resources Research* **3**(1967), No. 3.

9 H. A. Thomas, Jr., and R. P. Burden, *Operations Research in Water Quality Management*, Report PH 86-62-140, Harvard, 1963.

10 R. Dorfman, "Mathematical Models: The Multistructure Approach," in *Design of Water-Resource Systems* (A. Maass *et al.* principal authors), Chapter 13. Harvard University Press, Cambridge, Massachusetts, 1962.

11 R. Dorfman, "Mathematical Analysis: Design of the Simple Valley Project," *Economics of Watershed Planning*, Chapter 14B. Iowa State University Press, 1961.

12 H. A. Thomas, Jr., and P. Watermeyer, "Mathematical Models: A Stochastic Sequential Approach," in *Design of Water Resource Systems*, Chapter 14. Harvard University Press, Cambridge, Massachusetts, 1962.

13 A. S. Manne, "Product Mix Alternatives: Flood Control, Electric Power and Irrigation," *Intern. Economic Review* **3**(1962), No. 1.

14 A. S. Manne, "Linear Programming and Sequential Decisions," *Cowles Foundation Paper* No. 148, Yale University, New Haven, Connecticut, 1960.

15 A. S. Manne, "Product-Mix Alternatives: Flood Control, Electric Power and Irrigation," *Cowles Foundation Paper* No. 95, Yale University, New Haven, Connecticut, 1960.

16 H. A. Thomas, Jr., and R. P. Burden, *Indus River Basin Studies*, Harvard University, Cambridge, Massachusetts, 1965 (mimeographed).

17 *Diagnosis and Improvement of Saline and Alkali Soils*, Agriculture Handbook No. 60, United States Department of Agriculture, 1954.

18 G. E. P. Box and K. B. Wilson, "On the Experimental Attainment of Optimum Conditions," *J. Roy. Statist. Soc.* **B13**(1951), 1.

19 J. Dracup, *The Optimum Use of a Ground Water and a Surface Water System*, University of California, Water Resources Center, Contribution No. 107, 1966.

Chapter 6

# DYNAMIC PROGRAMMING

## A. SEQUENTIAL DECISION PROCESSES

Dynamic programming is a way of viewing a problem. The problems that lend themselves best to analysis and solution through the application of dynamic programming are those which can be considered as a sequence of steps. These steps, which may occur in real time or in three-dimensional space, involve decisions that affect the behavior of the system or the outcome of the process, or both. And here, a word of warning should be sounded: although the dynamic programming technique is ideally suited for solving many types of such problems, not all problems involving sequential decision making can be solved by dynamic programming.

One way in which problems involving sequential decision-making processes could be solved is by considering the effects of each decision independently. In water resources engineering, as in many other fields, it is not at all clear that the overall effect from a procedure optimizing each individual step in the development of the resource (or optimizing each use to which water might be allocated) is the best that can be attained. Dynamic programming enables us to investigate the conditions under which an overall "best" can be achieved.

Looking closer at processes of this kind, we observe that in the course of time (or in space) a system may undergo changes. Translating this observation into the more precise language of mathematics, we say that the system is subject to *transformation*. When the process and/or the system allows us the choice of the transformation that may be applied at any time, such a transformation is defined as a *decision*. Each decision is equivalent to a distinct transformation. If there is a single decision to make, that is, the problem is restricted to choosing once and for all one alternative from a set of admissible alternatives, it is a *single-stage process*. If a series of decisions have to be made, it is a *multistage process*. Each sequence of choices is termed a *policy*.

## Dynamic Programming

An important quality of dynamic programming is that it not only facilitates numerical computation of problems involving sequential decision processes, but also gives an indication as to the *structure* of the optimal policy. Instead of determining the optimal sequence of decisions starting from a *fixed* state of the system, dynamic programming determines the optimal decision to be made at any state of the system. Since the outcome of the decision does not appear as a point solution but as a "functional" (to borrow a term from the calculus of variations), we can also estimate the price of policies other than optimal. In such a manner we gain an insight into the intrinsic structure of the solution. This property of dynamic programming is of particular interest in water resources engineering, where the utilization of water is subject to criteria that are not always quantitatively describable.

## B. RECURRENCE RELATIONSHIPS

Consider the following problem, which is typical of many situations in water resources engineering. A conduit has to be constructed to convey a given quantity of water from source $A$ to a demand area $B$. Whereas the starting point of the conduit can be located usually with a high degree of accuracy, the location of the other extremity of the conduit may often present a number of alternative choices. In addition to this, the terrain between source $A$ and demand area $B$ (its topography, geology, land use, etc.) may present a variety of alternative routes, each involving different levels of outlay (expressed as either investments or annual costs). This is

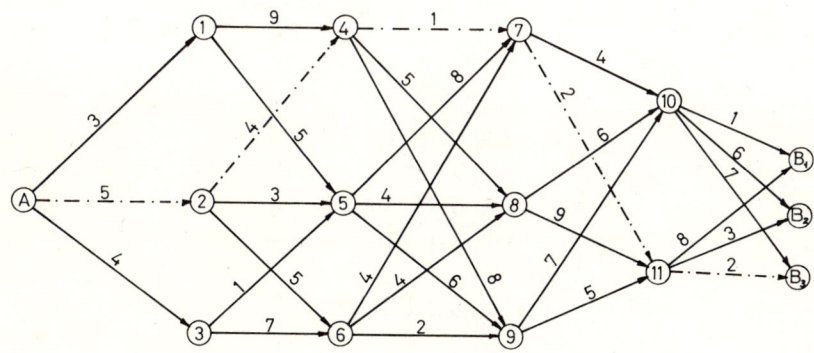

FIGURE 6.1. Alternative routes for the conduit $AB$.

## Scientific Allocation of Water Resources

shown graphically in Figure 6.1. In this figure, the water conduit (open channel or pipeline) must link $A$ with either of the three terminal points $B_1$, $B_2$, or $B_3$. The possible points through which the conduit may pass are numbered from ① through ⑪, and the digit appearing on each link joining these various points represents the expenditure connected with the construction of this link (in monetary units). The problem is to find the path linking $A$ with $B_i$ ($i = 1, 2, 3$) requiring the minimum expenditure.

The problem, as shown by Figure 6.1, appears to involve flows in networks and may be solved by any of the methods developed by the graph theory [1, 2]. However, we choose to view this problem as a multistage (sequential) decision process, in the hope that (a) the computational effort involved is smaller, and (b) a better insight into the structure of the solution is possible. The following stages will be, therefore, defined.

Stage 1: from $A$ to either of the points (nodes) ①, ②, ③.
Stage 2: from ①, or ②, or ③ to either ④, ⑤, or ⑥.
Stage 3: from ④, ⑤, or ⑥ to either ⑦, ⑧, or ⑨.
Stage 4: from ⑦, ⑧, or ⑨ to either ⑩ or ⑪.
Stage 5: from either ⑩ or ⑪ to $B_1$, $B_2$, or $B_3$.

Now, the information regarding the expenditures connected with the construction of the different links of the conduit may be summarized in a set of payoff matrices, as shown below.

|   | ① | ② | ③ |
|---|---|---|---|
| $A$ | 3 | 5 | 4 |

|   | ④ | ⑤ | ⑥ |
|---|---|---|---|
| ① | 9 | 5 | — |
| ② | 4 | 3 | 5 |
| ③ | — | 1 | 7 |

|   | ⑦ | ⑧ | ⑨ |
|---|---|---|---|
| ④ | 1 | 5 | 8 |
| ⑤ | 8 | 4 | 6 |
| ⑥ | 4 | 4 | 2 |

|   | ⑩ | ⑪ |
|---|---|---|
| ⑦ | 4 | 2 |
| ⑧ | 6 | 9 |
| ⑨ | 7 | 5 |

|   | $B_1$ | $B_2$ | $B_3$ |
|---|---|---|---|
| ⑩ | 1 | 6 | 7 |
| ⑪ | 8 | 3 | 2 |

## Dynamic Programming

In the ensuing analysis we shall use the following convenient notation [3].

| | |
|---|---|
| $n$ | number of stages ($n = 1, 2, 3, 4, 5$); |
| $s$ | state variable: the node number at which the process is in any stage; |
| $x_n$ | a decision variable: the immediate node toward which the process will progress when there are $n$ stages to go; |
| $f_n(s, x_n)$ | the total cost for the last $n$ stages, given that the process is in state $s$ and decision $x_n$ is made; |
| $c_{sx_n}$ | the cost of constructing the link joining $s$ with $x_n$, as shown in the payoff matrices; |
| $x_n^*$ | the decision $x_n$ that minimizes $f_n(s, x_n)$; |
| $f_n^*(s)$ | the corresponding minimum value of $f_n(s, x_n)$ when $x_n^*$ is adopted; thus |

$$f_n^*(s) = f_n(s, x_n^*). \tag{6.1}$$

Assume now that the conduit construction reached, with minimum costs, either node ⑩ or node ⑪, and there is one more stage in the decision process. For $n = 1$, the obvious solution is the following.

$n = 1$

| $s$ | $f_1^*(s)$ | $x_1^*$ |
|---|---|---|
| ⑩ | 1 | $B_1$ |
| ⑪ | 2 | $B_3$ |

In other words,

$$f_1^*(s) = \min_{x_1}\{c_{sx_1}\}. \tag{6.2}$$

Let us now go back one step in the sequential decision process and consider the situation when there are two more stages to go. The conduit construction reached, with least costs, node ⑦, or ⑧, or ⑨, and has to proceed further. The equation to be solved now is

$$f_2^*(s) = \min_{x_2}\{c_{sx_2} + f_1^*(x_2)\}, \tag{6.3}$$

and its solution is as follows.

*Scientific Allocation of Water Resources*

$$n = 2$$

| s | $x_2$ $f_2(s, x_2) = c_{sx_2} + f_1^*(x_2)$ | | $f_2^*(s)$ | $x_2^*$ |
|---|---|---|---|---|
|   | ⑩ | ⑪ | | |
| ⑦ | 4 + 1 = 5 | 2 + 2 = 4 | 4 | ⑪ |
| ⑧ | 6 + 1 = 7 | 9 + 2 = 11 | 7 | ⑩ |
| ⑨ | 7 + 1 = 8 | 5 + 2 = 7 | 7 | ⑪ |

So far, it seems clear that if the conduit reaches either ⑦ or ⑨, the best policy is to proceed to ⑪ and then to $B_3$; if, however, the conduit is at ⑧, the least-cost solution leads us through ⑩ on to $B_1$.

The next two stages are analyzed and solved in a similar manner:

$$f_3^*(s) = \min_{x_3}\{c_{sx_3} + f_2^*(x_3)\}. \tag{6.4}$$

$$n = 3$$

| s | $x_3$ $f_3(s, x_3) = c_{sx_3} + f_2^*(x_3)$ | | | $f_3^*(s)$ | $x_3^*$ |
|---|---|---|---|---|---|
|   | ⑦ | ⑧ | ⑨ | | |
| ④ | 1 + 4 = 5 | 5 + 7 = 12 | 8 + 7 = 15 | 5 | ⑦ |
| ⑤ | 8 + 4 = 12 | 4 + 7 = 11 | 6 + 7 = 13 | 11 | ⑧ |
| ⑥ | 4 + 4 = 8 | 4 + 7 = 11 | 2 + 7 = 9 | 8 | ⑦ |

If in the previous stages the alternative $B_2$ was discarded, now node ⑨ seems to be off the optimal path. For either ④ or ⑥ lead us to ⑦ → ⑪ → $B_3$, while ⑤ points out in the direction of ⑧ → ⑩ → $B_1$.

$$f_4^*(s) = \min_{x_4}\{c_{sx_4} + f_3^*(x_4)\}. \tag{6.5}$$

$$n = 4$$

| s | $x_4$ $f_4(s, x_4) = c_{sx_4} + f_3^*(x_4)$ | | | $f_4^*(s)$ | $x_4^*$ |
|---|---|---|---|---|---|
|   | ④ | ⑤ | ⑥ | | |
| ① | 9 + 5 = 14 | 5 + 11 = 16 | — | 14 | ④ |
| ② | 4 + 5 = 9 | 3 + 11 = 14 | 5 + 8 = 13 | 9 | ④ |
| ③ | — | 1 + 11 = 12 | 7 + 8 = 15 | 12 | ⑤ |

Now node ⑥ is discarded from a possible minimum-cost solution. This leaves the alternatives: either from ① or ② to ④ → ⑦ → ⑪ → $B_3$, or from ③ to ⑤ → ⑧ → ⑩ → $B_1$. Superficially, it may appear that the choice between nodes ① and ② is simple: the link $A$–① involves a smaller expendi-

## Dynamic Programming

ture than the link $A-\textcircled{2}$. We shall see, however, that this argument does not stand the test of rigorous analysis:

$$f_5^*(s) = \min_{x_5}\{c_{sx_5} + f_4^*(x_5)\}. \tag{6.6}$$

$n = 5$

| s | $x_5$ | $f_5(s, x_5) = c_{sx_5} + f_4^*(x_5)$ | | | $f_5^*(s)$ | $x_5^*$ |
|---|---|---|---|---|---|---|
| | | ① | ② | ③ | | |
| $A$ | | $3 + 14 = 17$ | $5 + 9 = 14$ | $4 + 12 = 16$ | 14 | ② |

Now we have an unequivocal least-cost path: $A \to \textcircled{2} \to \textcircled{4} \to \textcircled{7} \to \textcircled{11} \to B_3$. The cost is 14 monetary units. This solution was made possible through the derivation of a recurrence relationship in which the solution of one stage is used in the analysis and solution of the next stage of the problem. In this example, the recurrence relationship had the form

$$f_n^*(s) = \min_{x_n}\{c_{sx_n} + f_{n-1}^*(x_n)\}. \tag{6.7}$$

This formulation linked the optimal solution when $n$ stages remain in the process with that for $(n-1)$ remaining steps. As shown, the minimum-cost solution is composed of two parts: an immediate payoff $c_{sx_n}$, and the best solution of the remaining stages. The minimum-cost overall solution is attained through the selection of the decision variable $x_n$.

In order to obtain a complete solution, an additional condition of the type of equation (6.2) is necessary. In another context, this may indicate terminal or boundary conditions of the process.

### C. THE PRINCIPLE OF OPTIMALITY

The foregoing example illustrates how a multistage decision process, which is an optimization problem with at least as many unknowns as there are stages, can be transformed into a sequence of simpler problems, each with one (or a few) unknowns. This computational simplification was made possible by the recurrence relationship. However, a recurrence equation alone does not guarantee the optimum. This is attained through the application of the principle of optimality. To quote [4, page 83]: "An optimal policy has the property that whatever the initial state and initial decisions are, the remaining decisions must constitute an optimal policy with regard to the state resulting from the first decision."

How was this principle applied in our example? Consider equation (6.7). The system is in state $s$ with $n$ stages to go in the decision process. The decision $x_n$ has a double effect: (a) it yields an immediate payoff $c_{sx_n}$; (b) it transforms the state of the system into $x_n$. But starting with this new state and with $(n-1)$ remaining stages, we have determined already what the optimal policy, in this case $f^*_{n-1}(x_n)$, should be. In this way, the value $x_n{}^*$ is selected, which optimizes the sum of both effects.

## D. ONE-DIMENSIONAL ALLOCATION PROCESSES

The class of problems involving this type of allocation processes can be best described by the following example. Consider $N$ users of water (farms, communities, districts, etc.) supplied by a conduit (open channel, closed aqueduct) carrying a flow of $q$ ft³/sec,

$$0 \leqslant q \leqslant Q. \tag{6.8}$$

Accept the following assumptions. (1) The water used by any user generates a return that is independent of the quantities allocated to other users; (2) water allocated to one user cannot be utilized by any other user.

The problem is to determine the allocation policy that maximizes the sum of the returns along the given channel. Define $f_N(q)$ to be maximum net return to $N$ users when the conduit carries a flow of $q$ ft³/sec in its upper reach and an optimal allocation policy is followed, and $x_i$ to be the portion of the flow carried by the conduit allocated to the $i$th user ($i = 1, 2, \ldots, N$).

Clearly, no allocation can exceed the total available flow

$$0 \leqslant x_i \leqslant q, \tag{6.9}$$

nor can the sum of all allocations exceed $q$:

$$\sum_{i=1}^{N} x_i \leqslant q. \tag{6.10}$$

Let the net return to each user be a function of the quantity of water allocated to it and be expressible as $v_i(x)$. The sum to be summarized is

$$\sum_{i=1}^{N} v_i(x). \tag{6.11}$$

## Dynamic Programming

If there is only one user to which water is allocated, then

$$f_1(q) = \max_{0 \leq x \leq q} \{v_1(x)\}. \tag{6.12}$$

A typical net benefit function often encountered in water resources engineering is shown in Figure 6.2. This function, reflecting faithfully the law of diminishing returns, has a maximum when $x = a$. Equation (12) and

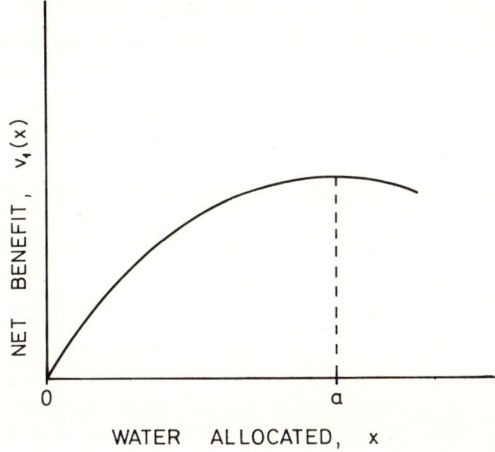

FIGURE 6.2. A typical net benefit function for water.

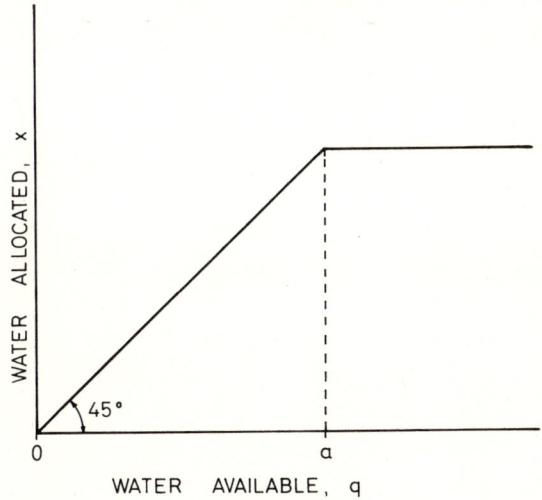

FIGURE 6.3. The allocation $x$ as a function of $q$ when the net benefit function is $v_1(x)$.

Figure 6.2 indicate that for $0 \leq q \leq a$, all water should be allocated to user 1. However, for $q > a$, the allocation $x$ that maximizes $v_1$ (thus yielding $f_1$) is $x = a$, the excess water $q - x$ (if any) being spilled. The dependence between $x$ and $q$ is shown in Figure 6.3. Incidentally, Figure 6.3 illustrates also that the solution of equation (6.12) is not a unique point, but a functional relating the allocation to the amount of resource available and to the return (net benefit) function $v$.

Suppose now that two users exist along the conduit. Allocating to user 2 $x$ ft³/sec, $(q - x)$ ft³/sec are left for user 1. The returns (or net benefits) are $v_2(x)$ and $f_1(q - x)$, respectively. Observe that if $f_1$ is defined by equation (6.12), then

$$f_2(q) = \max_{0 \leq x \leq q} \{v_2(x) + f_1(q - x)\}. \tag{6.13}$$

The net benefit function $v_2(x)$ may be similar to $v_1(x)$ or different from it: it is immaterial, and dynamic programming can handle both cases. For example, if $v_2(x)$ has a slope on its rising limb less than that of $v_1(x)$ (see Figure 6.4), then water will be allocated to user 1 until the slope of its return function is less than that of user 2; then the available water will be allocated to user 2.

For the case of three users,

$$f_3(q) = \max_{0 \leq x \leq q} \{v_3(x) + f_2(q - x)\}, \tag{6.14}$$

which indicates that after allocating $x$ ft³/sec to user 3, we obtain the net

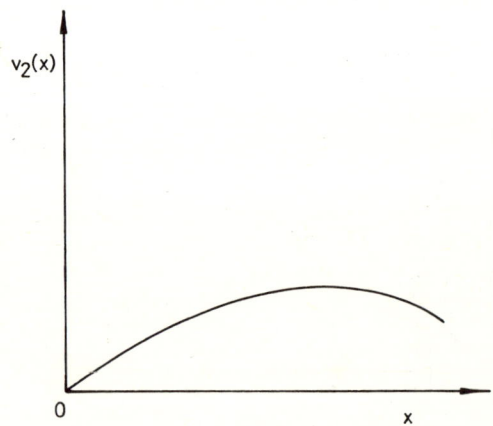

FIGURE 6.4. Net benefit function for user number 2.

## Dynamic Programming

benefit $f_2$ of the remaining users if we proceed optimally in allocating the amount of water $(q - x)$ among them, as shown by equation (6.13).

In general,

$$f_N(q) = \max_{0 \leqslant x \leqslant q} \{v_N(x) + f_{N-1}(q - x)\}. \tag{6.15}$$

This is the desired result, yielding the optimal allocation that maximizes the sum (6.11).

The foregoing example illustrates the following important points.

(a) A particular problem involving a specific amount of water to be allocated among a number of users is imbedded into a general class of problems dealing with a variable resource $(0 \leqslant q \leqslant Q)$ to be allocated among any number $N$ of users.

(b) The allocation process is described by only one state variable $(q)$ and is, therefore, a one-dimensional process.

(c) The mathematical model (equation (6.15)) yields a functional: $f_N(q)$ is given for the entire range of values that allocation $x$ admits.

(d) The solution of the general equation (6.15) includes the optimal policy to be followed, as well as the return (net benefit, in this case) at each stage of the allocation process.

## E. MULTIDIMENSIONAL ALLOCATION PROCESSES

An important problem in water resources engineering is that of efficient delivery of water from a number of reservoirs to several demand points. In general, this problem can be viewed as a Hitchcock–Koopmans transportation problem, and can be formulated in terms of dynamic programming. What follows is a paraphrase in terms of water resources engineering of a rigorous exposition of the dynamic programming approach to this problem as given by Bellman and Dreyfus [5].

Assume that there are two reservoirs $R_1$ and $R_2$ having active storage capacities $X_1$ and $X_2$, respectively. Within the same system, there is an arbitrary number of irrigation demand points $P_j$, $j = 1, 2, \ldots, N$. At the beginning of the irrigation season, the reservoirs contain $x_i$ volume units of water,

$$0 \leqslant x_i \leqslant X_i, \quad i = 1, 2. \tag{6.16}$$

The seasonal irrigation demand at the different points is $d_j$. In order to satisfy this demand, it is necessary to convey an amount of water $x_{ij}$ from reservoir $i$ to demand point $j$. This is accomplished at a cost $g_{ij}(x_{ij})$. Obviously

$$x_{ij} \geqslant 0, \qquad (6.17)$$

$$\sum_{j=1}^{N} x_{ij} \leqslant x_i, \qquad (6.18)$$

$$\sum_{i=1}^{2} x_{ij} = d_j. \qquad (6.19)$$

The unknown quantities in this problem are the amounts of water $x_{ij}$ to be supplied, such that the total cost of their delivery should be minimum:

$$Z = \min \sum_{i=1}^{2} \sum_{j=1}^{N} g_{ij}(x_{ij}). \qquad (6.20)$$

Define $f_N(x_1, x_2)$ to be the cost of supplying the demands $d_1, d_2, \ldots, d_N$ using an optimal policy starting with the quantities of water $x_1$ and $x_2$ at the reservoirs $R_1$ and $R_2$, respectively.

Supplying the demand at the $N$th point, the cost incurred will be

$$g_{1N}(x_{1N}) + g_{2N}(x_{2N}), \qquad (6.21)$$

and the amount of water stored in the reservoirs will be reduced to $x_1 - x_{1N}$ and $x_2 - x_{2N}$. Applying the principle of optimality, we obtain the following recurrence

$$f_N(x_1, x_2) = \min_{[D_N]} \{g_{1N}(x_{1N}) + g_{2N}(x_{2N}) + f_{N-1}(x_1 - x_{1N}, x_2 - x_{2N})\} \qquad (6.22)$$

for $N \geqslant 2$, and where $D_N$ is a two-dimensional region defined by

$$x_{1N} + x_{2N} = d_N, \qquad (6.23)$$

$$0 \leqslant x_{1N} \leqslant x_1, \qquad (6.24)$$

$$0 \leqslant x_{2N} \leqslant x_2. \qquad (6.25)$$

For $N = 1$, the optimum is given by

$$f_1(x_1, x_2) = g_{11}(x_{11}) + g_{21}(x_{21}). \qquad (6.26)$$

The extension of this formulation to several reservoirs presents no difficulties. However, the problem becomes computationally intractable when

## Dynamic Programming

the number of reservoirs exceeds four and if formulated as a straightforward dynamic programming. Nevertheless, there are available a few techniques that can be applied to overcome this obstacle [6].

## F. OPTIMIZATION IN SPACE

Consider a typical problem in water resources engineering: the design of an aqueduct that has to serve a number of geographical districts located in sequence along the supply line. The aqueduct has to contribute to the overall (economic) growth of the region—otherwise it would make no sense to construct it; but its effect in each district will be different. Specifically, the beneficial returns (however defined) from the irrigation districts will be nonlinear functions of the quantity of water delivered. Furthermore, the overall amount of water carried by the aqueduct may vary from year to year, sometimes being less than the maximum demand. The problem, therefore, is that of allocating optimally a variable quantity of water to a number of irrigation districts, in order to determine the sizes of the various reaches of the aqueduct. The solution sought is that which maximizes the excess of beneficial returns from the irrigation districts over the cost of the aqueduct serving them. In mathematical terms, find $R$ such that

$$R = \max \left\{ \sum_{i=1}^{N} R_i(q_i) - c(q_1, q_2, \ldots, q_n) \right\} \qquad (6.27)$$

subject to

$$\sum_{i=1}^{n} q_i \leqslant Q \qquad (6.28)$$

where $R$ is the total net return; $R_i(q_i)$ the beneficial return from the $i$th irrigation district when a quantity of water $q_i$ is supplied; $c$ the cost of the aqueduct; and $Q$ the maximum available amount of water.

The problem can be analyzed and solved by dynamic programming, the optimization being carried out along the supply line (in space). All costs and returns are discounted to present value. The analysis proceeds as follows.

Suppose that all irrigation districts were given optimum allocations of water, except the last one downstream. With one more district to be supplied, the situation is that (a) an amount of water $q$ is available; (b) an amount $q_1$, $0 \leqslant q_1 \leqslant q$, will be allocated to this district; (c) the corresponding return will be $r_1(q_1)$; (d) the costs involved in conveying the amount $q_1$ from the next-to-the-last district to the last one are $l_1 c_1(q_1)$, where $l_1$ is the length of the reach and $c_1$ is a unit cost function.

The net return will be, then,

$$f_1(q) = \max\{r_1(q_1) - l_1 c_1(q_1)\} \tag{6.29}$$

subject to

$$0 \leqslant q_1 \leqslant q, \tag{6.30}$$

$$0 \leqslant q \leqslant Q. \tag{6.31}$$

When two districts (last downstream) remain to be supplied optimally with irrigation water, the net return is

$$f_2(q) = \max_{\substack{0 \leqslant q_2 \leqslant q \\ 0 \leqslant q \leqslant Q}} \{r_2(q_2) - l_2 c_2(q) + f_1(q - q_2)\}. \tag{6.32}$$

(Observe that the cost of conveying $(q - q_2)$ to district 1 (last downstream) is included in $f_1$.)

For any number of districts $n$

$$f_n(q) = \max_{\substack{0 \leqslant q_n \leqslant q \\ 0 \leqslant q \leqslant Q}} \{r_n(q_n) - l_n c_n(q) + f_{n-1}(q - q_n)\}. \tag{6.33}$$

A numerical example worked out in detail can be found elsewhere [7].

## G. OPTIMIZATION IN TIME

In the context of water resources engineering, optimization in time reflects problems of systems operating policies. Here decisions must be made sequentially in time, in an optimal manner.

### 1. A Typical Illustration

Consider a water resources system consisting of a surface reservoir $A$ and an aquifer $B$ supplying water to a group of consumers $C$ (see Figure 6.5). The surface reservoir (which is Lake Kinneret in northern Israel) receives a net variable inflow $Y$, which is the net amount of water that may be used beneficially. A detailed analysis of the inflows into Lake Kinneret was presented elsewhere [8].

Now, the quality of water to be delivered to consumers is of importance, particularly to agriculture. The quality, in this case, is represented by the

## Dynamic Programming

concentration of chloride ion Cl⁻. The situation in Lake Kinneret was such that the chloride concentration was fairly high (around 350 ppm), while the limits acceptable by irrigated agriculture are considerably lower. It is decided, therefore, that a certain amount $H$ be diverted from surface runoff and introduced directly into the main conduit, bypassing the lake altogether, thus leaving as net total inflow into Kinneret the quantity $Y - H$. In this manner, water of higher quality can be delivered to the consumer. The amount to be diverted $H$ has to be determined as part of the optimal operating policy.

A certain amount of water $S_A$ ($S_A \geqslant 0$) may leave the system through overflow or spill. These losses of water, which have a probability distribution,

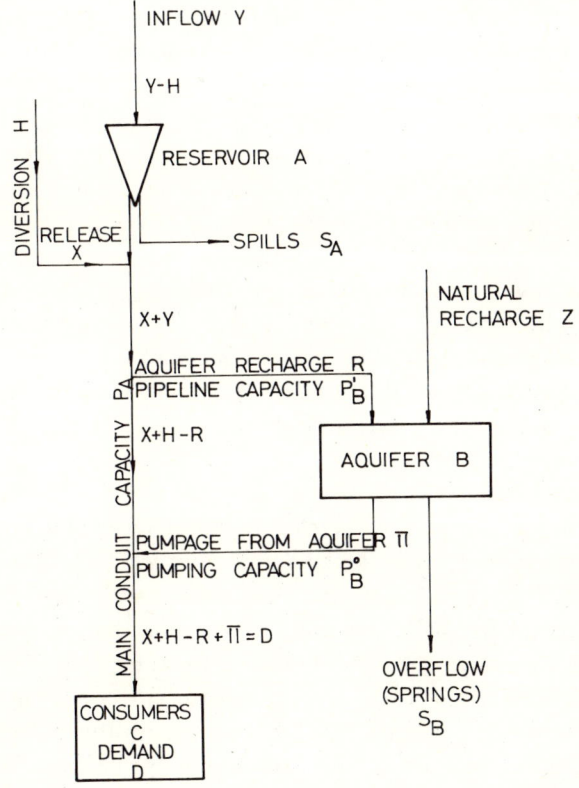

FIGURE 6.5. Schematic representation of a complex water resources system.

are outflows through a weir at the southern extremity of the lake in periods of high inflows and high water levels in the lake. The active storage of the surface reservoir is $V_A$ million cubic meters (Mm³).

The aquifers that are exploited in conjunction with the main conduit are lumped together for the purpose of this analysis and considered as a single reservoir, $B$, with an active storage capacity $V_B$. They are replenished naturally by an inflow $Z$. When the groundwater table exceeds a certain elevation, there is an overflow $S_B$ in the form of discharge of the surface springs. As contrasted with the overflows $S_A$, the discharge $S_B$ of these springs can be utilized beneficially. The reservoir $A$ and the aquifer $B$ have to supply the consumer $C$, whose demand $D$ is given.

The aquifer $B$ is linked to the main conduit by a pipeline through which an amount $R$ can pass for the artificial replenishment of the aquifers, and by a number of wells that pump an amount $\pi$, delivered into the main conduit. The capacity of the main conduit is $P_A$ Mm³/season; that of the replenishment facility, $P_{B_0}$ Mm³/season; and the aggregate pumping capacity from the aquifer, $P_B$ Mm³/season.

The system is operated principally by releasing water from the surface reservoir, and by pumping from the aquifer. Since Lake Kinneret is below mean sea level (its mean elevation is about $-212$ m), the "release" from it is also pumped. If we denote by $X$ the amount extracted from the lake, the quantity $H$ diverted from surface runoff will be added to $X$, so that the main conduit will carry $(X + H)$ Mm³/season. A portion $R$ of this surface water is stored in the aquifer $B$, and an amount $\pi$ is pumped from the groundwater and added to the main conduit. The main conduit, therefore, will convey to the consumers $C$ an amount equal to $X + H - R + \pi$, which must satisfy the demand $D$.

Now, any manipulation of the sources of water affects the quality of water stored or delivered. Thus the diversion $H$ will decrease the annual amount of high quality water entering the lake and will tend to increase the salinity of the amount $X$ extracted from it. However, the amount $H$ added to $X$ in the main conduit will have the effect of reducing the concentration of Cl⁻ in the water delivered to consumers or used for the artificial replenishment of the aquifer. Similarly, the salinity of the water introduced into the aquifer is higher than the salt concentration of the groundwater, which creates the risk of degrading the quality of the water pumped from it $\pi$. It follows that in addition to the difficulties usually encountered in the conjunctive utilization of a surface reservoir and an aquifer [9], the operation of the present system

## Dynamic Programming

has the complication of the quality considerations of the water stored and/or supplied. These complications stem primarily from the inadequate quantitative representation of the water quality. The question of how much 1 ppm $Cl^-$ in water is worth (or, how much damage it creates) has not been yet satisfactorily answered.

Regarding demand, projections were made with respect to its magnitude and monthly distribution. The monthly demand figures are given in graphical form in Figure 6.6.

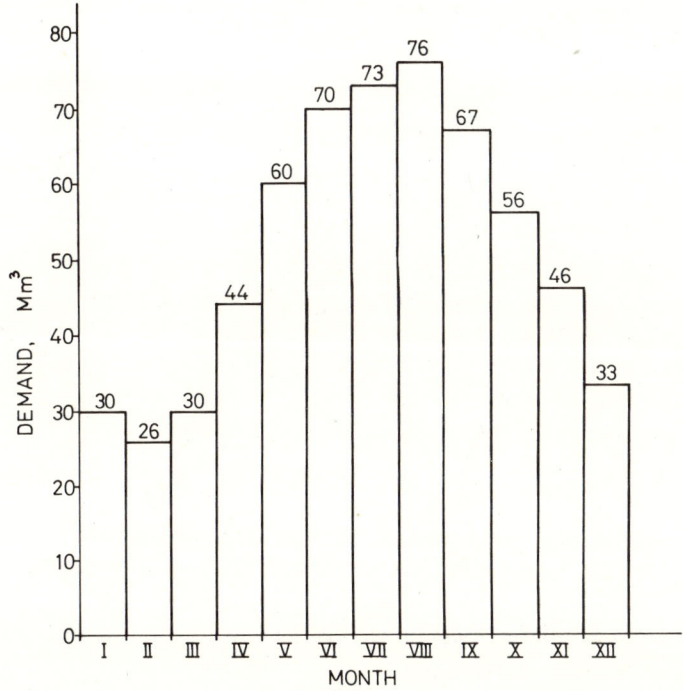

FIGURE 6.6. Projected monthly demand of consumers $C$.

We are now in a position to formulate the objectives of the optimization: it is desired to derive a policy for the operation of the system that will satisfy the demands at minimum costs. Hence, the optimization is principally in time.

## 2. The Mathematical Model

(i) *State Variables.* The state of the system is completely described by a vector composed of three elements: $Q$, the amount of water stored in reservoir $A$,

$$0 \leqslant Q \leqslant V_A; \tag{6.34}$$

$G$, the amount of water stored in the aquifers $B$,

$$0 \leqslant G \leqslant V_B; \tag{6.35}$$

and $S$, the salinity of water in reservoir $A$ expressed as the concentration of $Cl^-$ in parts per million,

$$150 \leqslant S \leqslant 400. \tag{6.36}$$

It is considered that the active storage of Lake Kinneret does not exceed 600 Mm³. Optimal policies are to be derived at the following levels of storage: $Q = 0, 200, 400, 600$ Mm³.

Regarding the active storage of the aquifers $V_B$, it became apparent during the early stages of this work that due to their considerably larger storage capacity (as compared to $V_A = 600$ Mm³), the state variable $G$ dominates the other two in the determination of the optimal policy. Preliminary computer runs indicated that as long as there was an ample supply available in the aquifers, no water should be diverted from the lake and demand $D$ should be satisfied entirely by pumpage. The question, however, remained regarding the optimal operation of the system when water levels in the aquifers approach the limits of economic pumping. It was assumed, therefore, that $V_B = 200$ Mm³ and that $G = 0$ represented the depth limitation of pumping. Optimal operating policies were, therefore, derived at the following points within the range given by relation (6.35): $G = 0, 50, 100, 150, 200$ Mm³.

The salinity variable was introduced into the optimization process at three levels: $S = 150, 250, 350$ ppm $Cl^-$.

(ii) *Constraints.* We distinguish between two kinds of constraints:

*Natural constraints.* The releases from Lake Kinneret cannot exceed the amount in storage,

$$0 \leqslant X \leqslant Q; \tag{6.37}$$

The pumpage cannot exceed the amount of water available in the groundwater aquifer. There is a fixed relationship between pumpage $\pi$ and demand $D$:

## Dynamic Programming

$$\pi = D - (X + H - R). \tag{6.38}$$

Assuming that the quantity of water recharged into the aquifer $R$ is immediately available for pumpage, the statement above can be expressed mathematically as

$$0 \leqslant \pi \leqslant G + R. \tag{6.39}$$

Substituting equation (6.38) into the relationship (6.39) we obtain

$$0 \leqslant D - X - H \leqslant G. \tag{6.40}$$

*System constraints* include limitations imposed by the capacity of the main conduit,

$$0 \leqslant H + X \leqslant P_A; \tag{6.41}$$

limitations imposed by the capacity of the groundwater recharge facility,

$$0 \leqslant R \leqslant P_B; \tag{6.42}$$

limitations imposed by the aggregate pumping capacity from the aquifer,

$$0 \leqslant \pi \leqslant P_B^0. \tag{6.43}$$

(iii) *Cost Functions.* There are several cost functions.

*Pumping costs.* The unit cost of pumping water from Lake Kinneret $\alpha$ is a function of the quantity pumped $\alpha(X)$. Thus, for $0 \leqslant X \leqslant 27$ Mm³/month, $\alpha = 0.04$ million Israeli pounds (MI£)/Mm³; for $27 < X \leqslant 47$, $d\alpha/dX = 0.001$ MI£/Mm³.

*The cost of diversion H.* The unit cost of diverting water from surface runoff and introducing it directly into the main conduit is constant, $\beta = 0.015$ MI£/Mm³.

*Aquifer pumping costs.* Ordinarily, the cost of pumping water from aquifers varies with the amount pumped and the depth of pumping. In this case, however, it is considered that the unit costs are fixed for all quantities pumped and for all possible states of the aquifer (as reflected by the depth to the water table), $\gamma = 0.010$ MI£/Mm³.

*"Spills" from Lake Kinneret.* The stochastic nature of the inflow gives rise to the possibility that water may flow uncontrolled out of Lake Kinneret and thus be lost to the system. Since it is considered that water is valuable, it is desirable to minimize the likelihood of these spills. A preliminary investigation [8] indicated "control" limits of water levels in the lake within

which spills will occur with given probabilities. In this analysis, the spills will be minimized if an expression equivalent to their unit cost is introduced into the optimization criterion. In order to do so, it is necessary to evaluate the worth of 1 cubic meter of water flowing out of the lake. Such an evaluation was done elsewhere [10], but its conclusions cannot be readily transferred to conditions in Israel. The "negative benefit" derived from the outflow of water from Lake Kinneret was arbitrarily set at $\delta = 1.000$ MI£/Mm³.

*Losses from aquifers.* The aquifers, which are lumped in this analysis into one element (reservoir $B$), are intersected by the land surface at several points. These intersection points are in fact springs through which some of the groundwater contained in the aquifer may flow out of it. Water discharged through these springs may leave the system, thus again generating a "negative benefit." At some of these springs, however, facilities are provided for the capture of the water discharged and its conveyance to the main distribution network. The cost of this operation is $\varepsilon = 0.020$ MI£/Mm³. It is considered that the discharge of the Yarqon springs $S_B$ expressed in million cubic meters per month, bears a definite relationship to the amount in storage in aquifer $B$:

$$\frac{S_B}{G - 500} = \frac{1}{80}. \tag{6.44}$$

*The salination of Lake Kinneret due to the extraction $X$.* A varying "penalty" $C_1(X)$ is introduced into the cost function reflecting the deterioration of the quality of the lake water due to the amount extracted from it. The penalty varies between 0.02 MI£/Mm³ and 0.08 MI£/Mm³, being zero at times when the lake is spilling.

*Damages due to the salinity of water in the main conduit.* No "negative benefits" are assessed to salinities up to 170 ppm Cl⁻. From this point onward, it is considered that costs up to I£300 per ton Cl⁻ should be imputed to the increasing salinities of water in the main conduit. The maximum charge is related to the maximum admissible salinity of 400 ppm Cl⁻. This concentration of chlorides is equivalent to 400 tons Cl⁻ per million cubic meters, which sets the maximum "negative benefit" at 0.120 MI£/Mm³. Thus the cost due to the salinity of the water in the main conduit $C_2(S_c)$ is zero for $0 \leqslant S_c \leqslant 170$, and increases linearly up to 0.120 MI£/Mm³ when $S_c = 400$ ppm.

*Effect of the surface runoff diversion on the salinity of Lake Kinneret.* The negative benefits $C_3(H)$ increase linearly from 0.04 MI£/Mm³ to 0.16 MI£/Mm³ when $H$ increases from zero to 15 Mm³/month.

## Dynamic Programming

The cost function $\Phi$ can now be written, by adding its eight components discussed above.

$$\Phi(X, H, S_c, \pi) = \alpha(X)X + \beta H + \gamma\pi + \delta S_A + \varepsilon S_B + C_1(X)X$$
$$+ C_2(S_c)X + C_3(H)H. \qquad (6.45)$$

Remembering that $\pi = D - (X + H - R)$ and collecting terms, we can write the cost function, which has to be minimized,

$$\Phi(X, R, D, S_c) = X[\alpha(X) + C_1(X) + C_2(S_c)] + H[\beta + C_3(H)]$$
$$+ \gamma[D - (X + H - R)] + \delta S_A + \varepsilon S_B. \qquad (6.46)$$

(iv) *Decision Variables.* As previously mentioned, the system is operated by extracting water from Lake Kinneret, by pumping from the southern aquifers, and by diverting surface runoff into the main conduit. The following variables are defined.

$X$ amount of water extracted from reservoir $A$ (Lake Kinneret). Part of this water is allocated to consumer $C$, while the balance is stored in reservoir $B$ (aquifer replenishment). This variable admits the values $X = 0, 18, 27, 37, 47$ Mm³/month.

$R$ portion of quantity $X$ stored in reservoir $B$. These values are admitted: $R = 0, 9, 18, 27, 37, 47$ Mm³/month.

$H$ amount of water diverted from surface runoff directly into the main conduit, $H = 0, 3, 6, 9, 12, 15$ Mm³/month.

$\pi$ pumpage from the reservoir $B$ (southern aquifers).

It should be emphasized that $\pi$ is not an independent decision variable because of the fixed relationship existing with respect to demand $D$, as expressed by equation (6.38).

(v) *Dynamic Programming Formulation.* In deriving an operating policy for the main conduit, it is considered that the system will be operated during $N$ consecutive monthly stages. We shall define, therefore, $f_N(Q, G, S) = $ the minimum expected total cost of operating the system during $N$ consecutive stages, starting in state $(Q, G, S)$ and pursuing an optimal policy. Thus if the system has to be operated only during one (last) stage,

$$f_1(Q, G, S) = \min_{\substack{X \\ R \\ H}} \left\{ \int_{-\infty}^{\infty} \Phi(X, R, H, D, S, Y) h(Y) \, dY \right\} \qquad (6.47)$$

where $h(Y)$ is the probability distribution function of this inflow $Y$ into the lake.

Now, following the operation of the system during one stage, a change occurs in the state of the system and the state vector $(Q, G, S)$ is transformed into $(Q', G', S')$. Specifically, during this stage the lake gains a net total inflow of $(Y - H)$, while an amount $X$ is extracted from it for beneficial use. Thus,

$$Q' = Q + Y - H - X. \tag{6.48}$$

Similarly, the aquifer $B$ gains $Z$ Mm³ as natural recharge and $R$ Mm³ as artificial replenishment, while the quantity $\pi$ Mm³ is pumped in order to satisfy demand $D$.

$$G' = G + Z + R - \pi = G + Z - D + X + H. \tag{6.49}$$

In order to determine the transformation of state variable $S$ into $S'$, we have to perform, in fact, the salt balance of the lake. The factors affecting the salinity of Lake Kinneret are (a) the total volume of water in the lake; (b) the salinity (salt concentration) of the inflowing water; (c) the contribution of certain saline springs discharging into the lake. Since the total volume of Lake Kinneret is $(4 \times 10^3 + Q)$ Mm³, the contribution of the saline springs 6700 tons/month, and denoting by $S_Y$ the salinity of the inflowing water, then

$$S' = \frac{S[(4 \times 10^3) + Q - X] + S_Y(Y - H) + 6700}{(4 \times 10^3) + Q'}. \tag{6.50}$$

Applying the principle of optimality [4], we can now write the minimum cost operation rule for the (last) two stages of operation:

$$f_2(Q, G, S) = \min_{\substack{X \\ R \\ H}} \left\{ \int_{-\infty}^{\infty} [\Phi(X, R, H, D, S_c; Y) + f_1(Q', G', S')] h(Y) \, dY \right\}. \tag{6.51}$$

Observe the equation (6.51) assumes only one probability distribution function $h(Y)$ for both stochastic variables $Y$ and $Z$; it is considered that both surface and groundwater flows are normally distributed.

By mathematical induction, the model for an $N$-stage process is

$$f_N(Q, G, S) = \min \left\{ \int_{-\infty}^{\infty} [\Phi(X, R, H, D, S_c; Y) + f_{N-1}(Q', G', S')] h(Y) \, dY \right\}. \tag{6.52}$$

## 3. Computational Aspects

In order to program for computer solution equations (6.47) and (6.52), it is necessary to discretize the continuous probability distribution function $h(Y)$. Assume, therefore, that the variables $Y$ and $Z$ admit only a finite number of values $Y_j$ and $Z_j$, $j = 1, 2, \ldots, M$, each of which may occur with probability $P_j$:

$$\sum_{j=1}^{M} P_j = 1. \tag{6.53}$$

Then, equations (6.47) and (6.52) may be expressed as

$$f_1(Q, G, S) = \min_{\substack{X \\ R \\ H}} \left\{ \sum_{j=1}^{M} P_j \Phi(X, R, H, D, S_c; Y) \right\}, \tag{6.54}$$

$$f_N(Q, G, S) = \min_{\substack{X \\ R \\ H}} \left\{ \sum_{j=1}^{M} P_j [\Phi(X, R, H, D, S_c; Y) + f_{N-1}(Q', G', S')] \right\}. \tag{6.55}$$

The values of $P_j$ used were $P_j = 0.1, 0.2, 0.4, 0.2, 0.1$.

Equations (6.54) and (6.55) were programmed for the IBM 1620 digital computer using the FORTRAN II language. However, the IBM 1620, being a relatively slow computer, is hardly adequate for the solution of dynamic programming problems. Therefore, in order to reduce somewhat the execution time, part of the program was coded in the SPS II language. The flow chart of the computer program can be found elsewhere [11].

## 4. Results and Their Analysis

The computer printout appeared in tabular form, one table for each stage (month) of operation. An example is given in Table I, and in graphical form in Figure 6.7. The computer calculations were continued until one set of twelve monthly tables was no different with regard to optimal policies from that of the preceding twelve months. In other words, it was attempted to reach policies that would not be affected by the terminal stages of the process, as formulated in "backward" dynamic programming.

Let us assume that the system under consideration is capable of existing at any particular time in any of a finite number of states $i$, $i = 1, 2, \ldots, N$. The probability that the system will change from state $j$ at time $t$ ($t =$

0, 1, 2, ...) to state $i$ at time $(t + 1)$ is given by the transition matrix $\mathbf{A} = (a_{ij})$. However, the matrix $\mathbf{A}$ is not fixed for all monthly stages, but runs over a set of values $\mathbf{A}(q)$. Defining $f_i(T)$ as the probability that the system will be in a given state at time $T$, starting in state $i$ and using an optimal policy,

$$f_i(T) = \max_q \left\{ \sum_{j=1}^{N} a_{ji}(q) f_j(T-1) \right\}. \tag{6.56}$$

Note that the elements of $\mathbf{A}(q)$ are written as $a_{ji}(q)$, since we count backward in time.

Now, if we associate with each transition from state $j$ to state $i$ a return $r_{ij}(q)$, then the problem becomes that of maximizing the expected return over a $T$-stage process. Redefining $f_i(T)$ as the expected return obtained from a $T$-stage process, starting in state $i$ and using an optimal policy, we get

$$f_i(T) = \max_q \left\{ \sum_{j=1}^{N} a_{ji}(q) [r_{ji}(q) + f_j(T-1)] \right\}, \tag{6.57}$$

$$f_i(0) = 0.$$

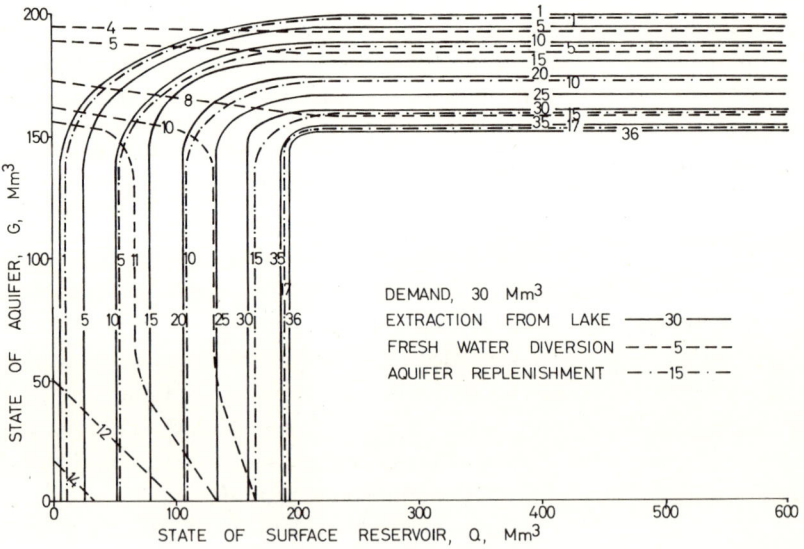

FIGURE 6.7. Optimal policies, January.

## Dynamic Programming

### Table I. Computer Results for the Month of January

| States | | | Decisions | | | Results | | | | | | |
|---|---|---|---|---|---|---|---|---|---|---|---|---|
| Q | G | $SAL^a$ | X | H | R | $PHI^b$ | $SA^c$ | $SB^d$ | $SDAS^e$ | $SC^f$ | $FN^g$ | |
| 0.0   | 0.0   | 150.0 | 0.0  | 15.0 | 0.0  | 15.0 | 0.0 | 0.0 | 146.6 | 0.0   | 7.9252 | 03 $ |
| 0.0   | 0.0   | 250.0 | 0.0  | 15.0 | 0.0  | 15.0 | 0.0 | 0.0 | 242.9 | 0.0   | 7.9252 | 03 $ |
| 0.0   | 0.0   | 350.0 | 0.0  | 15.0 | 0.0  | 15.0 | 0.0 | 0.0 | 339.1 | 0.0   | 7.9252 | 03 $ |
| 0.0   | 50.0  | 150.0 | 0.0  | 12.0 | 0.0  | 18.0 | 0.0 | 0.0 | 146.6 | 0.0   | 7.3063 | 03 |
| 0.0   | 50.0  | 250.0 | 0.0  | 12.0 | 0.0  | 18.0 | 0.0 | 0.0 | 242.7 | 0.0   | 7.3063 | 03 |
| 0.0   | 50.0  | 350.0 | 0.0  | 12.0 | 0.0  | 18.0 | 0.0 | 0.0 | 338.8 | 0.0   | 7.3064 | 03 |
| 0.0   | 100.0 | 150.0 | 0.0  | 12.0 | 0.0  | 18.0 | 0.0 | 0.0 | 146.6 | 0.0   | 6.8764 | 03 |
| 0.0   | 100.0 | 250.0 | 0.0  | 12.0 | 0.0  | 18.0 | 0.0 | 0.0 | 242.7 | 0.0   | 6.8764 | 03 |
| 0.0   | 100.0 | 350.0 | 0.0  | 12.0 | 0.0  | 18.0 | 0.0 | 0.0 | 338.8 | 0.0   | 6.8765 | 03 |
| 0.0   | 150.0 | 150.0 | 0.0  | 12.0 | 0.0  | 18.0 | 0.0 | 0.0 | 146.6 | 0.0   | 6.5321 | 03 |
| 0.0   | 150.0 | 250.0 | 0.0  | 12.0 | 0.0  | 18.0 | 0.0 | 0.0 | 242.7 | 0.0   | 6.5321 | 03 |
| 0.0   | 150.0 | 350.0 | 0.0  | 12.0 | 0.0  | 18.0 | 0.0 | 0.0 | 338.8 | 0.0   | 6.5321 | 03 |
| 0.0   | 200.0 | 150.0 | 0.0  | 3.0  | 0.0  | 27.0 | 0.0 | 0.0 | 146.3 | 0.0   | 6.3820 | 03 |
| 0.0   | 200.0 | 250.0 | 0.0  | 3.0  | 0.0  | 27.0 | 0.0 | 0.0 | 242.2 | 0.0   | 6.3820 | 03 |
| 0.0   | 200.0 | 350.0 | 0.0  | 3.0  | 0.0  | 27.0 | 0.0 | 0.0 | 338.2 | 0.0   | 6.3821 | 03 |
| 200.0 | 0.0   | 150.0 | 37.0 | 9.0  | 18.0 | 2.0  | 0.0 | 0.0 | 146.6 | 120.6 | 6.8148 | 03 |
| 200.0 | 0.0   | 250.0 | 37.0 | 9.0  | 18.0 | 2.0  | 0.0 | 0.0 | 242.8 | 201.0 | 6.8167 | 03 |
| 200.0 | 0.0   | 350.0 | 37.0 | 9.0  | 18.0 | 2.0  | 0.0 | 0.0 | 339.0 | 281.5 | 6.8209 | 03 |
| 200.0 | 50.0  | 150.0 | 37.0 | 9.0  | 18.0 | 2.0  | 0.0 | 0.0 | 146.6 | 120.6 | 6.4680 | 03 |
| 200.0 | 50.0  | 250.0 | 37.0 | 9.0  | 18.0 | 2.0  | 0.0 | 0.0 | 242.8 | 201.0 | 6.4700 | 03 |
| 200.0 | 50.0  | 350.0 | 37.0 | 9.0  | 18.0 | 2.0  | 0.0 | 0.0 | 339.0 | 281.5 | 6.4742 | 03 |
| 200.0 | 100.0 | 150.0 | 37.0 | 9.0  | 18.0 | 2.0  | 0.0 | 0.0 | 146.6 | 120.6 | 6.2014 | 03 |
| 200.0 | 100.0 | 250.0 | 37.0 | 9.0  | 18.0 | 2.0  | 0.0 | 0.0 | 242.8 | 201.0 | 6.2033 | 03 |
| 200.0 | 100.0 | 350.0 | 37.0 | 9.0  | 18.0 | 2.0  | 0.0 | 0.0 | 339.0 | 281.5 | 6.2073 | 03 |
| 200.0 | 150.0 | 150.0 | 37.0 | 9.0  | 18.0 | 2.0  | 0.0 | 0.0 | 146.6 | 120.6 | 6.0190 | 03 |
| 200.0 | 150.0 | 250.0 | 37.0 | 9.0  | 18.0 | 2.0  | 0.0 | 0.0 | 242.8 | 201.0 | 6.0210 | 03 |
| 200.0 | 150.0 | 350.0 | 37.0 | 9.0  | 18.0 | 2.0  | 0.0 | 0.0 | 339.0 | 281.5 | 6.0236 | 03 |
| 200.0 | 200.0 | 150.0 | 0.0  | 3.0  | 0.0  | 27.0 | 0.0 | 0.0 | 146.4 | 0.0   | 5.9314 | 03 |
| 200.0 | 200.0 | 250.0 | 0.0  | 3.0  | 0.0  | 27.0 | 0.0 | 0.0 | 242.6 | 0.0   | 5.9317 | 03 |
| 200.0 | 200.0 | 350.0 | 0.0  | 3.0  | 0.0  | 27.0 | 0.0 | 0.0 | 338.7 | 0.0   | 5.9922 | 03 |
| 400.0 | 0.0   | 150.0 | 37.0 | 9.0  | 18.0 | 2.0  | 0.0 | 0.0 | 146.7 | 120.6 | 6.4366 | 03 |
| 400.0 | 0.0   | 250.0 | 37.0 | 9.0  | 18.0 | 2.0  | 0.0 | 0.0 | 243.1 | 201.0 | 6.4388 | 03 |
| 400.0 | 0.0   | 350.0 | 37.0 | 9.0  | 18.0 | 2.0  | 0.0 | 0.0 | 339.5 | 281.5 | 6.4436 | 03 |
| 400.0 | 50.0  | 150.0 | 37.0 | 9.0  | 18.0 | 2.0  | 0.0 | 0.0 | 146.7 | 120.6 | 6.1233 | 03 |
| 400.0 | 50.0  | 250.0 | 37.0 | 9.0  | 18.0 | 2.0  | 0.0 | 0.0 | 243.1 | 201.0 | 6.1255 | 03 |
| 400.0 | 50.0  | 350.0 | 37.0 | 9.0  | 18.0 | 2.0  | 0.0 | 0.0 | 339.5 | 281.5 | 6.1303 | 03 |
| 400.0 | 100.0 | 150.0 | 37.0 | 9.0  | 18.0 | 2.0  | 0.0 | 0.0 | 146.7 | 120.6 | 5.8716 | 03 |
| 400.0 | 100.0 | 250.0 | 37.0 | 9.0  | 18.0 | 2.0  | 0.0 | 0.0 | 243.1 | 201.0 | 5.8737 | 03 |
| 400.0 | 100.0 | 350.0 | 37.0 | 9.0  | 18.0 | 2.0  | 0.0 | 0.0 | 339.5 | 281.5 | 5.8783 | 03 |
| 400.0 | 150.0 | 150.0 | 37.0 | 9.0  | 18.0 | 2.0  | 0.0 | 0.0 | 146.7 | 120.6 | 5.7185 | 03 |

## Table I (continued)

| | States | | | Decisions | | | Results | | | | |
|---|---|---|---|---|---|---|---|---|---|---|---|
| Q | G | SAL[a] | X | H | R | PHI[b] | SA[c] | SB[d] | SDAS[e] | SC[f] | FN[g] |
| 400.0 | 150.0 | 250.0 | 37.0 | 9.0 | 18.0 | 2.0 | 0.0 | 0.0 | 243.1 | 201.0 | 5.7297 03 |
| 400.0 | 150.0 | 350.0 | 37.0 | 9.0 | 18.0 | 2.0 | 0.0 | 0.0 | 339.5 | 281.5 | 5.7237 03 |
| 400.0 | 200.0 | 150.0 | 0.0 | 3.0 | 0.0 | 27.0 | 0.0 | 0.0 | 146.6 | 0.0 | 5.6504 03 |
| 400.0 | 200.0 | 250.0 | 0.0 | 3.0 | 0.0 | 27.0 | 0.0 | 0.0 | 242.9 | 0.0 | 5.6506 03 |
| 400.0 | 200.0 | 350.0 | 0.0 | 3.0 | 0.0 | 27.0 | 0.0 | 0.0 | 339.2 | 0.0 | 5.6513 03 |
| 600.0 | 0.0 | 150.0 | 37.0 | 9.0 | 18.0 | 2.0 | 126.3 | 0.0 | 150.9 | 120.6 | 6.1784 03 |
| 600.0 | 0.0 | 250.0 | 37.0 | 9.0 | 18.0 | 2.0 | 126.3 | 0.0 | 250.1 | 201.0 | 6.1809 03 |
| 600.0 | 0.0 | 350.0 | 37.0 | 9.0 | 18.0 | 2.0 | 126.3 | 0.0 | 349.3 | 281.5 | 6.1857 03 |
| 600.0 | 50.0 | 150.0 | 37.0 | 9.0 | 18.0 | 2.0 | 126.3 | 0.0 | 150.9 | 120.6 | 5.8920 03 |
| 600.0 | 50.0 | 250.0 | 37.0 | 9.0 | 18.0 | 2.0 | 126.3 | 0.0 | 250.1 | 201.0 | 5.8945 03 |
| 600.0 | 50.0 | 350.0 | 37.0 | 9.0 | 18.0 | 2.0 | 126.3 | 0.0 | 349.3 | 281.5 | 5.8993 03 |
| 600.0 | 100.0 | 150.0 | 37.0 | 9.0 | 18.0 | 2.0 | 126.3 | 0.0 | 150.9 | 120.6 | 5.6433 03 |
| 600.0 | 100.0 | 250.0 | 37.0 | 9.0 | 18.0 | 2.0 | 126.3 | 0.0 | 250.1 | 201.0 | 5.6458 03 |
| 600.0 | 100.0 | 350.0 | 37.0 | 9.0 | 18.0 | 2.0 | 126.3 | 0.0 | 349.3 | 281.5 | 5.6507 03 |
| 600.0 | 150.0 | 150.0 | 37.0 | 9.0 | 18.0 | 2.0 | 126.3 | 0.0 | 150.9 | 120.6 | 5.5110 03 |
| 600.0 | 150.0 | 250.0 | 37.0 | 9.0 | 18.0 | 2.0 | 126.3 | 0.0 | 250.1 | 201.0 | 5.5136 03 |
| 600.0 | 150.0 | 350.0 | 37.0 | 9.0 | 18.0 | 2.0 | 126.3 | 0.0 | 349.3 | 281.5 | 5.5184 03 |
| 600.0 | 200.0 | 150.0 | 0.0 | 3.0 | 0.0 | 27.0 | 169.3 | 0.0 | 152.1 | 0.0 | 5.4606 03 |
| 600.0 | 200.0 | 250.0 | 200.0 | 250.0 | 0.0 | 27.0 | 169.3 | 0.0 | 252.1 | 0.0 | 5.4638 03 |
| 600.0 | 200.0 | 350.0 | 0.0 | 3.0 | 0.0 | 27.0 | 169.3 | 0.0 | 352.1 | 0.0 | 5.4694 03 |

[a] $SAL$: salinity of reservoir $A$ (the lake) at the beginning of this stage.
[b] $PHI$: pumpage from reservoir $B$ (the aquifer).
[c] $SA$: maximum spills from reservoir $A$ (with probability $P \leqslant 0.1$).
[d] $SB$: maximum spills from reservoir $B$ (with probability $P \leqslant 0.1$).
[e] $SDAS$ salinity of reservoir $A$ at the end of this stage.
[f] $SC$: salinity of water delivered to consumers $C$.
[g] $FN$: the minimum costs involved in operating the system. The sign $ indicated that at this state, (0, 0, S), there is no water to satisfy the demand. Hence, water must be provided from an alternative, more expensive source.

Since the process with which we are concerned is not a terminal control process, it is reasonable to assume that as $T \to \infty$, $f_i(T)$ will tend asymptotically to

$$f_i(T) \sim aT + \Phi_i \qquad (6.58)$$

where $a$ is independent of the initial state and the term $\Phi_i$ is dependent upon $i$. This convergence is proven by Bellman [12], using standard Markov chain theory [13].

## Dynamic Programming

It should be noted that in this model the monthly inflows into the reservoir $A$ were considered as independent stochastic variables. From a strict hydrological point of view, however, we should take into account also the serial correlation exhibited by the inflows in successive months. Better than this, the data indicate also a certain degree of correlation between inflows in alternate months, and also correlation of lag three or more [14]. If the serial correlation were introduced into the model, the inflows of the preceding month would have become part of the state vector, thus increasing the dimensionality of the problem. Indeed, a model taking into account this additional information was proposed [15].

Optimal policies were sometimes independent of the salinity of the reservoir $A$, as shown by Figure 6.7; at other times they differed markedly, as indicated by Figures 6.8, 6.9, and 6.10.

## H. CONCLUSION

The problem of optimal operation of a water resources system was approached from the point of view of systems engineering [16]. It involves the planning and design of a system for the performance of functions or

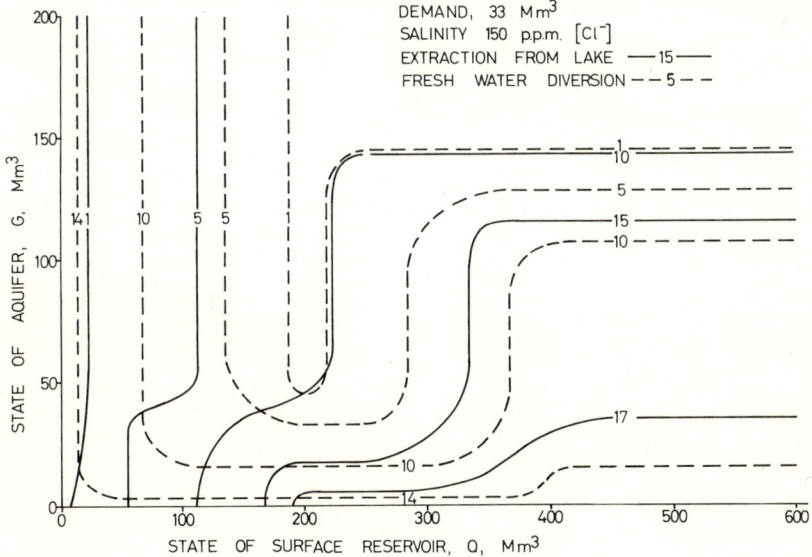

FIGURE 6.8. Optimal policies, December.

*Scientific Allocation of Water Resources*

services never before performed: the development and utilization of a significant amount of fresh water, and the integration of the regional water

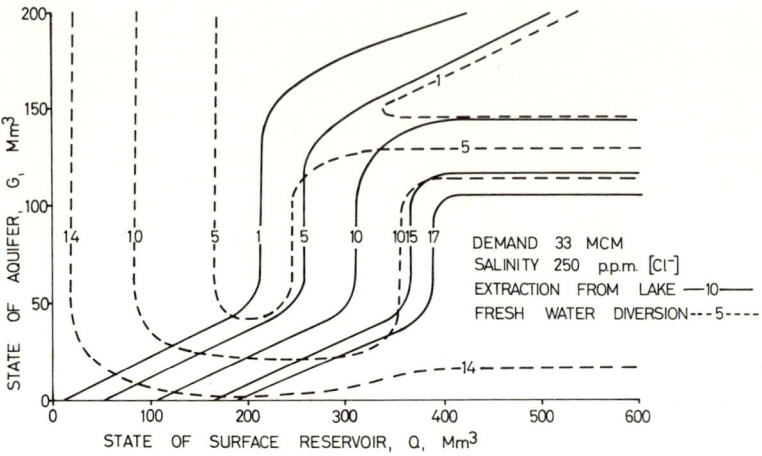

Figure 6.9. Optimal policies, December.

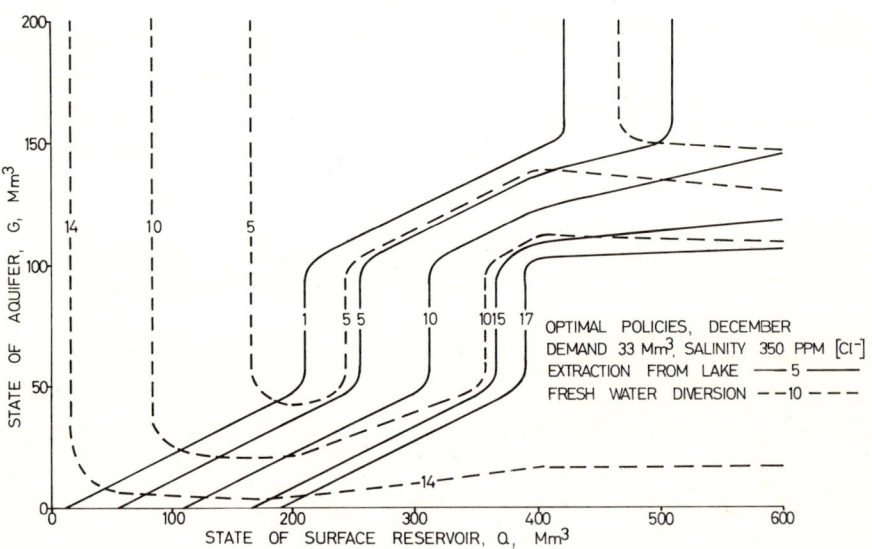

Figure 6.10. Optimal policies, December.

supply system into one overall scheme. It should be emphasized that the design process includes not only the determination of the dimensions of the physical elements to be constructed, but also the derivation of operating policies. The operating policies involved a sequence of decisions, to be optimized over time. The optimization was performed through the application of dynamic programming.

**REFERENCES**

1. C. Berge, *Théorie des Graphes et ses Applications*. Dunod, Paris, 1958.
2. L. R. Ford, Jr., and D. R. Fulkeson, *Flows in Networks*. Princeton University Press, Princeton, New Jersey, 1962.
3. F. S. Hillier and G. J. Lieberman, *Introduction to Operations Research*. Holden-Day, San Francisco, 1967.
4. R. E. Bellman, *Dynamic Programming*. Princeton University Press, Princeton, New Jersey, 1957.
5. R. E. Bellman and S. E. Dreyfus, *Applied Dynamic Programming*. Princeton University Press, Princeton, New Jersey, 1962.
6. R. E. Larson, *State Increment Dynamic Programming*. American Elsevier, New York, 1968.
7. W. A. Hall, "Aqueduct Capacity Under an Optimum Benefit Policy," *Proc. Amer. Soc. Civil Engineers* 87(1961), No. 3, paper No. 2923.
8. B. V. Dean and N. Buras, *Effective Control and Economic Scheduling of Lake Kinneret Pumping Operations*, Tahal (Water Planning for Israel, Ltd.), Tel Aviv, P.N. 282, 1963.
9. N. Buras, "Conjunctive Operation of Dams and Aquifers," *Proc. Amer. Soc. Civil Engineers* 89(1963), No. HY6, 111–131.
10. E. F. Renshaw, "Value of an Acre-Foot of Water," *J. Amer. Water Works Assoc.* 50(1958), 303–309.
11. N. Buras, "Operation of a Complex Water Resource Utilization System," *Intern. Conf. Water for Peace*, Washington, D.C., 1967.
12. R. E. Bellman, *Adaptive Control Processes: A Guided Tour*. Princeton University Press, Princeton, New Jersey, 1961.
13. E. Parzen, *Modern Probability Theory and its Applications*. Wiley, New York, 1960.
14. S. Yagil, "Generation of Input Data for Simulation," *IBM Systems J.* 2(1963), 288–296.
15. N. Buras, "Conjunctive Operation of a Surface Reservoir and a Groundwater Aquifer: 1. Conceptual Framework," *Symposium on Surface Waters*, Publication No. 63, International Association of Scientific Hydrology, Gentbrugge, Belgium, 1963, pp. 492–501.
16. A. D. Hall, *A Methodology of Systems Engineering*. Van Nostrand, Princeton, New Jersey, 1962.

Chapter 7

# APPLICATIONS OF DYNAMIC PROGRAMMING IN WATER RESOURCES ENGINEERING

## A. GENERAL

Previous discussions have shown several characteristic properties of water resource system optimization: (i) the stochastic nature of water inputs; (ii) the time effects (i.e., seasonal effects, development by stages, limited planning horizon, and hydrological trends); (iii) the nonlinearity of economic objective functions and operational constraints; (iv) the large number of technological economic, and other variables involved in the overall optimization of complex multistructure multipurpose systems. These factors cannot all be treated at once by probabilistic methods or by linear programming without the use of simplifications and/or by increasing overwhelmingly the computational burdens.

Other important aspects of real-life water resource systems, not mentioned yet, are the lack of adequate data and the adaptive nature of operational policies. Often few hydrological data are available at the time of planning. This means that as data accumulate, better estimations of probabilities of streamflow (and of rainfall) are possible, including any serial correlation and trends that may exist in consecutive periods. Operational decisions of a feedback nature need to be made on the basis of recently available data. If, in addition, changes are made (or expected) in cost functions, system benefits, and system components, long-range overall optimization is not possible by the previously discussed methods. Optimization of a multipurpose reservoir by linear programming cannot allow for increases or decreases in its capacity several years after construction. The coefficient matrix assumes that all seasons have the same constraints, while results relate to an infinite period of identical years. A set of optimal releases for each year (or stage) of the economic life of the project is very difficult to be derived, so as to allocate sufficient overyear storage in the "filling up period" and maximize at the same time the present value of expected benefits during the project's life. Although future returns may be discounted in a sequential stochastic linear model [1], any change in constraints requires the solution of a new problem. For this reason it is also important to understand the structure of the optimal solution, which may be stage dependent or may change when parameters vary.

The aspect of time, or the dynamic nature of water resources engineering, was stated (Chapter 3) by equation (3.1), as the transformation of a matrix describing the occurrence of the water and its properties to another matrix related to the objectives of the development project. Indeed, this transformation may be treated as a multistage decision process that seeks a sequence of decisions optimizing an economic objective function. Depending on the state of the system at each stage or period, a decision is made in the form of choice between alternative actions. Such a sequence of decisions is called the operating policy. These decisions may be made even if the components of the state vector are described by a probability distribution. Because of its multistage nature, dynamic programming seems to be an appropriate technique for dealing with water resource systems [2]. This approach, based on the "principle of optimality," has been extensively documented [3–5].

The advantages stemming from dynamic programming are numerous. It may be shown analytically that the method always yields an absolute optimum and in the case of stochastic processes converges to a stationary state solution. The accuracy of the result depends on the fineness of the grid of state values chosen. Constraints of the form $a_i \leqslant x_i \leqslant b_i$ present no difficulties; on the contrary, they reduce the number of state values and hence speed up computation. Discrete value sets simplify calculations. An important advantage is the use of tabulated values of the functions involved. Their analytical structure or shape need not be known at all, though in some cases their properties may be used to simplify a search process. Dynamic programming provides answers to such fundamental questions as: (a) How do the return and policy depend on initial conditions? (b) Using an optimal policy, what is the value of changing the initial state? (c) What is the effect of adding one more variable or carrying on the process for one more stage?

## B. GENERAL DESIGN APPLICATIONS

The usefulness of dynamic programming for water resources system optimization stems from the fact that river system development follows a hierarchical sequence of decisions that can be treated by the principle of optimality [2]. An example of the type of problem to be solved is that of determining an aqueduct's capacity, which is in effect a multistage allocation problem: each stage being the reach of the aqueduct in a particular geographic district [6, 7]. The general design problem may be stated as the maximization of overall net benefits generated by irrigation water supply, by deciding which districts to serve and the level of service to be provided. Thus, determine

$$\max \sum_{i=1}^{n} [V_i(q_i) - C(q_1, q_2, \ldots, q_n)] \tag{7.1}$$

subject to

$$\sum_{i=1}^{n} q_i \leqslant Q \tag{7.2}$$

where $V_i(q_i)$ is the annual net beneficial return to the $i$th district as a result of supplying $q_i$ units of water; $C(q_i, \ldots, q_n)$ the total annual aqueduct costs as a result of capacity $q_1, \ldots, q_n$; $i (= 1, 2, \ldots, n)$ the number of the district (numbered sequentially downstream); $Q$ the maximum amount of water available to the entire region per annum.

The actual form of $V_i(q_i)$ and $C(q_1, \ldots, q_n)$ is not important, provided that numerical values are known. The recurrence relationships are

$$f_n(q) = \max_{\substack{0 \leqslant q_n \leqslant q \\ 0 \leqslant q \leqslant Q}} \{v_n(q_n) - x_n C_n(q_n) + f_{n-1}(q - q_n)\} \tag{7.3}$$

$$f_1(q) = \max_{\substack{0 \leqslant q_1 \leqslant q \\ 0 \leqslant q \leqslant Q}} \{v_1(q_1) - x_1 c_1(q_1)\}$$

where $f_n(q)$ is the maximum annual net benefit resulting from allocating $q_n$ to district $n$; $c_n(q_n)$ the annual unit cost of aqueduct in district $n$; and $x_n$ the length of aqueduct between the outlet to district $(n - 1)$ and the outlet to district $n$.

The optimal solution of this problem may be refined [8] by including the cost–capacity relationship for a reservoir supplying the water, as well as the seasonal aspect of inflows into the dam. A linear programming solution is advocated assuming that mean monthly flows $Q_1, \ldots, Q_{12}$ are given; no overyear storage is needed; full regulation of the mean annual inflow is possible without waste; and the convex benefit function may be approximated by linear segments.

## Applications of Dynamic Programming

Assuming that the sizes of the aqueduct have been specified in the various reaches, the question of the optimal or cheapest route still remains. A preliminary optimization may be made using dynamic programming [9] by formulating the problem in terms of network of potential subroutes. It is assumed that the topography is a polyhedral surface composed of planes inclined at various angles to the horizontal. The optimum path is considered to be a combination of pumping lifts and gravity open-channel reaches. In this way second- and third-best routes are also evaluated using a special algorithm. The lift and reach across a typical plane inclined at an angle $\theta$ is shown in Figure 7.1.

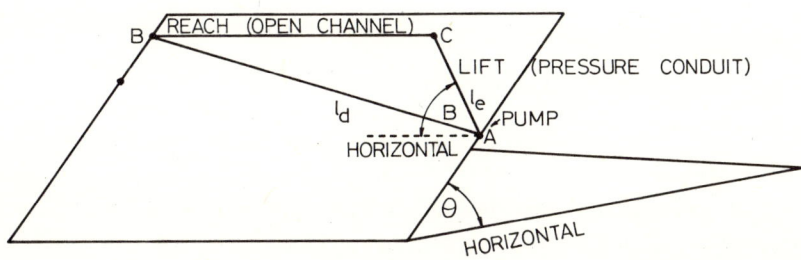

FIGURE 7.1. Lift and reach across a typical plane inclined at angle $\theta$ with respect to horizontal (after [9]).

The model assumes that the cost equation consists of pumping costs, conduit costs, and right of way costs. The cost of the aqueduct linking two nodes $i$ and $j$ is

$$c_{ij} = \left(h_g + \frac{8fq^2 l_1}{\pi^2 g d^5}\right)(v_1 + v_2)q + F + v_3 l_r + v_4 l_1 d^2 + v_5(w_r l_r + w_1 l_1) \quad (7.4)$$

where

$h_g =$ gravity head;
$f =$ friction factor of conduit;
$q =$ discharge to be transported;
$g =$ acceleration due to gravity;
$d =$ diameter of pressure conduit;
$l_1 =$ length of pressure conduit;
$l_r =$ length of open channel;

$v_1 =$ cost of energy per unit discharge per unit head;
$v_2 =$ variable cost of pumping installation per unit discharge per unit head;
$v_3 =$ cost of open channel per unit length;

## Scientific Allocation of Water Resources

$v_4$ = cost of pressure conduit per $d^2$;
$v_5$ = land value per unit area;
$F$ = fixed cost component of an aqueduct segment;
$w_l$ = width of land used for closed conduit;
$w_r$ = width of land used for open channel.

From the geometry of the model and the cost equation (7.4), it can be shown that the optimal angle $\beta$ that the closed conduit should make with the horizontal plane is a fixed angle $\beta_0$ diminished by an amount that varies with $\theta$:

$$\beta = \beta_0 - \sin^{-1}\left(\frac{s}{\sin \theta}\right) \tag{7.5}$$

where $s$ is the hydraulic slope of the conduit, and

$$\beta_0 = \frac{(v_1 + v_2)qs + v_3 + v_5 w_r}{(8fq^3/\pi^2 g d^5)(v_1 + v_2) + v_4 d^2 + w_5 w_l}. \tag{7.6}$$

The values of $\beta$ are calculated for each plane angle $\theta$ as well as for the unit costs of each conduit segment. Given a network of possible paths linking two points and unit costs of optimal reaches and lifts, a best route can be determined by a dynamic programming algorithm.

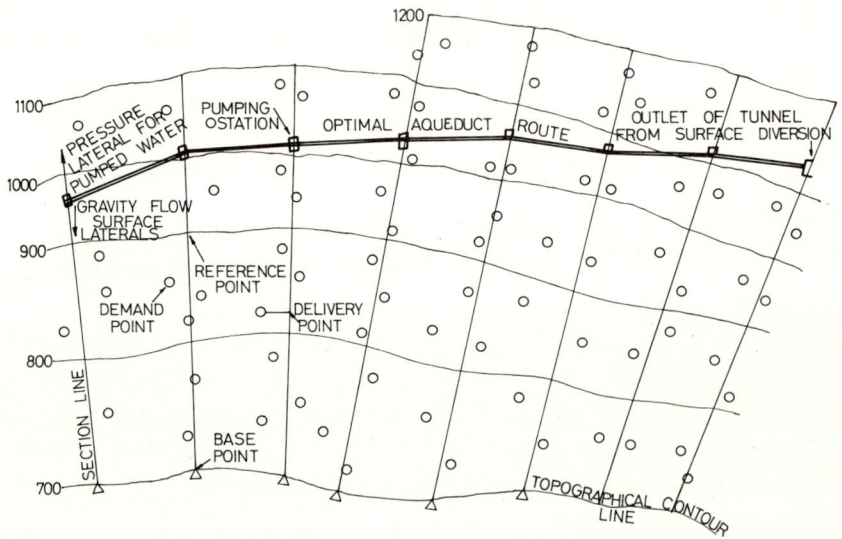

FIGURE 7.2. Schematic representation of an irrigation development project in Iran.

## Applications of Dynamic Programming

A somewhat different analysis was used in the optimization of a main aqueduct route in a development project in Iran [10]. In this project, a major conduit capable of conveying a maximum discharge of about 1100 ft$^3$/sec had to be designed in connection with the irrigation development of approximately 900,000 acres of gently sloping land. A schematic representation of the system is shown in Figure 7.2. In this sketch, the 300 or so villages scattered over the Ghazvin plain are represented by dots, the size of each dot being proportional to the irrigation demand for water. The optimal route of the main (open-channel) conduit should yield a minimum total cost for the complete system, including (1) the main aqueduct; (2) gravitational laterals sloping down from the main aqueduct; (3) pumping stations to lift water from the main aqueduct to higher demand points (villages); (4) pressure laterals for the delivery of the pumped water; (5) pumping energy.

As may be seen in Figure 7.2, the laterals follow some arbitrary lines crossing the topographical contours and called *section lines*. The intersections of section lines with topographical contours are termed *reference points*. There are $i_n$ ($i_n = 1, 2, \ldots, I_n$) reference points along any section line $n$ ($n = 1, 2, \ldots, N$). The location of a reference point is given by the vector $\mathbf{Z}_{in}$

$$\mathbf{Z}_{in} = (x_{in}, y_{in}, h_{in}) \tag{7.7}$$

where $x_{in}$, $y_{in}$ are plane coordinates and $h_{in}$ is the elevation above a common datum.

Let $g(Z_{i1})$ define the cost function of conveying water from any reference point $i1$ (on section line 1) to the delivery points on the same line. If $f(Z_{i1})$ is the function of minimum costs involved in conveying water along the same section line, then it is obvious that

$$f(\mathbf{Z}_{i1}) = g(\mathbf{Z}_{i1}). \tag{7.8}$$

Having denoted by number 1 the section line farthest downstream along the aqueduct, let us move one stage upstream to section line number 2. The cost of the aqueduct linking any reference point $\mathbf{Z}_{i2}$ on section line 2 with any reference point $\mathbf{Z}_{i1}$ on section line 1 is $c(\mathbf{Z}_{i2} - \mathbf{Z}_{i1})$, where $(\mathbf{Z}_{i2} - \mathbf{Z}_{i1})$ expresses both the distance and the difference in elevation between the two points. The cost function of conveying from any point $\mathbf{Z}_{i2}$ to delivery points along section line 2 is, accordingly, $g(\mathbf{Z}_{i2})$. Thus we can write the minimum cost function for the two-stage process of supplying irrigation water to the two last downstream laterals as

$$f(\mathbf{Z}_{i2}) = \min_{\substack{i2 \\ i=1,2,\ldots,I}} \{g(\mathbf{Z}_{i2}) + c(\mathbf{Z}_{i2} - \mathbf{Z}_{i1}) + f(\mathbf{Z}_{i1})\}. \tag{7.9}$$

Observe that the minimization here is performed on all reference points $i2$.

By induction, we reach the general expression for the recursive relationship describing the decision process:

$$f(\mathbf{Z}_{in}) = \min_{\substack{in \\ i=1,2,\ldots,I}} \{g(\mathbf{Z}_{in}) + c(\mathbf{Z}_{in} - \mathbf{Z}_{i,n-1}) + f(\mathbf{Z}_{i,n-1})\}. \tag{7.10}$$

The computational aspects of the algorithm included a number of details specific to the problem in hand:

1. Topographic computations for the establishment of three-dimensional coordinates of reference points and distances between them;
2. Economic velocities of flow in pipes, where pressure conduits were considered.
3. Friction losses in pipes were computed by the Hazen–Williams formula [11].
4. Hydraulic computations for open conduits were based on Manning's formula [12].
5. The cost function included (a) cost of concrete lining of canals, (b) cost of excavation and earth moving, (c) cost of an asphalt membrane placed under the concrete lining, (d) acquisition of right of way for the various conduits, (e) road crossings and footbridges made necessary by the irrigation water supply network.

These computational aspects were presented in great detail elsewhere [13]. The result of the computer runs (which were well below the $1000 mark, including programming), yielded a minimum-cost route for a major aqueduct (estimated investment $30,000,000). Of course, this optimal route is only a first approximation (and a pretty good one, at that) to the exact alignment of the aqueduct, which can be established only in the field.

Dynamic programming has also been applied to problems related to the long-range conversion of vegetative cover from brush to grass in watershed management, resulting in improved grazing facilities and greater water yield [14]. Let $x$ define the current state of the watershed and $q$ the decision vector, resulting in an immediate return $R_N(x, q)$, $N$ being the number of stages remaining in the revegetation process. If decision $q$ is made, the watershed is transformed into state $T(x, q)$ yielding a return $\phi[T(x, q)]$. If $f_N(x)$ is the total return from a watershed in state $x$ with $N$ stages remaining, then

*Applications of Dynamic Programming*

$$f_N(x) = \max_q \{R_N(x, q) + f_{N-1}[T(x, q)]\}. \tag{7.11}$$

The solution yields the decision $q$ to be carried out at each stage for each state $x$ of the watershed. An extension of the model is that of controlled burning of an area $u$ each year, with a probability $p$ that the burned area is converted to grass. Assume that $ax$ is the economic return from the brush area and the return from the grass area is $by$, if the latter is equal to $y$ acres and former is $x$. Then

$$f_N(x, y) = \max_{0 \leqslant u \leqslant x} \left\{ a(x - u) + by + \frac{1}{1 + i} [pf_{N-1}(x - u, y + u) \right.$$
$$\left. + (1 - p)f_{N-1}(x - u, y)] \right\} \tag{7.12}$$

where $1/(1 + i)$ is the annual discount factor for interest rate $i$ and $f_N(x, y)$ the present value of return from a watershed consisting of $x$ acres of brush and $y$ acres of grass, $N$ stages remaining, and pursuing an optimal policy of controlled revegetation.

## C. STORAGE REGULATION

An attempt has been made to utilize the Markovian nature of the reservoir problem to obtain a solution via dynamic programming [15]. The theory is based on a fundamental study of Markov processes and dynamic programming [16, 17]. An optimal policy of releases is determined as a function of the state vector, which includes initial storage, time of the year, and current inflows. Releases are determined at the beginning of each period, assuming that inflow is known. A transition matrix is provided for probabilities of inflow variations from year $i$ to year $i + 1$. In addition, the return as a function of draft $y_i$ is presented. A table lists the probabilities of going from state $i$ to state $j$ under policy (draft) number $k$, which are denoted as $p_{ij}^k$. These probabilities, which are only defined when transition is possible with the given policy, are equal to the transition probabilities of going from the inflow in the first state to the inflow in the next. The immediate expected reward $q_i^k$ from a single transition from state $i$ with policy number $k$ is given by

$$q_i^k = \sum_{j=1}^{N} p_{ij}^k r_{ij}^k \tag{7.13}$$

where $r_{ij}^k$ is the return from transition state $i$ to state $j$ under policy number $k$.

An iterative technique is used for solving the problem, starting with any feasible solution. A value determination operation is performed to find the relative value of being in each of the states with the assumed policy. The results are then used in a policy improvement routine, which determines a better policy if the chosen one is not optimal. The cycle is repeated until no change in policy is found. The value determination equations are

$$g + v_i = q_i + \sum_{j=1}^{N} p_{ij} v_j, \qquad i = 1, 2, \ldots, N, \qquad (7.14)$$

where $g$ represents average earnings per unit time with the given operating policy $= \sum_{i=1}^{N} \pi_i q_i$; $\pi_i$ the limiting state probability of state $i$; and $v_i$ the total expected reward from $n$ stages starting in state $i$ and following a given policy. For each state $i$, we find the policy $k$ that maximizes the test quantity $q_i^k + \sum p_{ij}^k v_j$, using the values $v_i$ and $v_j$ determined from the solution of equation (7.14). This process is repeated until the policy remains unchanged.

Solving models of the foregoing type enables us to approach multiseason storage regulation problems. Assume a single reservoir to be operated over two seasons. Inflow in both seasons can assume two possible values, while the dam can assume three possible values of storage. This results in twelve possible states for the system in both seasons. A transition matrix for changes in streamflow from season to season is given, as well as a table of benefits for possible releases in both seasons.

Specifying an operation procedure, a matrix of transition probabilities can be determined for the twelve states. The operating procedure $k$ is defined by a vector of policies for each state,

$$K = (K^W, K^D) = (k_1^W, k_2^W, \ldots, k_b^W; k_1^D, k_2^D, \ldots, k_b^D) \qquad (7.15)$$

where $k_i^W$ and $k_j^D$ are the policies of water releases in the $i$th state in the wet season and the $j$th state in the dry season, respectively. The matrix of state probabilities dependent upon the operation procedure $p(K)$ is written in partitioned form as

$$p(K) = \begin{array}{c} \\ W \\ D \end{array} \begin{array}{c} W \qquad\quad D \\ \left[ \begin{array}{c|c} 0 & \mathbf{A}(\mathbf{K}^W) \\ \hline \mathbf{B}(\mathbf{K}^D) & 0 \end{array} \right] \end{array}. \qquad (7.16)$$

The zeros indicate that no season can be skipped in transition. The submatrix $\mathbf{A}(\mathbf{K}^W)$ gives the set of transition probabilities from states in the wet season to states in dry season with a given operating procedure. The $i$th row of $\mathbf{A}(\mathbf{K}^W)$, $a_i(k_i^W)$, is the probability vector for transitions from the $i$th state in the wet season with policy (or release rule) $k_i^W$. If the policy for the $i$th state were changed, then the only change in the matrix $p(K)$ would be in the row $a_i$ of the submatrix $\mathbf{A}(\mathbf{K}^W)$. The same applies to $\mathbf{B}(\mathbf{K}^D)$.

The value determination technique would require a solution of 12 simultaneous equations. Had there been 12 months (instead of two seasons), there would have been 72 equations. A method of successive approximations is suggested, which attempts to find an optimal policy for one season of the year with policies for all the other seasons held fixed. This is done for each season until the cycle is completed. The process is then repeated until none of the policies change in any season. At any time that the method suggests a change in policy, the expected value of net benefits over the life of the system is increased. A key concept in the method is to regard the process as one that starts in one season and ends at the beginning of the same season after completing a cycle of operations. In effect, this means that seasonal transition matrices are multiplied as shown in equation (4.29). For example, the transition probability for going from the $i$th state in the wet season to the $L$th state in the wet season, given a specific set of policies, is

$$P_{iL}^W(k_i^W, K^D) = a_i(k_i) \cdot b^L(K^D) \qquad (7.17)$$

where $a_i(k_i)$ is the $i$th row of matrix $A(K^W)$ and $b^L(K^D)$ the $L$th column of matrix $B(K^D)$.

Using the foregoing approach, the immediate expected reward $q_i^{k_i^W}$ for a single transition from $i$ under policy $k_i^W$ needs to be defined. This is due to the fact that when the system makes a transition from state $i$ in the wet season under policy $k_i^W$, it can go to several different states in the dry season. The releases of water in these different states need not all be the same. This means that benefits from the release for each dry season state must be weighted by the probability of transition to the latter given the $i$th state in the wet season and policy $k_i^W$. The formula for $q_i^{k_i^W}$ is

$$q_i^{k_i^W} = r_i^W(k_i^W) + \sum_{j=1}^{n} p_{ij}^W(k_i^W) \cdot r_j^D(K^D) = r_i^W(k_i^W) + a_i(k_i^W) \cdot r^D(K^D) \qquad (7.18)$$

where $r^D(K^D)$ is the old (column) vector of direct rewards for the transition in the dry season under the given operation procedure. The value determination equations (equations (7.14)) are now applied iteratively. Although these equations are computationally simple, large computer storage is required even with a coarse grid for the range of system element values. A choice of reservoir capacity yielding maximum benefits would be made from solutions of these equations for a feasible range of reservoir capacities.

An important application of dynamic programming in water resources engineering is that of optimal design and operation of multiple-purposes reservoirs. Classical approaches to the solution of this problem are through the application of probability theory and linear programming. However, the serial correlation between streamflows in natural hydrological systems makes the application of probability theory to real problems rather complicated. It has been proposed, therefore, that the selection of the reservoir size maximizing the present value of expected net benefits could be made if an optimal operating policy could be determined for each value in a feasible range of reservoir sizes; this determination is best made by dynamic programming [18]. Some of the difficulties presented by the serial correlation of flows can be handled by the use of a synthetic (operational) hydrological record [19]. If the economic life of a surface reservoir is considered to be $N$ months, several sample records of $N$ months each are chosen from a synthetically derived time series of 500–1000 years. The sample set of records represents a number of equally likely sequences of inflow over the specified length of time required by the planning horizon. Thus the analysis using only one of the sample records will give one maximum return of a set of possible maximum returns from using optimal policies. The set of maximum returns so derived is then a sample of the population of maximum returns obtainable from the corresponding optimal policies.

For each record the functional equation technique of dynamic programming is applied. Given the reservoir capacity, releases are determined as a function of storage and recorded inflow, starting with the last time increment in the sample record. This leads to the set of equations

$$f_i(q_i, y_i) = \max_{0 \leqslant x_i \leqslant q_i + y_i} \left\{ v_i(x_i) + \frac{1}{1+r} f_{i-1}(q_{i-1}, y_{i-1}) \right\} \quad (7.19)$$

for

$$i = 1, 2, \ldots, n, \qquad x_i, y_i, q_i \geqslant 0, \qquad q_i \leqslant Q,$$

and given the continuity equation

$$q_i + y_i - x_i = q_{i-1}. \quad (7.20)$$

## Applications of Dynamic Programming

In these equations, $f_i(q_i, y_i)$ represents the maximum return obtainable when the storage at the beginning of the $i$th increment is $q_i$ and the inflow during the same increment is $y_i$; $v_i(x_i)$ is the benefit obtained from a release of water $x_i$ in the $i$th time increment; $r$ the interest rate; $Q$ the reservoir capacity; and $n$ the number of time increments considered.

Using the results derived from many such runs, an optimal dam size may be chosen on the basis of the expected present value of net returns, modified by considerations of the standard deviation of returns induced by the optimal operating policy. In this way, important risk considerations may be included in the decision process. Another important advantage of this approach is that different return functions and penalties for not meeting demand may be varied during the lifetime of the project. Although this problem could be solved also by a stochastic dynamic programming formulation, computation would be lengthy and complicated, especially when conditional probabilities were used to allow for serial correlation. Such a set of equations might be

$$f_i(q_i, y_i) = \max_{0 \leqslant x_i \leqslant q_i + y_i} \left\{ v_i(x_i) + \frac{1}{1+r} \sum_{k=1}^{m} p_k f_{i-1}(q_i + y_{ik} - x_i) \right\} \quad (7.21)$$

where $p_k$ are the probabilities of different values of inflow $y_k$ during period $i$.

Extending the reservoir model to treat multipurpose dam design problems leads to disadvantages inherent in the dynamic programming technique. One of them is the requirement that net benefits resulting from the allocation of regulated flow to a specific purpose or use must be independent of the benefits from all other users. Alternatively, it must be possible to arrange the uses sequentially so that no one use depends on any other allocation, except possibly those lower in time sequence. If "regulated flow" is defined as the provision of a specified quantity of water distributed according to a given demand pattern, then flood control releases are not considered "uses" of regulated flow. A method enabling allocation of regulated flow to different uses has been developed by the dynamic programming technique [20]. It was proposed that releases from the reservoir should be allocated to various activities (other than flood control), with the hypothetical assumption that water used for one purpose cannot be used for another. Once an optimal allocation of available water has been derived under these circumstances, yielding the greatest expected return, the restriction is relaxed. The size of the reservoir is now reduced to provide the same optimal benefits and allocations

## Scientific Allocation of Water Resources

as already determined but allowing for the multiple use of the same volume of water.

The allocation under the restrictive conditions is done as follows. Let $n$ be the number of single uses of mean regulated streamflow $X_h$ (volume units per year) that must be allocated to the $i$th activity such that quantities $x_i$, having returns $v_i(x_i)$, maximize the total gross return. The objective function of the hypothetical system, neglecting the cost of the structure $c(X_h)$, is

$$B_h = \max \sum_{i=1}^{n} v_i(x_i), \quad \sum_{i=1}^{n} x_i \leqslant X_h. \tag{7.22}$$

The recursive relationship used for the solution of this equation is

$$f_n(q) = \max_{\substack{0 \leqslant x_n \leqslant q \\ 0 \leqslant q \leqslant x_n}} \{v_n(x_n) + f_{n-1}(q - x_n)\}, \tag{7.23}$$

where $q$ represents the different quantities of regulated flow and $f_n(q)$ the total gross return from allocating water to various activities using an optimal policy, $n$ activities remaining in the allocation process.

Having allocated releases on an annual basis, the timing of the separate releases over an average year shows that overlapping occurs. An example is shown in Figure 7.3. It is seen that in practice only the regulated quantity represented by the upper heavy line needs to be released. This quantity is $X = X_h - D$, where $D$ is the quantity of water that serves two or more purposes and is shown by the shaded area of the diagram. The joint cost

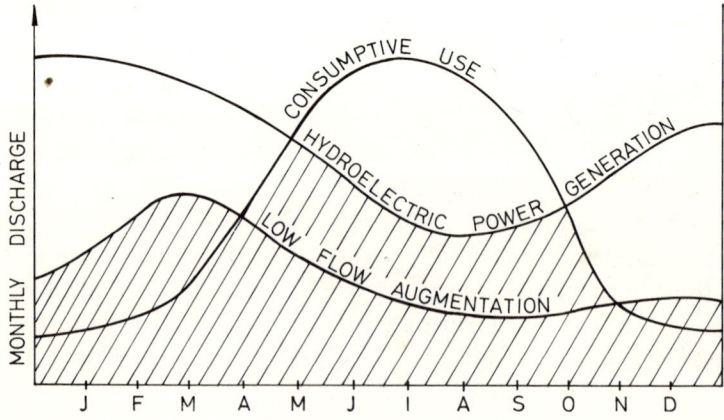

FIGURE 7.3. Timing of releases for different purposes during a year (after [20]).

of the dam is reduced to $c(x)$, enlarging the maximum net benefits while the optimal policy remains unchanged for the regulated streamflow.

The functional nature of a dynamic programming solution provides a set of optimal policies $x_i(q)$ and maximum returns $f_n(q)$ for all values that a hypothetical regulated flow $q$ might take in the range $0 \leqslant q \leqslant X_h$. To each $q$ and policy set $x_i(q)$ there is a corresponding use pattern resulting in a multiple-use volume $D(q)$. If $q$ takes on several upper limits $X_{h1}, X_{h2}, \ldots, \leqslant X_h$, there is an optimal policy set $x_{i1}, x_{i2}, x_{i3}, \ldots, x_{ih}$ and maximum benefit associated with each of these values. Using the various optimal policy sets, monthly demand patterns can be constructed for average years, giving a set of values $D_1, D_2, \ldots, D_h$. The latter are plotted versus $X_{h1}, X_{h2}, \ldots, X_h$. The value of $X_{hi}$ for any regulated flow $X$ is obtained graphically from this curve. As the gross benefit from the actual flow $X$, $B(X)$, equals that resulting from $X_h$, that is, $B_h = f_n(X_h)$, then $B(X) = f_n(X_h)$. The optimal return $V(X)$ is derived from

$$V(X) = B(X) - c(X) \qquad (7.24)$$

where $c(X)$ is the joint cost of a reservoir system needed to supply a mean regulated flow $X$ that is optimally allocated to several activities.

An extension using marginal analysis can be made to show to what extent the capacity of the reservoir has to be increased to provide flood control benefits.

## D. CONJUNCTIVE USE OF SURFACE AND GROUNDWATER RESOURCES

In semiarid regions, conjunctive use of surface and groundwater storage is often sought to offset deficits in the dry season and to enable storage and recharge of excess water in the wet season. An important function of aquifers is their capacity to allow demands to be met during periods having long cyclic variations in surface runoff. The problem of determining operational allocations to both forms of storage, as well as the capacity of surface storage required, is well suited to a solution using dynamic programming [21]. The storage allocation model assumes that demands (and also average benefits) are known over the life of the project. It follows that a minimization of storage costs is required, provided that the demand is met using an optimal policy of withdrawals from both types of storage. The problem may be stated as follows.

$$C_i = \min\left[c_{i1}(s_{i1}, q_i) + c_{i2}(s_{i2}, g_i)\right] \tag{7.25}$$

subject to

$$s_{i1} + s_{i2} = s_i, \tag{7.26}$$

$$0 \leqslant q_i \leqslant Q, \tag{7.27}$$

and

$$0 \leqslant g_i \leqslant G, \tag{7.28}$$

where $q_i$ is the storage in the surface reservoir of capacity $Q$ at the end of the $i$th month; $g_i$ the storage in the aquifer of capacity $G$ at the end of the $i$th month; $s_i$ the available water at the end of the $i$th month; $s_{i1}$, $s_{i2}$ the volumes from $s_i$ allocated to surface and groundwater storage, respectively; $c_{i1}$, $c_{i2}$ the unit storage costs for surface and groundwater, respectively.

It is shown that, given a reservoir of fixed size $Q$, surface storage capital costs are fixed, so that differential costs incurred in storing water above or below the ground depend upon $q_i$, $g_i$, and the inflow $y_i$. In the case of a multipurpose reservoir, differential costs (DC) are

$$\mathrm{DC} = \min \left\{ \begin{array}{c} \text{flood risks} - \text{hydroelectric benefits} \\ + \text{groundwater pumping costs} \end{array} \right\}. \tag{7.29}$$

Under such conditions, available water $s_i$ will be entirely allocated to either surface or groundwater storage.

Knowing that $s_i$ will be relegated to the surface reservoir or to the aquifer, the optimum surface storage capacity may be found by dynamic programming, assuming that demand $x_i$ and probable inflow $y_i$ are known. At each of the $n$ stages of operation, $q_i$ and $g_i$ must be selected so as to maximize the net benefit $v_i(q_i, g_i)$. In other words,

$$B = \max \left\{ \sum_{i=1}^{n} v_i(q_i, g_i) \right\} \tag{7.30}$$

subject to

$$0 \leqslant q_i \leqslant Q, \tag{7.31}$$

$$0 \leqslant g_i \leqslant G. \tag{7.32}$$

During the $i$th period, $s_i$ must be allocated to surface storage (alternative $a$) or groundwater storage (alternative $b$), resulting in benefits $B_{ai}$ or $B_{bi}$, respectively. For a multipurpose project

## Applications of Dynamic Programming

$$B_{ai} = v_i(x_i) + h_i(x_i, q_i) - c_{fi}(q_i + s_i) - c_{ai}(s_i) - F_a, \qquad (7.33)$$

$$B_{bi} = v_i(x_i) + h_i(y_i, q_i) + k_i s_i \left(H - \frac{g_i}{\sigma A}\right) c_{bi} s_i - F_b, \qquad (7.34)$$

where

$v_i(x_i)$ = return from consumptive use of water;
$h_i(x_i, q_i)$ = return from hydroelectric energy generated by release $x_i$ at a head determined by $q_i$;
$h_i(y_i, q_i)$ = return from hydroelectric plant by releasing $y_i$ at head determined by $q_i$;
$c_{fi}(q_i + s_i)$ = increase in flood hazard when flood control storage is reduced by $s_i$;
$c_{ai}(s_i)$ = cost of storage in the dam (operation charges);
$F_a$ = miscellaneous costs;
$k_i$ = price of energy needed for pumping from the aquifer;
$H$ = maximum economic lift;
$\sigma$ = specific yield of the aquifer;
$A$ = average cross-sectional area of the aquifer;
$c_{bi}(s_i)$ = cost of aquifer recharge;
$F_b$ = miscellaneous recharge costs.

Using these benefit functions, a recursive relationship for an $n$-stage process is given by

$$f_n(q_n, g_n) = \max_{\substack{0 \leq q_n \leq Q \\ 0 \leq g_n \leq G}} \begin{cases} a_i B_{an} + \left(\dfrac{1}{1+r}\right) f_{n-1}[q_{n-1} - e_n(q_n) + s_n, g_{n-1}] \\ b_i B_{bn} + \left(\dfrac{1}{1+r}\right) f_{n-1}[q_{n-1}, g_{n-1} + s_n - \varepsilon_n(g_n)] \end{cases} \qquad (7.35)$$

where $f_n(q_n, g_n)$ is the present value of total return from an $n$-stage process provided that $q_n$ and $g_n$ are allocated optimally in the remaining $n$ stages; $r$ is the current interest rate; $e_n(q_n)$ are evaporation and seepage losses from the surface reservoir in the $n$th stage; $\varepsilon_n(g_n)$ are unrecoverable groundwater losses.

The result is given as a function of $q_i$ and $g_i$ for each stage: for each of the possible combinations of the two variables, alternative $a$ or $b$ is specified, as well as the total benefit for the remaining $n$ stages when using an optimal policy.

## Scientific Allocation of Water Resources

The conjunctive use problem has been extended to deal with most major aspects of storage [22–24]. A fairly complex situation is presented in Figure 7.4 [25]. The system shown in this diagram is composed of two storage units: a surface reservoir of capacity $Q$ and a groundwater reservoir of capacity $G$, supplying water to two principal demand areas $DL$ and $D$. The interelement conveyance structures, well fields, and recharge facilities each have a maximum capacity determined by technical considerations. The monthly natural replenishment ($Z_j$) of the surface reservoir is small in relation to the latter's size and varies in relatively small increments. On the other hand, the monthly streamflow into the surface reservoir responds directly to winter rainfall and spring snowmelt. River flow fluctuates over a wide range, resulting in a standard deviation equivalent to 63% of its mean annual

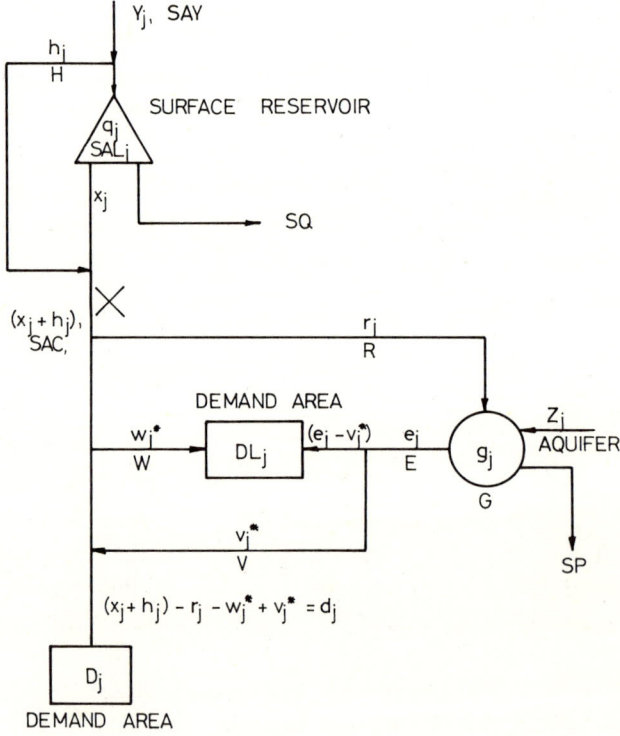

FIGURE 7.4. Schematic representation of a surface reservoir–aquifer system.

inflow [26]. For practical purposes, $Z_j$ may be regarded as a constant value in relation to $Y_j$, the monthly river flow.

When using monthly streamflows, analysis of existing data exhibits serial dependence between streamflow in any month $y_j$ and that of the preceding month $y_{j-1}$. A simple Markov chain relation is assumed, with monthly inflow probabilities normally distributed. The conditional probability function is given by a bivariate normal distribution of the form

$$f(y_j|y_{j-1}) = [(2\pi)^{1/2}\sigma_j(1-\rho_j^2)^{1/2}]^{-1} \exp\left\{-[2\sigma^2(1-\rho_j^2)]^{-1}\right.$$
$$\left.\cdot\left[y_j - \mu_j - \frac{\rho_j\sigma_j}{\sigma_{j-1}}(y_{j-1}-\mu_{j-1})\right]^2\right\} \qquad (7.36)$$

where $\rho_j^2$ is the serial correlation of two successive monthly inflows, $\sigma_j^2$ the variance of flows in month $j$, and $\mu_j$ the mean flow in month $j$.

A certain amount of water $SQ$ ($SQ \geq 0$) may leave the surface reservoir through overflow when net inflow exceeds available storage capacity. These losses should be minimized. Similar overflow via springs ($SP$) may occur when the storage in the aquifer exceeds $G$. This overflow, however, may be used locally. Physical and engineering considerations lead to the following constraints.

$$0 \leq h_j \leq \min(H, Y_j), \qquad (7.37)$$

$$0 \leq x_j + h_j \leq X, \qquad (7.38)$$

$$0 \leq x_j \leq \min(X, q_j), \qquad (7.39)$$

$$0 \leq e_j \leq \min(E, g_j + Z_j), \qquad (7.40)$$

$$0 \leq x_j + h_j - r_j - w_j^* + v_j^* = \min(D_j - d_j), \qquad (7.41)$$

$$e_j - v_j^* + w_j^* = DL_j, \qquad (7.42)$$

$$0 \leq q_j \leq Q, \qquad (7.43)$$

$$0 \leq g_j \leq G, \qquad (7.44)$$

$$0 \leq r_j \leq R, \qquad (7.45)$$

$$0 \leq w_j^* \leq W, \qquad (7.46)$$

$$0 \leq v_j^* \leq V, \qquad (7.47)$$

where

$h_j$ = the surface flow diverted in month $j$ bypassing the reservoir, $j = 1, 2, \ldots, 12$;
$H$ = capacity of surface flow bypass;
$Y_j$ = monthly surface flow;
$x_j$ = release from surface reservoir in month $j$;
$X$ = capacity of conduit connecting surface reservoir with demand area $D$;
$q_j$ = storage in surface reservoir at the beginning of month $j$;
$e_j$ = pumpage from aquifer in month $j$;
$E$ = pumping capacity of wells;
$g_j$ = amount of water available for pumping in aquifer at the beginning of month $j$;
$Z_j$ = monthly natural recharge of aquifer;
$r_j$ = artificial recharge of aquifer in month $j$;
$w_j{}^*$ = surface water delivered to demand area $DL$ if demand cannot be satisfied by groundwater;
$v_j{}^*$ = groundwater delivered to demand area $D$ if surface supply is insufficient;
$D_j$ = demand in area $D$ in month $j$;
$d_j$ = total monthly supply to area $D$ (from both surface and groundwater sources);
$DL_j$ = monthly water demand in area $DL$;
$Q$ = active storage in surface reservoir;
$G$ = maximum storage capacity of aquifer;
$R$ = capacity of recharge facilities;
$W$ = capacity of conduit supplying surface water to area $DL$;
$V$ = capacity of conduit supplying well water to area $D$.

Note that $v_j{}^*$ and $w_j{}^*$ are a special type of (decision) variable, such that $v_j{}^* = 0$ if $e_j \leqslant DL_j$ and $w_j{}^* = 0$ if $e_j \geqslant DL_j$.

An essential variable in the operation of the system is the quality of the water delivered to consumers, expressed by the concentration of chloride ions. The diversion of a certain part of the streamflow to bypass the surface reservoir is aimed at the introduction of high quality water directly into the main conduit that links the surface reservoir with demand areas. It follows that decisions concerning the magnitude of this diversion $h_j$ and the release from the surface reservoir $x_j$ must consider also their effect on the salinity of water. The chloride concentration of water delivered to consumers $SAC_j$ should be as low as possible.

## Applications of Dynamic Programming

The main objectives of operating the system are [27] (i) to ensure a firm annual supply according to a predetermined allocation; (ii) that the quality of water not be worse than a given standard; (iii) to meet the monthly demands; (iv) operation at least cost; (v) minimum losses of water (i.e., reduction of evaporation and spillage).

The cost function of monthly operation ($\Phi$) is composed of the following items.

(a) $\alpha(x_j)$, the unit cost (in million Israeli pounds per million cubic meters of water, MI£/Mm³) of extracting water from the surface reservoir, this is given by the function

$$\alpha_1(x_j)(x_j - 27)^* + \alpha_2(x_j)(27 - x_j)^*; \qquad (7.48)$$

(b) $\beta$, the unit cost of diverting water upstream from the surface reservoir (MI£/Mm³);

(c) $\gamma$, the unit cost of pumping water from the aquifer (MI£/Mm³);

(d) $\delta$, the unit "negative" benefit derived from spills $SQ$;

(e) $\varDelta$, the unit recharge costs (MI£/Mm³);

(f) $\varepsilon$, the unit cost of utilizing water from aquifer overflow $SP$;

(g) $C_1(x_j)$, a penalty for increase in salinity of the surface reservoir due to extraction $x_j$;

(h) $C_2(SAC_j)$, penalty for supplying water with more than a given chloride concentration to consumers in month $j$;

(i) $C_3(h_j)$, negative benefit as a result of diversion $h_j$;

(j) $I_1$, the unit cost of diversion $w_j^*$ (MI£/Mm³);

(k) $I_2$, the unit cost of diversion $v_j^*$ (MI£/Mm³).

The recurrence relation describing the monthly operation of the system is

$$F_N(q, g, SAL, y_{i,N+1}) = \min_{\substack{h \\ x \\ r \\ e}} \left\{ \sum_{j=1}^{s} p_{ij} \left[ \Phi(h, x, r, e) \right.\right.$$

$$\left.\left. + \frac{1}{1+b} F_{N-1}(q', g', SAL', y_{j,N}) \right] \right\} \qquad (7.49)$$

where $F_N(q, g, SAL, y_{i,N+1})$ is the minimum expected cost of operating the system during $N$ monthly stages beginning with $q$ Mm³ of water in surface storage, $g$ Mm³ in the aquifer, salinity $SAL$ of the water in the surface reservoir, an observed unflow $y_{i,N+1}$, during the preceding month, and pursuing an optimal policy; $p_{ij}$ are discrete conditional probabilities of inflow $y_j$ in month $N$, given an inflow $y_i$ in the previous month; $b$ is the current interest rate; and $q', g', SAL'$ the transformed state variables following the operation of the system during one stage.

This recursive equation represents a Markov decision process that has a completely ergodic transition matrix for each period in a 12-month cycle. This process will yield an optimal operating policy, or "pure strategy," for each month, given any admissible combination of state variables [28]. After a certain number of iterations, an optimal "stationary" policy manifests itself.

Equation (7.49) is a four-dimensional sequential decision problem, and its solution presents formidable computational difficulties, especially as regards high-speed memory requirements in electronic computers. In order to reduce significantly the high-speed memory requirement at the expense of some increase in the overall computing time, the return function $F_N(q, g, SAL, y_{i,N+1})$ was approximated by polynomials [29] of degree $M$. Specifically, Chebychev polynomials were used [30], which are defined recursively over the range (0, 1) as

$$T_0(x) = 1, \tag{7.50}$$

$$T_1(x) = 2x - 1, \tag{7.51}$$

$$\vdots$$

$$T_{n+1}(x) = (4x - 2)[T_n(x)] - T_{n-1}(x). \tag{7.52}$$

In general, a function of a single variable is approximated polynomially by

$$f_N(x) \cong \sum_{j=0}^{M} a_j^{(N)} \pi_j(x) \tag{7.53}$$

where $\pi_j(x)$ is a polynomial of degree $j$ in $x$, and $a_j^{(N)}$ is (in the case of an $N$-stage decision process) the $N$th-stage $j$th coefficient. These coefficients are found from a least squares approximation which minimizes the integral

$$\int_0^1 \left[ f_N(x) - \sum_{j=0}^{M} a_j^{(N)} \pi_j(x) \right]^2 dx = J[a_0^{(N)}, a_1^{(N)}, \ldots, a_M^{(N)}]. \tag{7.54}$$

The variable $x$ is measured so that an upper bound on $x$ is unity: the functions $\pi_i(x)$ and $\pi_j(x)$ are orthonormal on the interval (0, 1):

## Applications of Dynamic Programming

$$\int_0^1 \pi_i(x)\pi_j(x)\,dx = \begin{cases} 0 & \text{if } i \neq j, \\ 1 & \text{if } i = j. \end{cases} \tag{7.55}$$

It may be shown that the coefficients $a_j^{(N)}$ that minimize the mean square deviation are

$$a_j^{(N)} = \int_0^1 f_N(x)\pi_j(x)\,dx \qquad (j = 0, 1, 2, \ldots, M). \tag{7.56}$$

Calculation of the coefficients $a_j^{(N)}$ with great accuracy demands a fine grid. To evade this, a Gaussian quadrature formula may be used, which replaces the integral by a weighted sum of $R$ values of the integrand at certain points. The weights $w_i$ and the points of evaluation $\bar{x}_i$ can be determined so that the formula is exact for polynomials of degree up to $(2R - 1)$. Then

$$a_j^{(N)} = \int_0^1 f_N(x)\pi_j(x)\,dx = \sum_{i=1}^R w_i f(\bar{x}_i)\pi_j(\bar{x}_i). \tag{7.57}$$

Returning to the orthogonal Chebychev polynomials (equations (7.50), (7.51), and (7.52)), we can find their roots by

$$\bar{x}_i = \cos i\frac{\pi}{R}, \qquad i = 0, 1, 2, \ldots, R. \tag{7.58}$$

The approximation (7.53) then becomes

$$f_N(x) \cong \frac{a_0^{(N)}}{2} + \sum_{k=1}^M a_k^{(N)} T_k(x) \tag{7.59}$$

where $a_M^{(N)}$ is weighted by $\tfrac{1}{2}$ if $M = R$. Trigonometric interpolation may be used to calculate the coefficients $a_k^{(N)}$,

$$a_k^{(N)} = \frac{2}{R} \sum_{i=0}^R{}' f_N(\bar{x}_i) T_k(\bar{x}_i), \qquad k = 0, 1, 2, \ldots, M, \tag{7.60}$$

where the prime on the summation sign indicates that the coefficients $a_0^{(N)}$ and $a_m^{(N)}$ used in equation (7.59) are weighted by $\tfrac{1}{2}$.

Returning to our problem, equation (7.49) can now be written as

$$f_N(q, g, SAL, y_{i,N+1}) = \sum_{u=0}^M{}' \sum_{v=0}^M{}' \sum_{w=0}^M{}' \sum_{z=0}^M{}' a_{uvwz}^{(N)} T_u[\xi(q)] \cdot T_v[\xi(g)] \cdot T_w[\xi(SAL)]$$
$$\cdot T_z[\xi(y_{i,N+1})] \tag{7.61}$$

where $\xi$ is a function that normalized the variables $q$, $g$, $SAL$, and $y_{i,N+1}$ over the range $(0, 1)$. The coefficients $a_{uvwz}^{(N)}$ are calculated from

$$a_{uvwz}^{(N)} = \frac{16}{R^4} \sum_{u=0}^{R}{}' \sum_{v=0}^{R}{}' \sum_{w=0}^{R}{}' \sum_{z=0}^{R}{}' f_N \left[ \frac{\bar{m}_u}{\xi(q)}, \frac{\bar{n}_v}{\xi(g)}, \frac{\bar{o}_w}{\xi(SAL)}, \frac{\bar{p}_z}{\xi(y_{i,N+1})} \right]$$
$$\cdot T_u(\bar{m}_u) \cdot T_v(\bar{n}_v) \cdot T_w(\bar{o}_w) \cdot T_z(\bar{p}_z) \qquad (7.62)$$

where $\bar{m}_u$, $\bar{n}_v$, $\bar{o}_w$, $\bar{p}_z$ are the $u$th, $v$th, $w$th, and $z$th roots, respectively, of the Chebychev polynomials calculated by equation (7.58). The prime on the summation signs in equations (7.61) and (7.62) indicates that the coefficients $a_{uvwz}^{(N)}$, which have to be computed and stored at every stage $N$, have to be weighted as given in Table I.

**Table I. Weights for Polynomial Coefficients in a Four-Dimensional Sequential Optimization Problem**

| Coefficient | Weight | Coefficient | Weight |
|---|---|---|---|
| $a_{0000}^{(N)}$ | $\frac{1}{16}$ | $a_{000z}^{(N)}$ | $\frac{1}{8}$ |
| $a_{u000}^{(N)}$ | $\frac{1}{8}$ | $a_{uMMM}^{(N)}$ | $\frac{1}{8}$ |
| $a_{uv00}^{(N)}$ | $\frac{1}{4}$ | $a_{uvMM}^{(N)}$ | $\frac{1}{4}$ |
| $a_{u0w0}^{(N)}$ | $\frac{1}{4}$ | $a_{uMwM}^{(N)}$ | $\frac{1}{4}$ |
| $a_{u00z}^{(N)}$ | $\frac{1}{4}$ | $a_{uMuz}^{(N)}$ | $\frac{1}{2}$ |
| $a_{u0wz}^{(N)}$ | $\frac{1}{2}$ | $a_{uMMz}^{(N)}$ | $\frac{1}{4}$ |
| $a_{uvw0}^{(N)}$ | $\frac{1}{2}$ | $a_{uvwM}^{(N)}$ | $\frac{1}{2}$ |
| $a_{uv0z}^{(N)}$ | $\frac{1}{2}$ | $a_{uvMz}^{(N)}$ | $\frac{1}{2}$ |
| $a_{uvwz}^{(N)}$ | $1$ | $a_{MvMM}^{(N)}$ | $\frac{1}{8}$ |
| $a_{0v00}^{(N)}$ | $\frac{1}{8}$ | $a_{MvwM}^{(N)}$ | $\frac{1}{4}$ |
| $a_{0vw0}^{(N)}$ | $\frac{1}{4}$ | $a_{MvMz}^{(N)}$ | $\frac{1}{4}$ |
| $a_{0v0z}^{(N)}$ | $\frac{1}{4}$ | $a_{Mvwz}^{(N)}$ | $\frac{1}{2}$ |
| $a_{0vwz}^{(N)}$ | $\frac{1}{2}$ | $a_{MMwM}^{(N)}$ | $\frac{1}{8}$ |
| $a_{00w0}^{(N)}$ | $\frac{1}{8}$ | $a_{MMMz}^{(N)}$ | $\frac{1}{8}$ |
| $a_{00wz}^{(N)}$ | $\frac{1}{4}$ | $a_{MMMM}^{(N)}$ | $\frac{1}{16}$ |

Finally, equation (7.49) becomes

$$f_N(q, g, SAL, y_{i,N+1}) = \min_{\substack{h \\ x \\ r \\ e}} \left\{ \sum_{j=1}^{s} p_{ij} \left[ \Phi(h, x, r, e) + \frac{1}{1+b} \sum_{u=0}^{M}{}' \sum_{v=0}^{M}{}' \sum_{w=0}^{M}{}' \sum_{z=0}^{M}{}' \right. \right.$$

## Applications of Dynamic Programming

$$\cdot a^{(N-1)}_{uvwz} \cdot T_u[\xi(q')] \cdot T_v[\xi(g')]$$

$$\cdot T_w[\xi(SAL')] \cdot T_z[\xi(y'_{i,N+1})]\Big]\Big\}. \qquad (7.63)$$

In this way, a considerable saving in high-speed memory requirement is achieved. For if the approximation is with polynomials of degree $M = R = 3$, then the number of coefficients to be stored is $4^4 = 256$. An additional bonus in terms of reduced memory requirement is afforded by the fact that many of these coefficients are alike. Indeed, for $R = 3$, the number of coefficients that are different from each other is $(R + 4)!/(R!4!) = 35$. Of course, this saving is obtained at the expense of computer time, which, even if it may be substantial, is still within reasonable bounds.

It would be unjust to conclude the discussion on the conjunctive use of surface and groundwaters without a quick excursion into the domain of coastal aquifers and their utilization; for the operation of such hydrogeological formations is almost always in close connection with an extraneous (surface) water source. As an example, consider the situation shown in Figure 7.5 [31]. In this situation, a key detail is the fact that as increased pumping causes the seaward gradient of the water table to be reduced, so decrease fresh water losses to the sea $(Q_s)$. However, excess pumping may cause seawater intrusion, with the resulting degradation of the aquifer. It follows that an optimal policy over time ($N$ stages) is required regarding pumping from the aquifer $(Q_p)$ and its recharge from external sources $(Q_r)$.

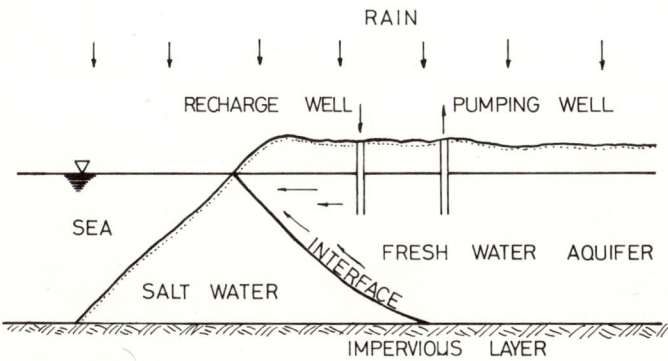

FIGURE 7.5. Sketch of a coastal aquifer cross section.

If the state of the aquifer can be described by the vector $S$, and $S'(N, S; Q_p, Q_r)$ is the new state resulting from the decisions $Q_p$ and $Q_r$ such that

$$S' = S + R + Q_r - Q_s - Q_p \qquad (7.64)$$

where $R$ is an average value of the effective natural recharge (rainfall), then the total cost of an $N$-stage operating process starting in state $S$ and pursuing an optimal policy $f_N(S)$ is given by

$$f_N(S) = \min_{\substack{0 \leq Q_p \leq P_c \\ 0 \leq Q_r \leq R_c}} \{P_N(S; Q_p, Q_r) + f_{N-1}(S + R + Q_r - Q_s - Q_p)\} \qquad (7.65)$$

where $P_N(S; Q_p, Q_r)$ is the cost of the first stage of a process of length $N$ starting in state $S$ and using decisions $(Q_p, Q_r)$; $P_c$ the maximum pumping capacity; and $R_c$ the maximum recharge capacity. The cost function is

$$P_N(S; Q_p, Q_r) = \Phi(Q_p) + U(Q_d - Q_p)^+ - W(Q_p - Q_d)^+ + C(Q_r) \qquad (7.66)$$

where $\Phi(Q_p)$ is the cost of pumping water; $U(Q_d - Q_p)^+$ the cost of meeting demand $Q_d$ from sources outside the region; $W(Q_p - Q_d)^+$ the benefit realized from exporting water outside the system; and $C(Q_r)$ the cost of artificial recharge.

It has been pointed out that conjunctive use planning is complicated by the fact that the unit period for surface water management is about one month, while that for groundwater is a year or more [32]. This means that available supplies should be stated for a 5-year period to enable advance planning of irrigated agriculture. Differences between surface water supply and consumptive use are made up by withdrawals from groundwater reserves. The analysis begins with consideration of a simple model consisting of an aquifer supplied by water from a surface reservoir whose probability distribution of release is known in advance. A dynamic programming formulation of the optimal withdrawal policy that maximizes expected net benefits over an $N$-stage period is

$$f_N(S_i) = \max_k \left\{ B_N{}^k(S_i) + (1 + r)^{-1} \sum_{j=1}^N P_{ij}^k f_{N-1}(S_j) \right\} \qquad (7.67)$$

where $S_i$ is the quantity of water in storage; $p_{ij}^k$ the probability of transition of $S_i$ to $S_j$ for a release of water $x^k$; $r$ the interest rate; and $B_N{}^k(S_i)$ the immediate benefit from a release $k$ when surface reservoir contains $S_i$.

It is pointed out that the decision rule converges to a constant policy when the net benefit function is invariant over stages. Computational improvements are introduced by testing the optimal policy for convergence after several stages have been processed.

If equation (7.67) is written in matrix form, the value determination technique of equation (7.14) can be used. Equation (7.67) then becomes

$$\mathbf{f(n)} = \max_q \{\mathbf{b}_n(\mathbf{q}) + \beta \mathbf{P}(\mathbf{q})\mathbf{f}(n-1)\}, \tag{7.68}$$

where

$\mathbf{f(n)} = n$-component column vector with $i$th component $f_n(S_i)$;

$\mathbf{q} = n$-component column vector with components of magnitudes $k$ representing possible water releases;

$\mathbf{b}_n(\mathbf{q}) = n$-component column vector with $i$th component $B_n{}^k(S_i)$;

$\mathbf{P(q)} = n \times n$ matrix elements $p_{ij}^k$, where $k$ for the $i$th row is determined by the $i$th component of $\mathbf{q}$;

$\beta = (1 + r)^{-1} < 1$, discount factor.

The convergence test requires the solution of $N$ linear equations of expected present value of net benefits over an infinite planning horizon, under a constant policy and net benefit function; that is, the solution of matrix equation

$$[\mathbf{I} - \beta \mathbf{P}]\mathbf{X} = \mathbf{b} \tag{7.69}$$

where $\mathbf{b}$ is a vector of constant values $\mathbf{b}_n(\mathbf{q})$; $\mathbf{P}$ is a matrix of constant values $\mathbf{P(q)}$; $\mathbf{I}$ is an identity matrix; $\mathbf{X}$ is an $N$-component unknown vector equivalent to $\lim_{n \to \infty} \mathbf{f(n)}$.

The computation requires that equation (7.68) be solved iteratively till convergence of policy is established. Equation (7.69) is then solved for $X$. If the value of $X$ and the total expected return evaluated previously are equal, convergence has been proven, that is,

$$\lim_{n \to \infty} \mathbf{q(n)} = \mathbf{q}^*. \tag{7.70}$$

If returns are not equal, a new policy is sought by the solution of further stages. This method is very useful for evaluating the effect of project life on the optimal policy.

An analytical solution for the choice of an optimal safe yield of aquifers has also been tried [33]. The analysis is based on the assumption that water in storage must be abundant relative to the optimal periodic rate of use and that cost of increased pumping depths limits groundwater mining. If, in the limit, as $n \to \infty$,

$$f_{n+1}(S) = f_n(S) = f(S), \tag{7.71}$$

then

$$f(S) = \max_{\mathbf{X}} \left\{ B(\mathbf{X}, S) + \beta \int_0^\infty f(S + w - \mathbf{X}) h(w, S)\, dw \right\}, \tag{7.72}$$

where $h(w, S)\, dw$ is the probability density function for $w_n$. If additions to groundwater reserves are independent of quantity in stock, it appears that the yield of aquifer can be expended safely "to a point where marginal net output with respect to current consumption of the resource is equal to the present value of a perpetual annuity equal in value to marginal net output with respect to quantity of resource in stock" [33, page 83]. It was found that numerical results using an analytical model with some simplifying assumptions closely approximated those obtained from the iterative analysis.

Given the optimal withdrawal policy for the transient states, as well as the steady state solution where policies and returns have converged, the structure of matrix $\mathbf{P}$ of equation (7.69) enables the variance of the returns (outputs) to be derived [34]. The stationary probability distribution of states, and hence of withdrawals and of economic returns, is approximated by a vector of stationary probabilities $\boldsymbol{\alpha} = (\alpha_1, \alpha_2, \ldots, \alpha_m)$. Each state $i$ has an optimal withdrawal $k(i)$ which implies an expected net return $B(X^k, S) = B_i^{k(i)}$. The asymptotic mean net return is then

$$E(B) = \sum_{i=1}^m \alpha_i B_i^{k(i)}. \tag{7.73}$$

The variance for a specified return is

$$V(B) = \sum_{i=1}^m \alpha_i [B_i^{k(i)}]^2 - [E(B)]^2. \tag{7.74}$$

However, the mean and variance could be computed for each stage of the process. If $\pi(n)$ is a probability vector for storage at the $n$th stage, then

$$E(B_n) = \sum_{i=1}^m \pi_i(n) B_{ni}^{k(i,n)}, \tag{7.75}$$

$$V(B_n) = \sum_{i=1}^m \pi_i(n) [B_{ni}^{k(i,n)}]^2 - [E(B_n)]^2. \tag{7.76}$$

The variance may be utilized as a decision criterion by restricting changes in $X$ when passing from stage $n$ to stage $n - 1$. This is done by introducing an additional variable into the functional equation, which is the quantity of water $X$ withdrawn in the previous stage. The functional equation is then

$$f_n(X, Z) = \max_X \{B_n(X, S) + \beta E f_{n-1}(S + w - X)\}, \qquad (7.77)$$

$$z - \delta \leqslant X \leqslant z + \delta, \qquad (7.78)$$

where $\delta$ is an arbitrary limit on successive period use rates. As $\delta \to 0$, variance declines. The resulting variance values offer additional evaluation of decisions.

The technique of dynamic programming often presents computational difficulties. A unique "closed form" type of solution to a complex operational problem in groundwater utilization has been proposed, based on the combination of marginal analysis and dynamic programming [35]. The physical model in Figure 7.6 shows the storage $S_t$, the pumping and recharge facilities $P_t$ and $R_t$, and an amount of leakage $Q_t$ that is a function of $h_t$, the groundwater elevation above the leakage outlet. The aquifer is operated over a number of discrete periods $t$ per year, the storage being determined by the following transformation equation for any period $t$.

$$S_{t+1} = \min\left\{\beta S_i + \frac{\beta}{\gamma N_t} - \frac{\beta}{\gamma}(P_c - R_c), SM\right\} \qquad (7.79)$$

where

$$\beta = \frac{2-\alpha}{2+\alpha}, \qquad (7.80)$$

$$\gamma = \frac{2-\alpha}{2}, \qquad (7.81)$$

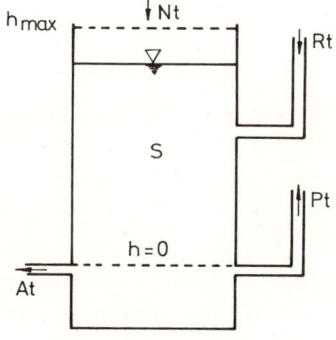

FIGURE 7.6. Physical model of a simple one-cell aquifer.

$SM$ is maximum aquifer capacity, $\alpha$ = aquifer constant, and $N_t$ is the natural aquifer recharge period in $t$. The economic aspects of finding an optimal pumping and recharge policy over a finite period $T$ are based on a water demand function, a cost function, and an interest rate on invested capital $r$. The benefit function $B_t(P)$ from supplying an amount $P$ is expressed as

$$B_t(P) = \int_0^P \delta_t(\eta)\,d\eta + B_0, \qquad B_0 \leqslant 0, \tag{7.82}$$

where $\delta_t(\eta)$ is a demand function for an amount of water $\eta$ ($\eta$ is a dummy variable of integration), and $B_0$ a fine imposed if $P = 0$ (i.e., water cannot be supplied from the aquifer).

The cost of pumping $C(P_t)$ depends on the amount pumped, so that

$$C(P_t) = a_1 P + a_2 P^2 + a_3 P^3 \tag{7.83}$$

where $a_1$, $a_2$, $a_3$ are constants.

The recharge cost function has a similar structure. The objective function to be maximized may now be written as

$$V = E\left\{\sum_{t=1}^T (D)^{t-1}\hat{U}_t(P_t, R_t) + (D)^T U_{sv}(S_v)\right\} \tag{7.84}$$

subject to

$$P_t - R_t \leqslant \gamma S_t + N_t', \tag{7.85}$$

$$0 \leqslant P_t \leqslant P_M, \tag{7.86}$$

$$0 \leqslant R_t \leqslant R_M, \tag{7.87}$$

where

$$D = (1 + r)^{-1}; \tag{7.88}$$

$$\hat{U}_t = B_t(P) - C(P_t)P + C(R_t)R; \tag{7.89}$$

$U_{sv}(S_v)$ = the salvage value of water in storage ($S_v$) at the end of the operation cycle $T$;

$P_M$, $R_M$ = maximum pumping and recharge capacitives, respectively;

$N_t'$ = minimum amount of natural replenishment expected in period $t$;

$C(R_t)$ = cost of recharge of groundwater in period $t$.

The optimization problem may be solved using the recursive approach of dynamic programming stated as follows.

*Applications of Dynamic Programming*

$$V_n{}^*(S) = \max_{P,R} \left\{ \hat{U}_n(P, P-y) + D \int_0^\infty V_{n-1}^* \left[ \beta S + \frac{\beta}{\gamma v} - \frac{\beta}{\gamma}(y); SM \right] dF_n(v) \right\},$$

(7.90)

given

$$-RM \leqslant y \leqslant PM, \qquad (7.91)$$

where $V_n{}^*(S)$ is the maximum expected value of returns from operating the system optimally with $n$ periods remaining until end of period $T$;

$$Y = P - R; \qquad (7.92)$$

$v$ is the random magnitude of natural recharge $N$; and $\hat{U}_n(P, P-y) = $ returns from $P$ and $P-y$ at the $n$th stage.

This formulation reduces the dimensionality of the problem to one: it is required only to find optimal pumping rates $P_t{}^*$ for constant values of $y$, thus yielding also optimal recharge rates $R_t{}^*$.

Marginal analysis may be applied to the optimization of $V_n{}^*(S)$. An insight into the general structure of the optimal policy can also be obtained.

## E. MULTISTRUCTURE AND MULTIPURPOSE SYSTEMS

The analysis of multiunit multipurpose water resource systems presents considerable difficulties, both in the design of such systems and in their operation. Although the design problem still awaits a rigorous approach, in the operational direction we can point out some encouraging beginnings [36]. To be sure, the problem of a single-structure multiple-purpose reservoir has been analyzed [20], as has that of multistructure single-purpose systems [37, 38]. The more general situation, in which complex water resources systems have to satisfy a number of complementary and/or competing demands, often requires the combined forces of several analytical methods.

Consider the northern half of the California water scheme, as shown diagrammatically in Figure 7.7 [39]. It has to provide irrigation water (locally and for delivery in the southern half of the scheme); it generates power at a large number of hydro plants; it must ensure the navigation of certain vessels up to a given point on the Sacramento River; and it has to maintain fish life in its various rivers and creeks. Since most of the elements of the system have been constructed (or were under construction), the problem was (a) to estimate the maximum amount of firm water and firm power generated by the system, and (b) to derive an operating policy maximizing returns. The problem was stated so, in order to stress two important details: (a) The agency operating the system, as well as the buyers of power and water, are interested in maximizing the amount of firm, dependable power and water; (b) water released and power generated in excess of firm quantities may be sold (at prices lower than those of firm water and power). These

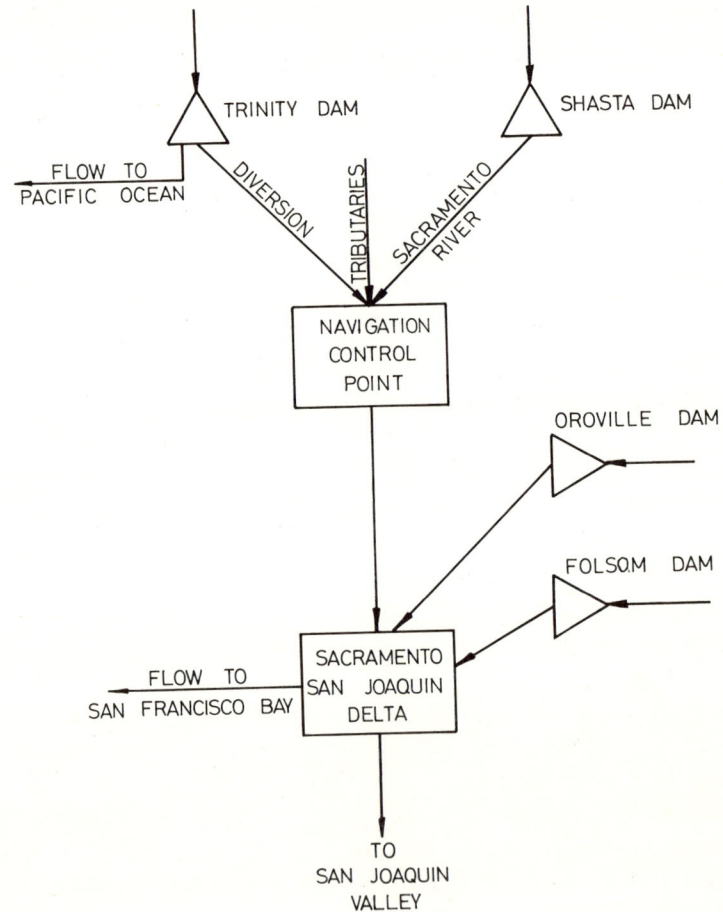

FIGURE 7.7. Schematic representation of the northern part of the California water scheme.

extra amounts of water and power are limited only by the power-generating capacity of the system and by the capacity of water conveyance facilities.

In order to estimate the maximum amount of firm water and power, a 10-year period (from a 40-year hydrological trace) was selected such that it included the lowest flows on record. The argument in favor of this selection was that firm quantities supplied during a critical period will most probably be delivered also during times of relative water abundance.

In the analysis of this complex multistructure multipurpose system, the "principle of decomposition" [40] was applied. The entire system was considered to be composed of four subsystems: Trinity, Shasta, Oroville, and Folsom. The operation of each subsystem was optimized during the critical period by the application of dynamic programming, while a master linear program controlled the operation of the whole complex for the overall maximization of net returns [41]. In the generalized mathematical model presented below, the following symbols are used.

$a$ = unit price of nonfirm water;
$\bar{a}$ = unit price of firm water;
$b$ = unit price of nonfirm power delivered during peak demand periods;
$b'$ = unit price of nonfirm power delivered during off-peak demand periods;
$\bar{b}$ = unit price of firm power;
$f_n(S_i)$ = total return from sale of water and power during the remaining $n$ months of operating the subsystem $i$ optimally in the critical period starting with a volume of water $S_i$ in storage, $i = 1, 2, 3, 4$; $n = 1, 2, \ldots, 120$;
$P_d$ = unit price of nonfirm power (used in the dynamic programming subproblem);
$P_w$ = unit price of water (used in the dynamic programming subproblem);
$q$ = evaporation and other reservoir losses (in month $n$);
$R$ = returns (to the system);
$U$ = monthly generation of firm power (by each subsystem);
$U_{in}$ = on-peak power generation by subsystem $i$ in month $n$;
$V$ = monthly nonfirm power generation;
$W$ = nonfirm water deliveries (by the system);
$\bar{W}$ = firm water deliveries (by the system);
$y$ = monthly releases of water by each subsystem;
$Z$ = nonfirm power delivered by the system in peak demand periods;

$Z$ = firm power delivered by the system;
$\alpha_n$ = proportion of yearly firm water to be supplied by the system in month $n$,

$$0 \leqslant \alpha_n \leqslant 1, \qquad (7.93)$$

$$\sum_{n=1}^{12} \alpha_n = 1; \qquad (7.94)$$

$\beta_n$ = proportion of yearly firm power to be supplied by the system in month $n$,

$$0 \leqslant \beta_n \leqslant 1, \qquad (7.95)$$

$$\sum_{n=1}^{12} \beta_n = 1; \qquad (7.96)$$

$\Phi_n$ = inflow (to each subsystem) in month $n$;
$\Phi_{\text{ncp}}$ = minimum flow required at the navigation control point.

Because of the difficulties encountered in defining firm and nonfirm water at the subsystem level, and since the monthly weights $\beta_n$ for *total* supplied firm power may not fit the power generation schedule of each subsystem, every one of the four subsystems was optimized by the following recursive relationship.

$$f_n(S_i) = \max_{\substack{y \\ U \\ V}} \{P_w y + \bar{b} U + P_a V + f_{n-1}(S_i + \Phi_n - y - q)\}, \qquad (7.97)$$

$$n = 1, 2, \ldots, 120.$$

The solutions of equations (7.97) yield an optimal schedule of releases, which can be introduced, after a certain amount of processing, into the master linear program:
Maximize

$$R = \bar{a}\bar{W} + aW + \bar{b}\bar{Z} + bZ + b'V, \qquad (7.98)$$

subject to

$$\sum_{i=1}^{4} y_{in} = \alpha_n \bar{W} + W_n, \qquad (7.99)$$

$$\sum_{i=1}^{4} U_{in} = \beta_n \bar{Z} + Z_n, \qquad (7.100)$$

## Applications of Dynamic Programming

$$y_{1n} + y_{2n} \geqslant \Phi_{\text{ncp}}, \qquad (7.101)$$

$$\sum_{i=1}^{4} V_{in} = V, \qquad (7.102)$$

and subject to technological constraints resulting from capacities of reservoirs, power stations, conduits, and so on.

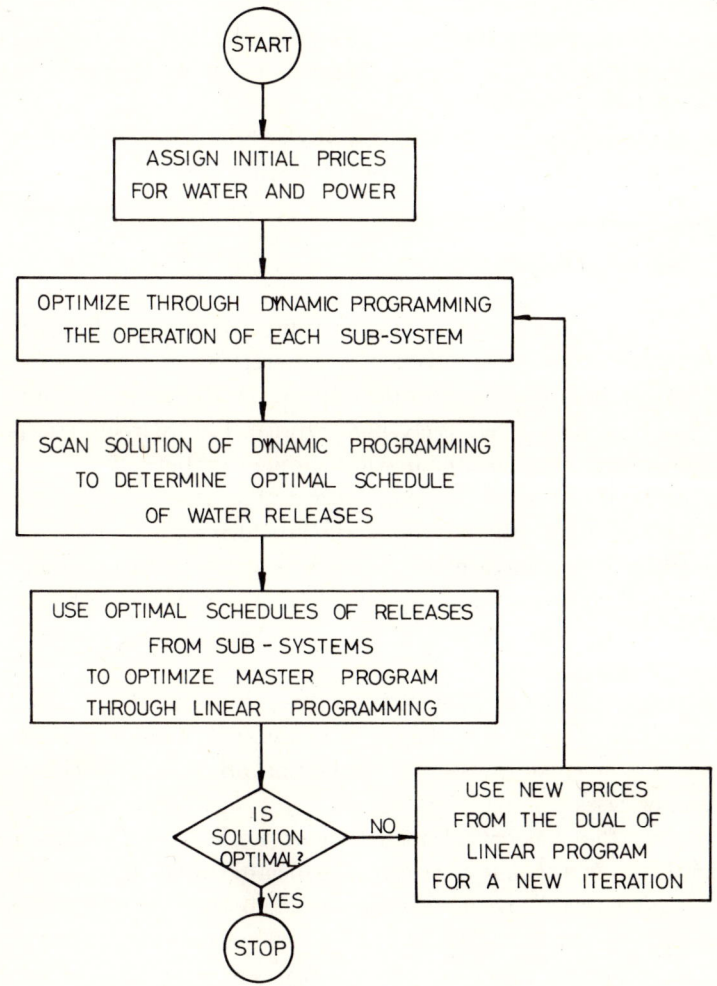

FIGURE 7.8. Flow chart for solution of multistructure multipurpose water resource system.

When the linear programming problem is solved, its dual yields a set of shadow prices that measure the value of changes in the outputs of the component subsystems. These prices are used in rerunning the dynamic programming optimizations of the four subsystems, which results in new schedules of releases and of water and power production. These quantities, which are treated as "resources" by the master linear program, are used in it for the determination of overall firm water and power and nonfirm outputs. Clearly, the procedure is iterative; it continues until the improvement in the value of $R$ is as small as desired. A schematic flow chart of the computation is shown in Figure 7.8.

The model presented and briefly discussed above was extended to include elements from the southern half of the California water scheme as well [42].

## F. PUMPED STORAGE

In order to increase the power output from a hydroelectrical installation, advantage is sometimes taken of existing differential price rates for electricity during peak demand hours and off-peak times. During hours of peak demand, when power is sold at a relatively higher price, the hydroelectric plant will usually generate power. Water flowing through turbines would be stored—in part, at least—at a convenient downstream reservoir, in order to be pumped back into the original impoundment during off-peak hours. In this way, relatively inexpensive power is used to augment the amount of water in storage in the power-producing reservoir, which can be used to increase the output during peak demand hours. This arrangement is usually known as *pumped storage*.

In the California Water Project there are a number of complex pumped-storage facilities. One of them has been analyzed in considerable detail [43], and this analysis can be transferred, with appropriate modifications, to many other similar cases.

Essentially, the conceptual model deals with a problem in resources allocation over time, where a return is associated with the used part of the resources, and where the resource is replenished both as a natural phenomenon at practically no cost and as a result of a given operating policy at a nonnegligible cost. Since the operating policy consists of a sequence of decisions (in time), the net return $r_i$ for any one time period is given by

$$r_i = f_i(A_j) - g_i(B_k) \qquad (7.103)$$

where the subscript $i$ refers to the state of the system (i.e., amount of water in storage in the power-producing reservoir) at the beginning of the time period; $f_i$ is the gross return associated with the quantity $A_j$ used for power production $j$; and $g_i$ is the cost of pumping back into the main reservoir the amount $B_k$. The maximum value of the net return, with the system in state $i$, is

$$R_i = \max_{\substack{A_j \\ B_k}} \{f_i(A_j) - g_i(B_k)\}. \tag{7.104}$$

For the last time period in the decision process, the maximum net return can be obtained from equation (7.104), where $R_i$ should be subscripted $R_{i1}$, to indicate a one-stage process. For the last two stages,

$$R_{i,2} = \max_{\substack{A_j \\ B_k}} \{f_i(A_j) - g_i(B_k) + R_{i',1}\} \tag{7.105}$$

where the transformation from state $i$ to state $i'$ is given by

$$i' = i - A_j + B_k + C; \tag{7.106}$$

here $C$ is the natural replenishment of the resource.

The maximum net return from the remaining $t$ periods in the process is

$$R_{i,t} = \max_{\substack{A_j \\ B_k}} \{f_i(A_j) - g_i(B_k) + R_{i',t-1}\}. \tag{7.107}$$

Of course, the maximization is subject to the availability of the resource (inflows into the reservoir) and to the physical limitations of the system (storage capacity, power generation capability, pumping capability). Additional constraints imposed on the system were (a) release of water from the reservoir for fishlife maintenance; (b) release of water for regional use (domestic, industrial, irrigation); (c) flood control storage capacity of the reservoir; (d) minimum number of hours (per month) during which power has to be generated; (e) maximum number of hours (per month) during which power can be purchased at off-peak rates and be used for pumping. A specific hydrological trace was used.

The results for the monthly period when $t = 59$ are shown in Figure 7.9. The inflow during this month was 340,000 acre-ft, the regional demand for water (mandatory releases) was 2100 acre-ft, and the flood control reservation in the reservoir (available for storing prospective flood flows) was 516,000 acre-ft. The returns were calculated on the basis of given prices of firm and off-peak power, and interest rate for present value discounting.

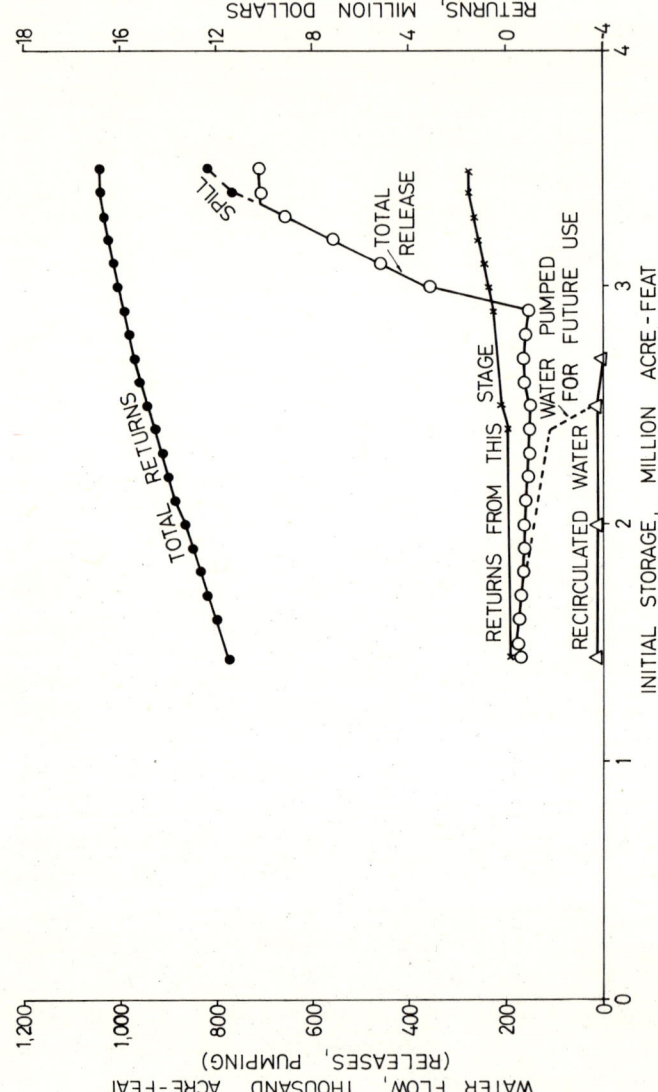
FIGURE 7.9. Optimal operation of a pumped storage system.

## REFERENCES

1. F. D'Epenaux, "A Probabilistic Production and Inventory Problem," *Management Science* **10**(1963), No. 1.
2. W. A. Hall and N. Buras, "The Dynamic Programming Approach to Water Resources Development," *J. Geophysical Research* **66**(1961), No. 2.
3. R. E. Bellman, *Dynamic Programming*. Princeton University Press, Princeton, New Jersey, 1957.
4. R. E. Bellman and S. E. Dreyfus, *Applied Dynamic Programming*. Princeton University Press, Princeton, New Jersey, 1962.
5. G. L. Nemhauser, *Introduction to Dynamic Programming*. Wiley, New York, 1966.
6. W. A. Hall, "Aqueduct Capacity under an Optimum Benefit Policy," *Proc. Amer. Soc. Civil Engineers* **87**(1961), No. IR3.
7. W. A. Hall, "A Method for Allocating Costs to a Water Supply Canal," *J. Farm Economics* **65**(1963), No. 4.
8. S. Ramaseshan, Discussion of [6], *Proc. Amer. Soc. Civil Engineers* **88**(1962), No. IR2.
9. W. A. Hall and J. S. Hammond, "Preliminary Optimization of an Aqueduct Route," *Proc. Amer. Soc. Civil Engineers* **91**(1965), No. IR1.
10. N. Buras and Z. Schweig, "Aqueduct Route Optimization by Dynamic Programming," *Proc. Amer. Soc. Civil Engineers* **95**(1969), No. HY5.
11. H. W. King and E. Z. Brater, *Handbook of Hydraulics*. McGraw-Hill, New York, 1963.
12. V. T. Chow, *Open-Channel Hydraulics*. McGraw-Hill, New York, 1959.
13. Z. Schweig, *An Application of the Dynamic Programming Method to the Planning of the Taleghan Conduct in Ghazvin, Iran*, M.S. Thesis, Technion, Haifa, 1966 (in Hebrew).
14. N. Buras, "Dynamic Programming Methods Applied to Watershed Management Problems," *Trans. Amer. Soc. Agricultural Engineers* **5**(1962), No. 2.
15. L. Falkson, *An Application of Howard's Policy-Alteration Method for the Solution of Sequential Decision Processes to the Problem of Determining the Optimal Operation Procedure of a Water Resource System*, Water Resources Group, Harvard University, Cambridge, Massachusetts, 1961.
16. R. A. Howard, *Dynamic Programming and Markov Processes*. Wiley, New York, 1960.
17. E. V. Denardo and L. G. Mitter, "Elements of Sequential Decision Processes," *J. Industrial Engineering* **18**(1967), No. 1.
18. W. A. Hall and D. T. Howell, "The Optimization of a Single Purpose Reservoir Design with Application of Dynamic Programming to Synthetic Hydrology Samples," *J. Hydrology* **1**(1963), 355–363.
19. M. M. Hufschmidt and M. B. Fiering, *Simulation Techniques for Design of Water Resource Systems*. Harvard University Press, Cambridge, Massachusetts, 1966.
20. W. A. Hall, "Optimum Design of a Multiple Purpose Reservoir System," *Proc. Amer. Soc. Civil Engineers* **90**(1964), No. HY4.
21. N. Buras and W. A. Hall, "An Analysis of Reservoir Capacity Requirements for Conjunctive Use of Surface and Groundwater Storage," Publication No. 57, pp. 556–563, International Association of Scientific Hydrology, Gentbrugge, Belgium, 1961.

22 N. Buras, "Conjunctive Operation of Dams and Aquifers," *Proc. Amer. Soc. Civil Engineers* **89**(1963), No. HY6.
23 N. Buras, "A Three Dimensional Optimization Problem in Water Resources Engineering," *Operations Research Quarterly* **16**(1965), No. 4.
24 N. Buras, "The Conjunctive Use of Surface and Ground Waters," *Reservoir Yield Symposium*, Paper No. 10, Oxford, 1965.
25 T. Herman and N. Buras, "Solution of Some Computational Problems Connected with the Design of Water Resource Systems," *Proc. Nat. Conf. Data Processing* (Jerusalem, 1968), pp. E117–E134.
26 N. Buras, "Conjunctive Operation of a Surface Reservoir and a Ground Water Aquifer," *Symposium on Surface Waters*, Publication No. 63, pp. 492–501, International Association of Scientific Hydrology, 1963.
27 R. Amir and Z. Kally, *A Model of the National Water Carrier as a Means of Designing its Operation*, Tahal, Water Planning for Israel, Tel Aviv, P.N. 355, 1963 (in Hebrew).
28 N. Buras, *Optimal Operation of a Water Resource System: An Application of Dynamic Programming*, European Meeting of Statisticians, London, 1966.
29 R. E. Bellman and R. Kalaba, *Polynomial Approximations and the Computational Solution of Dynamic Programming Problems*, Report RM-3046/II PR, The Rand Corporation, Santa Monica, California, 1962.
30 C. Lanczos, *Applied Analysis*. Prentice-Hall, Englewood Cliffs, New Jersey, 1961.
31 N. Buras and J. Bear, "Optimal Utilization of a Coastal Aquifer," *Proc. Sixth Intern. Congr. Agricultural Engineering*, Lausanne, 1964.
32 O. R. Burt, "The Economics of Conjunctive Use of Ground and Surface Water," *Hilgardia* **36**(1944), No. 2.
33 O. R. Burt, "Optimal Resource Use over Time with an Application to Ground Water," *Management Science* **11**(1964), No. 1.
34 O. R. Burt, "Economic Control of Ground Water Reserves," *J. Farm Economics* **48**(1966), 632–647.
35 O. Levin, *Optimal Use of an Aquifer as an Element in a Water Resource System*, D.Sc. (Tech.) dissertation, Technion, Haifa, 1966 (in Hebrew).
36 J. Bernier, *La Gestion des Réservoirs à Buts Multiples*, Electricité de France, Report No. HYD-66/No. 11, 1966.
37 W. L. Meier, Jr., and C. S. Beightler, "An Optimization Method for Branching Multistage Water Resource Systems," *Water Resources Research* **3**(1967), No. 3, 645–652.
38 S. Meyers, *Mathematical Models for Optimal Development of Water Storage Systems on Small Watersheds in Arid and Semi-Arid Regions*, M.S. thesis, Technion, Haifa, 1969.
39 N. Buras, *The Optimization of Large Scale Water Resource Systems: Operational Aspects*, Report to Water Resources Center, University of California, Los Angeles, 1965.
40 G. B. Dantzig, *Linear Programming and Extensions*. Princeton University Press, Princeton, New Jersey, 1963.
41 S. C. Parikh, *Linear Dynamic Decomposition Programming of Optimal Long Range Operation of a Multiple Multi-Purpose Reservoir System*, Report ORC 66-28, Operations Research Center, University of California, Berkeley, 1966.

42 W. A. Hall and R. W. Shephard, *Optimum Operations for Planning of a Complex Water Resources System*, Contribution No. 122, Water Resources Center, University of California, Los Angeles, 1967.

43 W. A. Hall and T. G. Roefs, "Hydropower Project Output Optimization," *Proc. Amer. Soc. Civil Engineers* **92**(1966), No. P01, 67–69.

Chapter 8

# SIMULATION METHODS FOR THE DESIGN OF WATER RESOURCE SYSTEMS

## A. INTRODUCTION

The appropriateness of a chapter on simulation in a monograph concerned primarily with analytical methods might be questioned. However, many of the situations encountered in planning projects and designing systems in the field of water resources engineering defy analysis by rigorous mathematical methods. For often the strict application of mathematical analysis may lead to either of two culs-de-sac: either the real problem is simplified to the extent of stripping it of a number of essential aspects so that its formulation would be analytically tractable; or the analytical model, attempting to reflect reality, is so complex as to become computationally hopeless. It is mostly in the latter cases that recourse is made to simulation methods.

Simulation has been defined, generally, as a process that "duplicate(s) the essence of a system or activity without actually attaining reality itself" [1]. This "duplication" can be attained by using analog computers, digital computers, or combinations of both (what are sometimes termed *hybrid computers*). In the present discussion, we limit ourselves to simulation methods using digital computers.

From its definition, we can see that simulation is both an art and a science [2]. It is an art since the setting up of a simulation model involves much insight into the real problem, intuition, and engineering judgment, but few hard and fast rules. It is a science since it uses principles derived from three areas belonging to mathematical sciences: (a) probability and mathematical statistics; (b) solution of partial differential equations; (c) operations research. The aspects of interest in water resources engineering are mostly those of probability and operations research.

The probabilistic study of models representing systems of particles moving partly regularly and partly at random (e.g., in nuclear reactors) gave rise to the idea that the partial differential equations describing the behavior of these particles be solved experimentally. The concept of "experiment" was extended to cover also conceptual experiments, that is, the introduction of arbitrary, judicious, or random data into the partial differential equations and the solution of these equations. The solutions so derived were likened to experimental results obtained for changed conditions. This method of simulating the behavior of natural systems was termed by von Neumann, in the nineteen-forties, the *Monte Carlo method*. More will be said about this method presently.

The operations research aspect of simulation is linked perhaps with the optimization of systems. The design of water resource systems involves the maximization (or the minimization) of a criterion function. Analytically, these are well-known methods for attaining global optima [3]. However, when the problem is (or appears to be) analytically intractable, simulation methods are used. Then there is no guarantee that a global optimum is attained: at most, local optima may be detected.

## B. THE MONTE CARLO METHOD

It was mentioned in the previous section that experiments may be physical (laboratory) or conceptual (mathematical). Incidentally, mathematical experiments are not as new as we might think: King Salomon, around 1000 B.C., made for his temple a copper basin "ten cubits from one brim to the other ... and a line of thirty cubits did compass it round about" (1 Kings vii.23): a pretty good approximation of the value of the constant $\pi$ (within 5%). The Monte Carlo method is concerned with mathematical experiments involving random numbers [4].

There are different kinds of Monte Carlo computations, the differences between them being in the degree of sophistication. Consider, for example, a rather unsophisticated kind. In evaluating a certain design in water resources engineering, a number of economic (benefits, costs) parameters are introduced. Let us assume that all these parameters are lumped into the parameter $y$, the true value of which is not known. However, a range of values is given for $y$. It would be not unreasonable to assume that $y$ is a random variable $(y_1, y_2, \ldots, y_n)$ rectangularly distributed within the standardized range $(0, 1)$. The payoff function of the system design,

$$f_i = f(y_i) \tag{8.1}$$

is, therefore, also a random variable with expectation $\theta$. By definition,

*Scientific Allocation of Water Resources*

$$\bar{f} = \frac{1}{n} \sum_{i=1}^{n} f_i \tag{8.2}$$

is an unbiased estimation of $\theta$. The variance of the estimator $\theta$ is

$$\frac{1}{n} \int_0^1 [f(x) - \theta]^2 \, dx = \frac{\sigma^2}{n}, \tag{8.3}$$

where $x$ is a dummy variable of integration and $n$ is the number of times that the function $f(y_i)$ is evaluated. The values $y_i$ are picked with the help of a table of random numbers.

In order to estimate the variance of the estimator $\theta$, we need the value of $\sigma^2$, which is the true variance of the random variable $f_i$. This, in turn, is estimated by

$$s^2 = \frac{1}{n-1} \sum_{i=1}^{n} (f_i - \bar{f})^2. \tag{8.4}$$

This variety of Monte Carlo technique, in which the dependent variable $y$ is estimated by substituting random numbers for the independent variable $x$ in a given (or known) functional relationship, is called *crude Monte Carlo*.

Referring to the sample example (rectangular distribution of parameter $y$), let us standardize also the payoff function $z = f(y)$

$$0 \leqslant f(y) \leqslant 1. \tag{8.5}$$

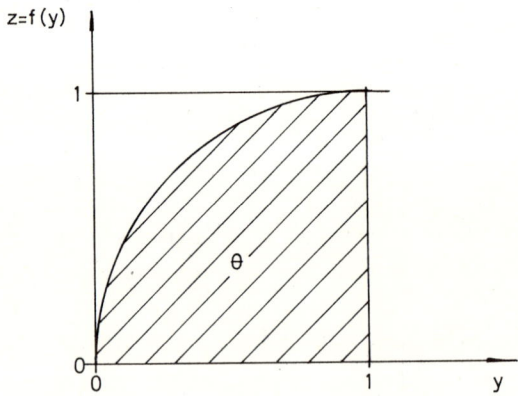

FIGURE 8.1. The standardized function $Z = f(y)$.

Plotting the curve $z = f(y)$ in the unit square $0 \leqslant y \leqslant 1$, $0 \leqslant z \leqslant 1$ (see Figure 8.1), the expectation of $f(y)$, which we called $\theta$, would be the proportion of the area beneath the curve. Formally,

$$f(y) = \int_0^1 g(y, z) \, dz, \tag{8.6}$$

where

$$\begin{aligned} g(y, z) &= 0 &&\text{if } f(y) < z, \\ &= 1 &&\text{if } f(y) \geqslant z. \end{aligned} \tag{8.7}$$

The expectation $\theta$ is given by double integral

$$\theta = \int_0^1 \int_0^1 g(y, z) \, dy \, dz \tag{8.8}$$

and may be estimated by

$$\bar{g} = \frac{1}{n} \sum_{i=1}^n g(x_{zi-1}, x_{zi}) = \frac{n^*}{n} \tag{8.9}$$

where $n^*$ is the number of times that $f(x_{2i-1}) \geqslant f(x_{2i})$. In other words, we take $n$ points at random in the unit square and determine the proportion of those falling below the curve $z = f(y)$. Observe that what is done in fact here is a sampling process from a binomial distribution, where the values that lie below the given curve in the unit square may be considered as "successes" with probability $p = \theta$. It follows that the variance of the estimator $\bar{g}$ is

$$\frac{p(p-1)}{n} = \frac{\theta(\theta-1)}{n}. \tag{8.10}$$

This variety of Monte Carlo technique, sometimes named *hit-or-miss Monte Carlo*, is even worse, in terms of computational effort necessary to achieve a desirable degree of accuracy, than the crude Monte Carlo. This can be shown by considering the difference between the two variances (equation (8.10) less equation (8.9)):

$$\frac{\theta(1-\theta)}{n} - \frac{1}{n} \int_0^1 [f(x) - \theta]^2 \, dx$$

$$= \frac{\theta}{n} - \frac{\theta^2}{n} - \frac{1}{n}\int_0^1 \{[f(x)]^2 - 2\theta f(x) + \theta^2\}\,dx$$

$$= \frac{\theta}{n} - \frac{\theta^2}{n} - \frac{1}{n}\int_0^1 [f(x)]^2\,dx + \frac{2\theta^2}{n} - \frac{\theta^2}{n} = \frac{\theta}{n} - \frac{1}{n}\int_0^1 [f(x)]^2\,dx$$

$$= \frac{1}{n}\int_0^1 \{f(x) - [f(x)]^2\}\,dx > 0. \tag{8.11}$$

This result is obvious, since $f(x) < 1$ and therefore $[f(x)]^2 < f(x)$. Hence the variance of the hit-or-miss method is larger than that of the crude Monte Carlo.

A technique having a variance smaller than that of the crude Monte Carlo is *stratified sampling*. In it we break the range of integration into $k$ segments defined by the abscissas $0 = \alpha_0 < \alpha_1 < \cdots < \alpha_j < \cdots < \alpha_k = 1$, and apply crude Monte Carlo with $n_j$ points in each $j$th segment. The estimate of $\theta$ is

$$t = \sum_{j=1}^k \sum_{i=1}^{n_j} (\alpha_j - \alpha_{j-1}) \frac{1}{n_j} f[\alpha_{j-1} + (\alpha_j - \alpha_{j-1})x_{ij}] \tag{8.12}$$

and its variance is

$$\sigma_t^2 = \sum_{j=1}^k \frac{(\alpha_j - \alpha_{j-1})}{n_j} \int_{\alpha_{j-1}}^{\alpha_j} [f(x)]^2\,dx - \sum_{j=1}^k \frac{1}{n_j}\int_{\alpha_{j-1}}^{\alpha_j} [f(x)\,dx]^2. \tag{8.13}$$

The estimator of the variance $\sigma_t^2$ is given by

$$s_t^2 = \sum_{j=1}^k \frac{(\alpha_j - \alpha_{j-1})^2}{n_j(n_j - 1)} \sum_{i=1}^{n_j} (f_{ij} - \bar{f}_j)^2, \tag{8.14}$$

where

$$f_{ij} = f[\alpha_{j-1} + (\alpha_j - \alpha_{j-1})x_{ij}] \tag{8.15}$$

and

$$\bar{f}_j = \frac{1}{n_j}\sum_{i=1}^{n_j} f_{ij}.$$

## C. GENERATION OF SYNTHETIC STREAMFLOW DATA

A particular area in water resources engineering in which simulation has been used in recent years is hydrology. Specifically, hydrological data from given gauging stations, which form basic information for the design of water resource systems, are viewed as samples from infinitely long time series. The sequence within the existing hydrological record has a probability very close to zero to repeat itself. What has a considerably greater probability is that any future sequence of hydrologic events will be different from the existing record. Since water resources systems are designed for the future, we are interested in estimating their performance (and behavior) with hydrological inputs statistically indistinguishable from the observed record, but with different internal patterns. We are interested, therefore, in generating a sequence of numbers that are statistically indistinguishable within anticipated sampling errors from the existing hydrological record [5].

Let us begin with a time series that can be represented by the function

$$q_t = f(t) + u_t \qquad (8.16)$$

where $q_t$ is the value of the time series at time $t$, $f(t)$ is a deterministic component, and $u_t$ is a random element. If the deterministic component is a constant, then the effect of time is reflected only through $u_t$. If, in addition, the time series is stationary, we can expect nonzero covariances between values (flows, discharges) $q_t$ at time $t$ and values $q_s$ at times $s$. Thus we can write the linear autoregressive relation

$$q_t = \beta_0 + \beta_1 q_{t-1} + \beta_2 q_{t-2} + \cdots + \beta_m q_{t-m} + w_t \qquad (8.17)$$

where $\beta_i$ are autoregression coefficients and $w_t$ an independent random error term. For $m = 1$, equation (8.17) becomes

$$q_t = \beta_0 + \beta_1 q_{t-1} + w_t. \qquad (8.18)$$

If we view $q_t$ as yearly flows and $q_t$ and $q_{t-1}$ as being derived from a bivariate normal population with means $\mu_t = \mu_{t-1} = \mu$ and standard deviations $\sigma_t = \sigma_{t-1} = \sigma$, then the expected value of $q_t$ when $q_{t-1}$ is known is

$$E\{q_t | q_{t-1}\} = \mu + \rho(q_{t-1} - \mu) \qquad (8.19)$$

where $\rho$ is the correlation coefficient. Similarly, the variance of this conditional variate is

$$\text{var}\{q_t | q_{t-1}\} = \sigma^2(1 - \rho^2). \qquad (8.20)$$

Substituting in equation (8.18) $(1 - \rho)$ for $\beta_0$, $\rho$ for $\beta_1$, and $v_t \sigma (1 - \rho^2)^{1/2}$ for $v_t$, we obtain an expression for $q_t$ that has the same mean and standard deviation as $q_{t-1}$:

$$q_t = \mu(1 - \rho) + \rho q_{t-1} + v_t \sigma (1 - \rho^2)^{1/2}$$
$$= \mu + \rho(q_{t-1} - \mu) + v_t \sigma (1 - \rho^2)^{1/2}, \qquad (8.21)$$

where $v_t$ is a normal random deviate with zero mean and unit variance. It is easy to show that $E\{q_t\} = \mu$ and that $E\{q_t^2\} - \mu^2 = \sigma^2$, which is exactly what we wanted. Equation (8.21), therefore, is a recursive relation by which we can generate a sequence of numbers $q_t$, starting with any one $q_{t-1}$.

To introduce seasonal (monthly) variations, define $q_{ij}$ to be the flow in period (season, month, etc.) $i$, which is the $j$th such period in a yearly cycle. For example, if $q_{ij}$ is used to describe monthly flows, $j$ runs from one through twelve, while $i$ takes values of $1, 2, \ldots, N$. Equation (8.21) is then modified to be

$$q_{ij} = \mu_j + \rho_j \frac{\sigma_j}{\sigma_{j-1}} (q_{i-1, j-1} - \mu_{j-1}) + t_j \sigma_j (1 - \rho_j^2)^{1/2}. \qquad (8.22)$$

Here $\rho_j$ is the correlation coefficient between flows in seasons $j$ and $j - 1$, and $\rho_j \sigma_j / \sigma_{j-1}$ is the same as the regression coefficient $\beta_j$. $t_j$ is a random variate with zero mean and unit variance. This recursive model does have the property of preserving the first two moments and the covariance, which is what is desired.

Equations (8.21) and (8.22) are sequential stochastic models of streamflow having a correlation of lag one; that is, they consider streamflows to be correlated only with those in the immediately preceding season (month). Actual data indicate, however, that monthly streamflows may be correlated also with those in the past two, three, and so on, months. These higher lag correlations decrease as the correlated month is further removed in the past. It appears desirable, sometimes, to construct streamflow generating models in which these multiple lag correlations are included. At least one such model is available [6], by which monthly flows exhibiting correlations up to (and including) lag 12 are included.

The models presented above assume to have their stochastic elements distributed in accordance with the Gaussian (normal) distribution. Models have been proposed [5] in which stochastic elements assumed to be distributed in accordance with other distributions were included.

## D. EXAMPLES OF SIMULATION STUDIES

Simulation analysis of water resources systems was carried out even before analytical methods were adapted for use in the field of water resources engineering. As an example of such an early work is the simulation study of the Nile Valley Plan [7].

The development of the Nile Valley presents complex problems of flow regulation through the operation of surface storage reservoirs. The system objectives are irrigation, navigation, and the generation of electricity, subject to social, political, and economic constraints. In addition, two natural factors affect any operating policy of the system: streamflows and evaporation losses. Thus, the operating policies of the surface reservoirs had to take into account not only seasonal fluctuations (dry season, wet season), but also long-term (overyear) storage so as to level out natural annual variations in river discharge. The problems regarding the size of the reservoirs and their operation were treated by simulation. Some of the problems will be briefly introduced below.

1. *Reservoirs "in Phase."* One control procedure that was tested was to ensure that certain adjacent reservoirs fill or empty together, that is, that they be "in phase." This means that the ratio of their contents is constant. Consider three points on the river, $P$, $Q$, $R$, in the direction of the flow. Dams are constructed at points $Q$ and $R$. The continuity equations at points $Q$ and $R$ are

$$Q_c{}^* = Q_c + C_{PR}P_d + Q_i - Q_0 - Q_e - Q_d, \qquad (8.23)$$

$$R_c{}^* = R_c + C_{QR}Q_d + R_i - R_0 - R_e - R_d, \qquad (8.24)$$

where

$Q_c{}^*, R_c{}^*$ = contents of reservoirs $Q$ and $R$, respectively, at the end of a given period of operation;
$Q_c, R_c$ = contents of reservoirs $Q$ and $R$, respectively, at the beginning of the same period of operation;
$C_{PQ}$ = percentage of flow $P_d$ passing point $P$ reaching reservoir $Q$;
$C_{QR}$ = percentage of release $Q_d$ from reservoir $Q$ reaching reservoir $R$;
$Q_i, R_i$ = inflow of tributaries directly into the reservoirs $Q$, $R$, respectively;
$Q_0, R_0$ = outflows (local abstractions) from reservoirs;
$Q_e, R_e$ = evaporation losses;
$Q_d, R_d$ = discharge from reservoirs during a given period of operation.

Reservoirs in phase should fulfill the condition

$$\frac{Q_c^*}{R_c^*} = \frac{Q_{c\,\max}}{R_{c\,\max}}. \tag{8.25}$$

Defining

$$Q' = Q_c + C_{PQ}P_d + Q_i - Q_0 - Q_e, \tag{8.26}$$

$$R' = R_c + R_i - R_0 - R_e - R_d, \tag{8.27}$$

we condense equations (8.23) and (8.24) to

$$Q_c^* = Q' - Q_d, \tag{8.28}$$

and

$$R_c^* = R' + C_{QR}Q_d.$$

It follows that the required condition becomes

$$(Q' - Q_d)R_{c\,\max} = (R' + C_{QR}Q_d)Q_{c\,\max}. \tag{8.29}$$

From here,

$$Q_d = \frac{Q'R_{c\,\max} - R'Q_{c\,\max}}{C_{QR}Q_{c\,\max} + R_{c\,\max}}. \tag{8.30}$$

Up to three reservoirs in series were analyzed using this approach.

2. *"Quota."* When a reach of the river is dominated by one reservoir, the control equation of this dam can lead to a small discharge so that the flow downstream could drop to undesirable levels at times of deficient rainfall. To prevent this happening, "quotas" were introduced. The quota was defined as a minimum desirable discharge, which may be less than a minimum permissible discharge. Denoting the quota for dam $P$ as $P_q$, and using the same notation as earlier, we have

$$P_q = \max \begin{cases} \dfrac{Q_0 + Q_{d\,\min}}{C_{PQ}} \\ \dfrac{Q_0}{C_{PQ}} + \dfrac{R_0 + R_{d\,\min}}{C_{PR}} \end{cases} \tag{8.31}$$

For the extreme cases when reservoirs at $Q$ and $R$ are empty, the continuity equations (8.23) and (8.24) indicate that in order to ensure the discharges $Q_d$ and $R_d$ as well as the offtakes $Q_0$ and $R_0$, the quotas $P_q$ and $Q_q$ must equal $P_d$ and $Q_d$, respectively.

## Simulation Methods for the Design

3. *Target Values.* Consider three reservoirs in series at points $A$, $B$, $F$. The controlled release (discharge) $B_d$ at point $B$ is linked with the target contents $A_{ct}$ of reservoir $A$, and with the target contents $F_{ct}$ of reservoir $F$, through the following equation.

$$B_d = B_{dt} + \alpha(A_c - A_{ct}) + \beta(F_{ct} - F_c), \tag{8.32}$$

where $B_{dt}$ is the target value of $B_d$; $A_c$ and $F_c$ are the actual contents of reservoirs $A$ and $F$, respectively; and $\alpha$ and $\beta$ are parameters. Simulation was used to determine the value of parameters $\alpha$ and $\beta$, as well as acceptable target values of reservoir contents and discharges.

4. *Irrigation Release Equations.* The yearly irrigation release $X$ from reservoir $A$ can be calculated on the basis of releases in the previous $n$ years:

$$X_{n+1} = \frac{1}{n} \sum_{i=1}^{n} X_i + \gamma(A_c - A_{ct}), \tag{8.33}$$

where $\gamma$ is a positive parameter (correction factor) connected with the deviations of the reservoir contents from their target value. The application of control equation (8.33) smoothed out the variations in the irrigation water supply from any one reservoir, as compared with the irrigation releases based on current inflows alone.

The operation of the reservoir created by the high dam at Aswan (Lake Nasser) was investigated by the application of the Monte Carlo method [8].

The utilization of a surface reservoir operated in conjunction with a groundwater aquifer was simulated in Israel using monthly intervals [9]. The situation was very similar to that shown in Figure 7.4. After having tested that the monthly inflows into the surface reservoir are normally distributed at an acceptable level of significance (0.05), the operation of the system was simulated in accordance with certain operating rules. Since the surface reservoir is a natural lake (Lake Kinneret), its active storage volume had to be determined in connection with its yield (annual abstractions) and annual inflows. The relation between these three variables was determined by simulation. In addition, average annual spills from the surface reservoir were estimated as functions of the active storage volume, with annual inflows as a parameter. The simulation model included qualitative (salinity) aspects of the surface water source.

The management and utilization of a complex hydrological stream–aquifer system was simulated in connection with the irrigation of a large area overlying the aquifer [10]. The Arkansas River valley in the state of Colorado was divided by an imaginary grid into a large number of square elements. In each element, a complete water balance was performed: deep percolation of precipitation and applied irrigation water; inflow from the stream or from adjacent elements; depletion of aquifer by wells (pumpage); evapotranspiration losses by crops and other vegetation (including phreatophytes). The results of the simulation were estimates of groundwater level changes during specific time intervals for given operating rules (rates of pumping) of the aquifer. These fluctuations of the water table can be used as criteria for evaluating groundwater operating rules.

The operation of multiple-purpose water resources systems, covering entire river basins, was studied using simulation techniques. The models, computer programs, results, and conclusions are presented *in extenso* elsewhere [11].

**REFERENCES**

1 R. L. Ackoff, *Progress in Operations Research*, Vol. 1. Wiley, New York, 1961.
2 K. D. Tocher, *The Art of Simulation*. The English Universities Press, London, 1963.
3 D. J. Wilde and C. S. Beightler, *Foundations of Optimization*. Prentice-Hall, Englewood Cliffs, New Jersey, 1967.
4 J. M. Hammersley and D. C. Handscomb, *Monte Carlo Methods*. Methuen, London, 1964.
5 M. B. Fiering, *Streamflow Synthesis*. Macmillan, New York, 1967.
6 S. Yagil, "Generation of Input Data for Simulation," *IBM Systems J.* 2(1963), 288–306.
7 D. A. Emery and B. L. Meek, "The Simulation of a Complex River System," in *Les Choix Economiques* (P. Rosenstiehl and A. Ghouila-Houri, eds.), pp. 237–255. Dunod, Paris, 1960.
8 H. E. Hurst, "A Monte Carlo Method Applied to the Future Regulation of the High Aswan Dam," *Proc. Reservoir Yield Symposium*, Water Research Association, Marlow, Bucks, U.K., Paper No. 11, 1965.
9 J. Gluck and C. Jusopovitch, *Monthly Simulation of a Water Supply System*, Publication No. 896, Tahal Consulting Engineers, Tel Aviv, 1969.
10 R. A. Longenbaugh, *Mathematical Simulation of a Stream–Aquifer System*, Report CER67-68AL22, Department of Civil Engineering, Colorado State University, Fort Collins, Colorado, 1967.
11 M. M. Hufschmidt and M. B. Fiering, *Simulation Techniques for Design of Water-Resource Systems*. Harvard University Press, Cambridge, Massachusetts, 1966.

Chapter 9

# CONCLUSION

The importance of water resources in many plans for regional development requires that the design of systems that supply water (and water derivatives) should be based on detailed and accurate analysis. An initial step in the design process of such systems is a clear definition of the objectives that the system has to meet: social, economic, and technological. This perhaps applies equally well to the development of all natural (renewable) resources. Water, however, seems to be such a basic element in any regional development plant that it can be easily compared with the independent variable in a complex mathematical relationship. For its availability, at the required location, at the desired time, in adequate quantity and of acceptable quality, affects directly the response of other important natural resources, such as land (soil) and vegetation (crops).

In many instances, however, development plans for water resources compete for funds with other development projects. In these cases, too, the design process has to provide answers to a number of questions: (a) what storage facilities should be developed; (b) what level of development should be chosen; (c) how should the system be operated; (d) what institutional arrangements must be made. The answers are arrived at through an iterative process in which the planners and the policy makers participate. Alternative designs, formulated by engineers and considered optimal for the specified objectives and constraints, are ranked, evaluated, and discussed with the appropriate agencies (ordinarily governmental authorities), who may demand changes and who will assign priorities through a political process, the analysis of which is outside the scope of design engineering.

The general design problem in water resources engineering is that of transforming a variable quantity of water, which has a certain probability distribution at given points in time, is located at a given site, and has a certain quality, into fixed quantities of water to be supplied at given times and locations and of a specific quality. The transformation necessary for the fulfillment of the requirements is achieved through a system. This system will comprise both hardware elements (dams, reservoirs, pumping stations, pipe lines, wells, etc.) and software (operating rules, institutional requirements, etc.). The creation of this system is, therefore, the realm of water resources engineering.

At the regional level, the design process considers first the various dam sites among which to select those which will fulfill best the development objectives. However, the optimal design of such structures must reflect the various purposes for which storage space is to be provided. The storage for a given purpose (irrigation, hydropower, etc.) must be in accordance with subregional demands for water and water derivatives, and these, in turn, should be the result of internal suboptimizations. In short, the regional development of water resources involves a sequence of decisions, from the individual farm system all the way through to the overall regional system. In order to analyze such complex problems, sophisticated analytical techniques have to be activated in the design process.

One of the salient features of water resource systems is the stochastic nature of the hydrological process. The first corollary of this observation is that streamflow has to be regulated in order to match the highly erratic supply to the more steady demand. Furthermore, such regulation should not only store water in the wet season for use in the dry period, but also should store it in years having above average flow so as to meet demands in lean years. Usually, there are limitations to the practical size of dams and reservoirs.

In analyzing storage problems, queuing theory is readily applicable. The stochastic inflow into the reservoir is comparable to the arrival rate at a service station, while the rule by which water is released through the dam is analogous to the service rate. The queue is the amount of water in storage. Given the probability distribution of the inflows and the operating rule, queuing theory enables the estimation of probabilities of given amounts in storage at specified times.

Probability analysis, in addition to queuing, was applied to establish safe draft rates from surface reservoirs. Fairly complex models, in which evaporation losses were accounted for, were set up in order to determine net yield–frequency curves for any reservoir capacity. These curves may be interpreted as the risk connected with a given reservoir size and mean draft, with respect to contingencies, such as inability to satisfy demand. The operation of surface storage facilities can be analyzed using Markov chain methods.

## Conclusion

Markov chain theory was applied also to the derivation of operating rules for multistructure systems, as well as to the analysis of problems connected with pollution transport in streams. Both these situations exhibit problems of considerable complexity, amenable to analysis when viewed as Markovian processes. In this manner, the mathematical models developed can treat multistage processes both in space (several dams along a river, a number of industrial plants discharging waste in a stream) and in time (yearly, monthly, weekly, and daily operation of these systems). The latter treatment often involves flows that are serially correlated.

Many problems in water resources development are multidimensional, in the sense that several economic activities (water supply, flood control, hydro power generation, recreation, etc.) compete for the same resource. The allocation aspect of the resource is then stressed, and linear programming is used for the analysis and solution of such problems. This technique is utilized extensively and it is most effective when all variables can be assumed to be deterministic in nature.

Linear programming methods were applied to a number of problems in water quality management. The range of these problems extended from the design of a single waste water treatment plant to the derivation of an investment schedule in regional water quality improvement. As may be expected, many of the objective, cost, and benefit functions are not linear. However, several approaches were suggested for the handling of such non-linearities in the linear programming formulation.

Linearized models of water resource systems have also been used in the design and operation of surface reservoirs. Here, too, there were great difficulties in considering the stochastic aspect of streamflows. Of course, averages were used. However, to indicate the seasonal variability, the hydrological year was divided into a number of seasons in each of which average flows were considered.

Attempts were made to introduce stochastic elements into linear programming models. Models ranged from single dam, single use, and single season with few possible values of inflow, to a multipurpose system with a multiperiod operating policy and a more detailed frequency distribution. The principle of decomposition of linear programming and parametric programming was used in the analysis and solution of these models.

Complex problems of aquifer management were analyzed through linear programming. The most notable of them is the optimization of an irrigation and drainage project in the Indus Valley of Pakistan. Quantity as well as quality constraints entered the model, and nonlinear functions were linearized with little loss in accuracy. The simplex method of solution was used iteratively, with a "steepest ascent" technique interposed between iterations.

The obstacles separating idealized models from reality, and which are handled with great difficulty by linear programming (stochastic aspects, time effects, nonlinearities), can be treated more conveniently with dynamic programming. This technique, which enables the analysis of sequential processes, is particularly useful in planning water resources development. Basic problems in watershed management, basin-wide questions of resource development planning, and general layout of major elements of a water resource system can be viewed as sequential decision processes and analyzed through dynamic programming.

Problems of storage regulation, which exhibit a distinct Markovian property, can be cast as dynamic programming models. Probability matrices govern the transition from one stage to the next, and the overall effect is composed of the expected immediate reward to which the total expected reward from the remaining stages of operation is added. It should be noted that models involving several structures and many seasons lead rapidly to computational difficulties. Thus approximation techniques, or a more efficient search for optimum, or both, should be applied.

The conjunctive development and utilization of surface storage and aquifers, especially in semiarid regions, were successfully analyzed through dynamic programming. Beginning with rather simple models, the analysis progressed to include stochastic inflows serially correlated, and more specific aquifer-oriented problems. One such model touched upon the important problem of optimal exploitation of a coastal aquifer, where the saltwater–fresh water interface has an important role. Another model analyzed in great detail the behavior of an aquifer, which has to satisfy certain demands for water and which is connected to the surface storage subsystem through its recharge facilities.

A wide variety of analytical methods were applied in the design of water resource systems. Most of them, however, pointed out the necessity of setting up stochastic sequential models, as the best approximations to the real situation. Dynamic programming seems to fill this need, with its variations and adaptations. However, the effectiveness of dynamic programming is limited by computational difficulties. Nevertheless, dynamic programming and its outgrowths (forward dynamic programming, state increment dynamic

## Conclusion

programming) have great promise in store for the analysis and solution of problems arising in the development and utilization of water resources.

Finally, simulation techniques were presented and briefly discussed. These techniques proved especially useful in cases where the water resources systems under consideration were too complex for analytical formulations. Of course, there were cases in which simulation was used even when it was known that an analytical solution was feasible: a matter of convenience.

Most simulation methods applied in water resources engineering were developed in other fields of technology. However, one method is specific to water resources: the generation of streamflow data or, as it is called by various authorities, *synthetic hydrology* or *operational hydrology*.

The various methods presented here, analytical and nonanalytical, each contribute from a slightly different angle to the same general problem: the scientific allocation of water resources. Only after the water resources of a region are allocated (among purposes, among uses, etc.) in a logical, rational manner, can we begin planning the further advancement—economic, social, and technological—of the region. In most regions of the world, the development projects tend to crystallize around a nucleus formed by water resources systems optimally designed [1].

**REFERENCE**

1 A. T. Ippen, "Water Resources Development, a Vital Responsibility of the Civil Engineer," *J. Boston Soc. Civil Engineers*, vol. 48(2): 83–96, 1961.

# AUTHOR INDEX

Ackerman, E. A., 50
Ackerman, W. C., 49
Ackoff, R. L., 28, 49, 113, 192
Aharoni, Y., 14
Amir, R., 180
Amoss, H. L., 13
Anis, A. A., 52, 81
Avi-Itzchak, B., 82

Bain, J. S., 14, 51
Bear, J., 180
Beightler, C. S., 180, 192
Bellman, R. E., 3, 13, 29, 123, 138, 141, 179, 180
Ben-Tuvia, S., 82
Berge, C., 141
Berman, R. R., 51
Bernier, J., 13, 50, 180
Bernoulli, Daniel, 2
Bhavnagri, V. S., 82
Biswas, A. K., 27
Borgman, L. E., 82
Bower, B. T., 48, 49, 50
Box, G. E. P., 113
Brater, E. Z., 179
Breuer, J., 13
Brown, G. J., 14
Bugliarello, G., 82
Buras, N., 13, 14, 28, 29, 49, 50, 83, 141, 179, 180
Burden, R. P., 14, 29, 82, 113
Burt, O. R., 180

Cahana, J., 50
Charnes, A., 113
Chézy, 2
Chorafas, N. 62
Chow, V. T., 2, 12, 28, 179
Chun, R. Y. D., 28

Clark, C. D., 14
Cole, J. A., 82
Conover, S., 83
Crawford, N. H., 49

d'Alembert, 2
Dantzig, G. B., 47, 50, 112, 180
Darcy, H., 2, 12
Davis, C. V., 14
Davis, R. K., 49
Dean, B. V., 29, 50, 83, 141
Deininger, R. A., 113
Denardo, E. V., 179
d'Epenaux, F., 179
De Wiest, R. J. M., 14, 49
Dixon, J. R., 28
Dorfman, R., 13, 28, 50, 82, 113
Dracup, J. A., 113
Dreyfus, S. E., 29, 123, 141, 179
Durant, W., 12

Eaton, J. M., 29
Eckstein, O., 14, 28, 49
Emery, D. A., 192
Evenari, M., 14

Fair, G. M., 13, 14, 28, 82
Falkson, L., 179
Feller, W., 52, 81
Fiering, M. B., 13, 49, 179, 192
Ford, L. R., Jr., 141
Fowler, L. C., 28
Fox, I. K., 49
Fulkerson, D. R., 141
Furness, L. W., 81

Gani, J., 83
Gazith, E., 29
Geyer, J. C., 14

Ghouila-Houri, A., 192
Ghulam, M., 28, 29
Gluck, J., 192
Gupta, S. K., 28, 49

Hadley, G., 28, 49, 112
Hall, A. D., 14, 28, 141
Hall, W. A., 3, 13, 14, 50, 141, 179, 181
Hammersley, J. M., 192
Handscomb, D. C., 192
Harder, J. A., 49
Hare, V. C., Jr., 28
Harris, R. A., 82
Hazen, A., 52, 81
Herman, T., 14, 180
Hillier, F. S., 141
Howard, R. A., 82, 179
Howell, D. T., 179
Hufschmidt, M. M., 12, 13, 28, 49, 50, 82, 179, 192
Hurst, H. E., 52, 81, 192

Ippen, A. T., 197
Irmay, S., 13

Jarvis, C. L., 82
Jusopovitch, C., 192

Kalaba, R., 180
Kally, Z., 180
Kindsvater, C. E., 49
King, H. W., 179
Kneese, A. V., 12, 13, 49, 50
Knetch, J. L., 49
Kohler, M. A., 14
Krutilla, J. V., 13, 14, 28, 49
Kubik, M. E., 81
Kuiper, E., 14, 50

Lahmi, H., 29
Lanczos, C., 180
Langbein, W. B., 81, 82
Larson, R. E., 141
Leopold, L. B., 81
Levin, O., 180
Lieberman, G. J., 141

Linsley, R. K., Jr., 14
Little, J. D. C., 50
Lloyd, E. H., 50, 52, 81, 82
Löf, G. O. G., 50
Logan, J. A., 113
Longenbaugh, R. A., 192
Loucks, D. P., 83
Lynn, W. R., 83, 113

Maass, A., 12, 13, 28, 50, 82
Manne, A. S., 113
Marglin, S. A., 13, 28, 82
Margolis, J., 13
Massé, P., 9
Matalas, N. C., 81
McCutchan, J. W., 49
McDonough, M., 14
McNickle, R. K., 13
Meek, B. L., 192
Meier, W. L., Jr., 180
Melentijevich, M. J., 50, 81
Meyers, S., 50, 180
Mido, K. W., 28
Minas, J. S., 28, 49
Mitchell, L. R., 28
Mitter, L. G., 179
Moran, P. A. P., 49, 82
Morris, R. A., 82

Nazir, A., 29
Nemhauser, G. L., 179
Nir, D., 82

Odoom, S., 82
Okun, D. A., 14

Parikh, S. C., 51, 181
Parzen, E., 141
Paulhus, J. L. H., 14
Pillsbury, A. F., 14, 27
Pollack, F. S., 13
Pollit, W. M., 49
Prabhu, N. U., 82

Ramaseshan, S., 179
Reedy, W. W., 50

Renshaw, E. F., 141
Revelle, R., 28
Rippl, W., 81
Roefs, T. G., 13, 181
Rosenstiehl, P., 192
Roux, H., 13

Schweig, Z., 179
Shanan, L., 14
Shephard, R. W., 181
Smith, S. C., 12, 13, 49, 50
Sobel, M. J., 113
Stall, J. B., 81

Tadmor, M., 14
Tahal, Water Planning for Israel, Ltd., 14, 51
Thomann, R. V., 113
Thomas, H. A., Jr., 13, 14, 28, 29, 82, 113
Tocher, K. D., 192
Todd, D. K., 13, 14, 50

Tyson, H. N., Jr., 28

Valantine, V. E., 28
Von Neumann, J., 183

Watermeyer, P., 113
Water Research Association, **4**, **13**
Weber, E. M., 28
White, G. F., 49
White, J. B., 82
Whitin, T. M., 49
Wiener, A., 83
Wilde, D. J., 192
Wilson, K. B., 113
Wiser, E. H., 82
Wolf, P. O., 29
Wolman, A., 83

Yagil, S., 141, 192
Yevdjevich, V. M., 49, 81
Young, G. K., Jr., 50

# SUBJECT INDEX

Agriculture
  irrigated, 127
Allocation, 121 (figure), 195
  optimal, 120, 123, 153
Allocation process, 120–125
Analytical techniques, 44
Annual inflow
  serial correlation, 54
Annual streamflow
  range of, 53
Approximation, 183
Aqueduct, 125
  capacity, 144
Aquifer, 23, 25, 26, 31, 128, 130, 132, 133, 134, 161, 166, 169, 192
  capacity, 170
  coastal, 165
  dynamic response of, 23
  hydrological parameters, 22
  management, 23, 24 (figure), 27, 105–112
  mining, 107
  operation, 22, 25
  pumping from, 131
  recharge, 40, 128, 131
  safe yield, 167, 168
  skimming, 107
  storage in, 79
  utilization, 21, 23, 27, 112
Arkansas River, 191
Autoregression, 63
  coefficient, 187
Availability, 47

Benefit function, 121, 122
Benefits
  evaluation, 34
  intangible, 34
  primary, 19
  secondary, 19
  tangible, 34
Biological oxygen demand (BOD), 69, 70, 85, 86
Budgetary constraints, 20, 92

California, 48
California Water Project, 11, 46, 171, 172 (figure), 176
Chebychev polynomial, 162, 163, 164
Chloride ion ($Cl^-$)
  concentration of, 127
Colorado, 191
Colorado River, 5, 111
Computational technique, 96
Computer
  digital, 23
  hybrid, 182
Conduit, 117, 118, 120, 122, 131
  alternative routes, 115
Conjunctive use, 155–171, 196
Correlation
  lag one, 188
  multiple lag, 188
Cost function, 133
Criteria
  design, 18
  operating, 18
  physical, 18
Current engineering, 17

Dam
  Aswan, 191
  Folsom, 173
  optimal size, 59
  Oroville, 173
  release rule from, 65
  Shasta, 173
  Trinity, 173

Data
  relative accuracy, 38
Decision, 114
Decision process, 120
  multistage, 116
Decision theory, 11
Decision variables, 25, 117, 133, 160
Decomposition principle, 47, 97, 100, 173, 195
Delaware River Basin, 90
Desalination, 33
  electrodialysis, 27
Design
  criteria, 37
  objectives, 37
  optimal, 17, 193
Development
  goals, 34
  level of, 105
  scale of, 17, 18
Development planning, 17
Development process, 30
Development project
  objectives of, 30
Discharge
  probability distribution, 60
Dissolved oxygen concentration (DO), 69, 70, 71, 90
Drainage, 10, 33
  surface, 25
Dynamic linear system, 90
Dynamic programming, 3, 42, 44, 46, 114–141, 143, 145, 146, 148, 149, 152, 153, 155, 156, 166, 169, 170, 173, 176, 196
  application to water resources development, 45
  application to water resources engineering, 142–181, 196
  state vector
    three-dimensional, 27
  stochastic, 153

Economic efficiency, 18, 19, 34
Economics, 11

Effluent, 71
Electricité de France
  Centre de Recherches et d'Essais, 4
Environment, 15, 92
Environmental factors, 32
Equalization fund, 60
Evaporation
  losses, 55
  reduction, 33
Evapotranspiration, 33

Feasibility study, 16
Feather River, 111
Flood control, 54, 153, 177
Flood damage, 60
  management, 35, 36
Flooding
  probability, 65
Flood prevention, 44
Forecasting
  methods, 35
  reservoir, 35
  river, 35
Full employment, 34
Functional, 122, 123
Functional equation, 169

Gaussian quadrature, 163
Graph theory, 116
Groundwater, 191
  exploitation, 7
  management, 21
  mining, 23, 167
  recharge, 111, 131
  table, 128
  *See also* Aquifer
Groundwater basin
  storativity, 22
  transmissibility, 22
Groundwater table, 23

Harvard University
  water resources program, 2, 23
Hazen–Williams formula, 148
Hitchcock–Koopmans transportation problem, 123

Hydraulic engineering, 8, 10, 11, 33
Hydrological cycle, 7, 33
Hydrological models, 35
Hydrology, 8, 11, 187
  parametric, 33
  stochastic, 33
  subsurface, 33
  surface, 33
Hydro power production, 44

Illinois, 55
Imperial Valley, 5
Income redistribution, 18, 20
Indus Valley, 5, 23–25, 48, 195
Inflows
  stochastic characteristics, 27, 39
Integer programming, 20, 89
International Association of Scientific Hydrology, 33
Inventory problem, 56
Inventory system, 39
Inventory theory, 42, 80
Iran
  Ghazvin plain, 147
Irrigation, 10, 33, 35, 44, 107, 123
  benefits, 144
  demand, 124
  district, 125
  system, 95
  water, 95, 101, 102, 107–109, 126
Israel, 25–27, 35, 48, 72, 126, 132, 191
  coastal plain, 33, 40
  national water scheme, 25
Israel Water Plan, 26

Kansas rivers, 54

Lake Kinneret, 43 (figure), 72, 73, 75–77, 126, 128, 130–134, 191
Lake Nasser, 191
Land reclamation, 10
Least-cost path, 119
Leontieff matrix, 35
Linear approximation, 93, 96
Linear interpolation, 96

Linearization weights, 96
Linear programming, 44, 45, 84–113, 144, 152, 173, 174, 176, 195
  dual, 111
  mixed integer, 91
  parametric, 90, 105, 111
Local optimum, 47
Los Angeles basin, 22
Low flow augmentation, 43

Manning's formula, 148
Markov chain, 56, 62, 64, 67, 138, 159, 194
Markovian process, 45, 56, 58, 149, 162, 195
Mass curve, 52, 54, 97
Mathematical experiment, 183
Mathematical induction, 134
Mathematical model, 15, 25
Maximum return, 34
Mean recurrence interval (MRI), 55
Model
  analytical, 39
  linear programming, 20
  multistructure, 93
  reservoir
    multiperiod, 103
  simulation, 39
  stochastic, 100 (figure), 103
    sequential, 103
Monte Carlo method, 183–186, 191
  crude, 184, 186
  hit-or-miss, 185, 186
Multipurpose project, 156
Multistage allocation problem, 144
Multistage decision process, 114, 119, 143

Natural replenishment, 158, 166, 171
Natural resources, 30
  development and utilization, 9, 11
  nonrenewable, 6, 7
  renewable, 6, 32
Navigation, 44
Negev, 7
Network, 146
  analog, 22

analyzer, 22
  flow, 116
  resistor-capacitor, 22
Nile Valley Plan, 189
Node, 117, 118

Objektive function, 154
  linearized, 109
    nonlinear, 95, 110
      separable, 96
Oceanography, 33
One-stage process, 177
Operating policy, 18, 22, 23, 41, 129, 141, 142, 143, 176, 189
  optimal, 17, 23, 32, 45, 104, 127, 130, 152, 162
  monthly, 27
Operating procedure, 104, 151
Operating rule, 42–44, 192
  criteria for, 43
  flexibility, 42
Operational hydrology, 39, 197
Operations research, 11, 27, 36, 183
Optimal operation, 139
Optimal path, 118, 145
Optimal policy, 123, 124, 133, 136, 139, 140 (figure), 155
  structure of, 115
Optimal return, 155
Optimal solution, 119
  structure of, 143
Optimization, 84, 142, 183
  graphical, 81
Optimization methods, 38
Optimizing criteria, 34, 132

Payoff matrix, 116, 117
Planning horizon, 152, 167
Poisson process, 60
Policy, 114
Policy improvement routine, 150
Pollutant
  routing of, 69
Pollutant transport, 67, 68
Pollution, 87
  load, 88

Polynomial approximation, 162, 165
Power
  dump, 44
  firm, 44, 47, 172, 173, 174
  thermal, 101, 102
Power plant, 95
  generating capacity, 101
Precipitation
  control and inducement, 33
Principle of optimality, 119, 120, 124, 143, 144
Probability, 44, 152
Probability distribution, 31
Probability vector
  initial state, 57
Process
  terminal control, 138
Programming
  combination of linear and dynamic, 45 (figure), 47
Pumped storage, 176–178

Quadratic programming, 92
Queuing model, 56, 92
Queuing theory, 42, 194

Reconnaissance survey, 16
Recreation, 34, 44
Recurrence relationships, 115, 119, 144, 148, 154, 157, 161, 174, 188
Regional development, 4, 30, 193
  planning, 34
Regional model
  input-output, 37
Regional planning, 30
Regional welfare
  maximization of, 17
Regulated flow, 153
Reservoir, 93–105, 123, 130, 139
  active storage, 42, 191
  dependent, 39, 40
  design, 61
  groundwater, 158
  independent, 39, 40
  in phase, 189
  irrigation release, 191

    multipurpose, 44, 152
    off-channel, 62
    operation, 61
    quota, 190
    spill from, 43
    surface, 128, 156, 158, 166, 191
    target output, 191
Reservoir model
    multiseason, 61, 62
Response surface, 18
Rippl diagram, 52
Risk, 60, 75, 153
Runoff, 128, 131, 132, 133

Sacramento River, 171
Salinity, 25, 107, 128, 130, 132
Salt balance, 25, 134
San Gabriel Valley, 111
Scale of development
    optimization of, 32
Scientific method, 16, 27
Seawater intrusion, 165
Sensitivity analysis, 111
Sequential decision problem, 27, 41
Sequential decision processes, 114, 115, 117
Sequential stochastic model, 188
Serial correlation, 44, 63, 67, 70, 139, 159
Settling basin, 41
Shadow price, 111, 176
Simplex method, 100, 110, 196
Simulation, 22, 25, 38, 44, 47, 182–192, 197
Single-stage process, 114
Sodium adsorption ratio (SAR), 107, 108
Soil conservation, 10
Southern California, 21–23, 111
Space
    multidimensional, 18
Spill, 75, 127, 131, 191
  loss, 77
  risk of, 76
  uncontrolled, 72
Spreading ground, 41
Springs, 132
  saline, 134

Stage, 117, 119, 120, 133, 134, 136
    terminal, 135
State, 120, 135, 136
State matrix
    transformation, 31
State variable, 117, 123, 130
State vector, 134
Stationary distribution, 62
Stationary probability, 58, 59
Steepest ascent, 109
Storage
    overyear, 40
    surface, 26, 161, 189
    underground, 26
Storage capacity, 54
Storage control curves, 74 (figure)
Storage control limit
    lower, 78, 80
    upper, 75
Storage regulation, 149–155
Storage required
    range of, 53
Storage-yield relationship, 103
Stratified sampling, 186
Streamflow
    persistence, 62
    serial correlation, 62
    stochastic, 99, 195
Streamflow regulation, 55, 194
Sustained gross yield, 55
Synthetic hydrology, 38, 39
Synthetic streamflow generation, 37, 187, 188
System
  components of
    optimal dimensions, 32
  multistructure and multipurpose, 171–176
Systems analysis, 36, 37
Systems approach, 15, 17, 27
Systems engineering, 15, 20, 21, 25, 27, 139
  functions of, 16
  phases of, 16

Target output, 41, 48
Technion—Israel Institute of Technology, 4
Tennessee Valley Authority, 5
Terminal conditions, 119
Transformation, 114, 193
Transition, 136
Transition probability, 57, 196
Transpiration, 33
Two-stage process, 147

Uncertainty, 11, 38
Uniform treatment policy, 90
Universities Council on Water Resources (UCOWR), 3
University of California
  Water Resources Center, 3
Urban hydrology, 33

Value determination operation, 150, 151, 167

Waste carrying, 44
Waste disposal, 35
Waste treatment plant, 69, 71, 85, 86, 88, 89, 91
Water
  class I, 47
  demand for
    distribution of, 31
  firm, 172, 173, 174
  nonfirm, 174
  shortage, 43, 75
  storage, 41
  transfer, 35
Water conservation, 10
Water derivatives, 31, 34
Water pricing, 37
Water quality, 35, 67, 126, 128, 160, 161
  biological, 31
  caloric, 31
  improvement, 43
  management, 85–92, 112
  mineral, 31

Water resources
  benefit functions, 37
  comprehensive planning, 36–38, 48
  development, 30, 32, 197
    policy issues, 36
  development planning, 9, 197
    factors, 9
    objectives, 9
  management, 5, 35
  model, 98 (figure)
  occurrence of, 30
  optimal development, 41
  regional development, 48, 144
  regional plan, 37
Water resources development, 34
  multipurpose project, 94 (figure)
Water resources engineering, 2, 8, 32, 47, 112, 114, 115, 123, 125, 182, 183, 187, 194
  interdisciplinary nature of, 9–12
  systems approach, 4
Water resources planning
  in metropolitan areas, 40, 41
Water resources projects
  multiple-purpose, 7
Water resources system, 139, 171, 187
  design of, 30
  multiple-purpose, 192
  operation of
    optimal procedure for, 44
  planning of, 30
Water supply, 44
Water treatment, 86
Watershed
  revegetation, 149
Watershed management, 10, 148
Wells, 192
West Pakistan
  irrigation, 105, 106 (figure)
  drainage, 105, 106 (figure)
Winter floods, 41

Yarqon springs, 132

$z$ transform, 58

# Nathan Buras

Since 1966, Dr. Buras has held the rank of Associate Professor at The Lowdermilk Faculty of Agricultural Engineering, Technion—Israel Institute of Technology, in Haifa. His affiliation with the Technion began, however, in 1962, with his appointment as Senior Lecturer in the teaching of water resources engineering. He has been awarded the degrees of B.S. in soil physics by the University of California, Berkeley (1949), M.S. in agricultural engineering by the Technion (1958), and Ph.D. in engineering by UCLA (1962).

Dr. Buras' professional and research experience includes academic and governmental positions on two continents. Beginning in the soil conservation service of the Israeli Ministry of Agriculture (1951-1952), he has served with Tahal, Ltd., in irrigation and drainage research and design (1952-1957), with UCLA in irrigation, soil science, and water resources research (1957-1962), with Tahal as a consultant (1962-1965), with the University of California, Berkeley, on research in water resources (1965), and with Stanford University, as Visiting Professor of Operations Research (1967).

As speaker at numerous international conferences, Dr. Buras has presented papers on water storage, optimal use of water resources, operations research as a problem-solving technique in water resources engineering and management, drainage system design, and the development of water resources. In 1964, he received the Lauréat du Congrès at the Sixth International Congress of Agricultural Engineering in Lausanne.

His memberships include international, U.S., and Israeli professional groups: International Association of Scientific Hydrology, International Water Supply Association, Commission Internationale du Génie Rural; AAAS, American Geophysical Union, American Society of Civil Engineers, American Society of Agricultural Engineers, and American Water Resources Association; and Israel Society of Geodesy and Geophysics, Israel Meteorological Society, Israel Association for Data Processing, Israel Association for Agricultural Engineering, and Israel Association for Operations Research.